THE SELF IN MORAL SPACE

ALSO BY DAVID PARKER

Ethics, Theory, and the Novel

Renegotiating Ethics in Literature, Philosophy, and Theory
(edited with J. Adamson and R. Freadman)

THE SELF
IN MORAL SPACE

Life Narrative and the Good

DAVID PARKER

CORNELL UNIVERSITY PRESS

ITHACA AND LONDON

Permission to reprint portions of poems by Seamus Heaney published
by Faber and Faber Ltd. in *Death of a Naturalist, Seeing Things,* and *The Haw Lantern*
has been granted by Faber and Faber Ltd. Permission to reprint portions of poems
by Seamus Heaney published in U.S. editions by Farrar, Straus and Giroux has been
granted by Farrar, Straus and Giroux.

First published 2007 by Cornell University Press

Printed in the United States of America

Library of Congress Cataloging-in-Publication Data

Parker, David.
The self in moral space: life narrative and the good / David Parker.
        p.   cm.
Includes bibliographical references and index.
ISBN 978-0-8014-4561-3 (cloth : alk. paper)
    1.   Autobiography—Moral and ethical aspects.
    2.   Identity (Psychology)—Moral and ethical aspects.
                I. Title.

CT25.P37   2007
920—dc22

2006039786

Cornell University Press strives to use environmentally responsible suppliers and
materials to the fullest extent possible in the publishing of its books. Such
materials include vegetable-based, low-VOC inks and acid-free papers that are
recycled, totally chlorine-free, or partly composed of nonwood fibers. For further
information, visit our website at www.cornellpress.cornell.edu.

Cloth printing   10   9   8   7   6   5   4   3   2   1

Contents

Acknowledgments

The conversations that have contributed to this book extend far and wide. One of my deepest debts is to Charles Taylor, whom I have met in person only once. But he has long been my interlocutor on the page, and his clarity, humanity, and wisdom have been my constant reference points. I thank John Eakin for introducing me to the rich possibilities of autobiography as an academic study. When he visited the Humanities Research Centre at the Australian National University in 1990, we began memorable talks about life narrative that have borne much fruit over the years. Richard Freadman and I have shared much, including many productive thoughts about the relations between life writing, literary theory, and moral philosophy. Among my ANU colleagues, the intellectual companionship of Simon Haines, Jane Adamson, Fred Langman, and Axel Clark has been of fundamental importance to me. I owe a great deal to my friends and former students, Rosamund Dalziell, Mary Besemeres, and Susan Tridgell, who manage to keep spurring me on. Joy Hooton is another member of the Canberra life writing circle whose work has been a stimulus to me. From beginning to end, Ian Donaldson and the HRC have been presences in my thinking, as have the ANU philosophers, who have together attracted visits to Australia by some of the best minds in the humanities. Of these, Michael Holquist, Martha Nussbaum, and Raimond Gaita have had direct bearing on the present book.

The International Auto/Biography Association (IABA) has been the setting for many formal and informal gatherings that have greatly enhanced my thinking about life narrative. I have particularly valued my conversations with John Barbour, Tom Couser, Tom Smith, Roger Porter, Margaretta Jolly, Gillian Whitlock, Susanna Egan, Gabi Helms, Sidonie Smith, Philippe Lejeune, Alfred Hornung, Maureen Perkins, Eugene Stelzig, Kay Schaffer, Zhao Baisheng, and Li Zhanzi. Among many other things, Craig Howes gave me canny advice about the shape of this project that helped it along no end. I also gained greatly from the colloquium on the Ethics of Life Writing held at Indiana University, Bloomington, in October 2002.

At The Chinese University of Hong Kong I have found stimulus in my talks with colleagues Peter Crisp, Peter Skehan, David Huddart, Michael Bond, Ambrose King, Kwan Tze Wan, and Jeff Cody, and with my graduate students Lily Chen, Spring Liao, Serena Xie, Winne Wong, Sally Cheung, Nicole Wong, Nancy Tsui, Chloe Li, Shi Huiwen, and Li Ou. My graduate and undergraduate students at CUHK never cease to inspire me.

This book would not have been possible without the support of The Chinese University of Hong Kong, which has an excellent library and which has generously funded my attendance at conferences in Vancouver, Xi'an, Boulder, Canberra, Fuzhou, Lyon, Beijing, Melbourne, Hawai'i, and Mainz; nor without the Australian National University, which supported my trip to the first IABA conference in Beijing. I thank David Smith of the Poynter Center for the Study of Ethics and American Institutions at Indiana University, along with the English Department at Indiana University, and John Eakin for inviting me to the colloquium on the Ethics of Life Writing in 2002 that has contributed so much to this book. Writing only began in earnest when The Chinese University of Hong Kong awarded me a Summer Research Grant to be a Visiting Scholar in July 2003 at the Institute for Advanced Study at Indiana University, Bloomington, for which I also thank Indiana University.

Portions of this book have appeared previously in somewhat different versions. I acknowledge them here. The original versions were: "'Between Two Worlds': Modes of Identification in Seamus Heaney's Autobiographies," *The Critical Review* 39 (1999), 46–60; "Multiculturalism and Universalism in *Romulus, My Father*," *The Critical Review* 41 (2001), 44–53; "Locating the Self in Moral Space: Globalisation and Autobiography," in *Selves Crossing Cultures: Autobiography and Globalisation,* ed. Rosamund Dalziell (Melbourne: Australian Scholarly

Publishing, 2002), 3–21; "Ethicism and the Aesthetics of Autobiography: The Relational Aesthetic of J.M. Coetzee's *Boyhood*," *Life Writing* 1, 1 (2004), 3–19; "Life Writing as Narrative of the Good: *Father and Son* and the Ethics of Authenticity," in *The Ethics of Life Writing*, ed. Paul John Eakin (Ithaca: Cornell University Press, 2004), 53–72; "Narratives of Autonomy and Narratives of Relationality in Autobiography," *a/b: Auto/Biography Studies* 19, 1 and 2 (Summer and Winter 2004), 137–155; "Nietzsche's Ethics and Literary Studies: A Reading of *Ecce Homo*," *The Cambridge Quarterly* 33, 4 (2004), 299–314.

At Cornell I am grateful to Bernie Kendler for his helpful initial advice and to John G. Ackerman for his support of the book and his efficiency in bringing it so swiftly to publication. I am also grateful to my research assistant Li Ou, who worked around the clock checking quotations and proofreading.

My family, Helen, Jean, Fabian, and Tim, have always been my most encouraging and challenging interlocutors.

DAVID PARKER

The Chinese University of Hong Kong

THE SELF IN MORAL SPACE

Life Narrative and the Good

This book is premised on a particular view of what it means to be a self or agent in the world. It begins with the notion that behind any autobiographical act[1] is a self for whom certain things matter and are given priority over others. Some of these things are not merely objects of desire or interest, but command the writer's admiration or respect. These are the key "goods" the writer lives by, shaping her acts of ethical deliberation and choice. Such goods may include ideals of self-realization, social justice, equality of respect, or care for certain others. We can say that commitment to these goods orients her morally, or, in the words of my title, constitutes her as a self in moral space.[2] Such goods also inevitably shape the stories she tells when she projects her future or construes her past or present. In short, these goods are at the heart of life narrative, necessary constituents of it.

To some extent my line of argument may be seen as part of the turn to ethics in literary studies and more recently in studies of life writing. "The Turn to Ethics in the 1990s" is the title of an introductory essay I wrote to a collection called *Renegotiating Ethics in Literature, Philosophy, and Theory* (1998). This turn included the work of literary critics such as Wayne C. Booth, Tobin Siebers, and S. L. Goldberg, moral philosophers such as Martha C. Nussbaum, Bernard Williams, and Alasdair MacIntyre, and literary theorists in the postdeconstructive mold, such as J. Hillis Miller, Simon Critchley, and Geoffrey Galt Harpham. This group represented a widely divergent range of approaches, at one extreme drawing on Aristotle and Matthew Arnold, at another on Jacques Derrida and Emmanuel Lévinas. What they shared was a belief that the

ancient connection between ethics and literature is perennially important. They shared something else too. When they took up literature, they
naturally turned, as the ancients had, to "poetry" in the widest sense,
that is, to imaginative literature, principally to fiction and drama.

Renegotiating Ethics broke new ground in including essays by Paul
John Eakin, Richard Freadman, and John Wiltshire on ethics and non-
fictional narrative, particularly life narrative. In Eakin's essay, the ethics
of life writing became a defined discursive space for the first time, to
be taken up in subsequent studies, such as the collection *Mapping the
Ethical Turn* (ed. Davis and Womack, 2001) in which G. Thomas Couser
contributed an essay on the ethics of collaborative life writing. However, the book that has most clearly established the importance of ethical approaches to life narrative is the collection of essays edited by Paul
John Eakin, *The Ethics of Life Writing* (2004). The collection includes essays on truth-telling in autobiography and biography, work on representing others, as well as a group of pieces telling "counter-stories" to
some dominant social narratives on disability, hereditary disease and
identity. In fact this last group is a reminder that, for all the novelty of
foregrounding ethics in life writing studies, the cultural politics of marginal identities—the mainstream approach of the 1980s—was always
implicitly ethical. Much the same is true of the essays on truth-telling:
they remind us that the questions by which the field of life writing studies originally constituted itself against the dominance of imaginative
modes were as much ethical questions as generic ones. As John Eakin
put it at a conference in 2000, "ethics is the deep subject of autobiographical discourse."[3]

Bringing the deep subject of life writing discourse to the surface
was important. Telling the truth, respecting privacy, and representing
others are among the first issues to come up in serious reflection on
writing stories about self and others. They all involve the question
of what it is right for a life writer to do. As I point out in my own
essay in the Eakin collection—which forms part of my argument in
this book (chapter 2)—the question, *What is it right to do?* has to be
significant in any philosophical account of ethics. And yet, on some
accounts, such as the one I draw on here, right action occupies only
part of the broader ethical domain, which is defined by the question
as it was posed by the ancient Greeks: *How should a human being live?*
This broader formulation contains another question, which I contend
is also at the heart of all written lives, *What is it good to be?*

Of course, the right and the good overlap and intersect in many different ways, but in the present context there are reasons to distinguish them. For one thing, as we see in the Eakin collection, the ethics of right action tends to give predominant emphasis to the agent's moral obligations *to others*—with injunctions against lying, invading privacy, exerting undue power over vulnerable subjects, misrepresenting former lovers, and judging parents harshly. Again, any account of the ethics of life writing must give due importance to such preoccupations. But, as I argue in chapter 2 with regard to Edmund Gosse's *Father and Son*, an ethics in which the goods of self-care and self-realization scarcely weigh in the scale against other-regarding imperatives can be a vehicle of oppression. This is one reason for paying strategic attention to the question, *What is it good to be?* Another emerges from the work of two important contributors to *The Ethics of Life Writing*, John Barbour and Richard Freadman, both of whom in the end incline more to an ethics of the right than of the good.[4] The monographs of these scholars have opened up significant areas of this field. Barbour's pioneering book, *The Conscience of the Autobiographer* (1992), explores conscience as both sponsor and monitor of the writing of life narrative. Barbour shows the centrality for autobiographers of such issues as the potential narcissism of self-scrutiny, self-deception, parading guilt as a virtue, appealing to conscience as a rhetorical strategy to win the reader's regard, and the wishful or willful distortion of the past. In all these ways, truthfulness—as opposed to theoretical issues of truth and fictionality—emerges as a major ethical problematic of life writing. Richard Freadman's *Threads of Life* (2001) focuses on volition and shows the importance to autobiography of such issues as moral luck, freedom, determinism, and weakness of will. Barbour and Freadman differ in significant ways. Barbour prefers to see ethical criticism of life writing as an untheorized practice, while Freadman sees the need, as I do, for a more systematic approach, grounded not in Theory as it is normally understood in literary studies, but in moral philosophy. For all of these differences, Barbour and Freadman share something significant; they both articulate a view of ethics that gives constitutive centrality to *moral deliberation and choice*.

Common sense is bound to ask at this point, what could conceivably be wrong with the view that ethics is all about deliberation and choice? The answer cannot be a short one, since it involves a claim that modernity has left us with a skewed and impoverished sense of the ethical. This is why it is not satisfactory simply to assume, as writers on ethics and life writing commonly do, that we all know what ethics is. As Iris Murdoch argues, what we laymen "know" in this case, and many contemporary philosophers as well, involves a severely attenuated view of the human. In *The Sovereignty of Good* (1970 [2001]) Murdoch attacks what we are calling the ethics of right action because it pictures the ethical life as a series of privileged deliberative and volitional moments, selected out of the flux of experience, while it gives no ethical import to the multitudinous moments in between: "What is 'inward', what lies in between overt actions, is either impersonal thought or 'shadows' of acts, or else substanceless dream. Mental life is, and logically must be, a shadow of life in public. Our personal being is the movement of our overtly choosing will. Immense care is taken to picture the will as isolated. It is isolated from belief, from reason, from feeling, and is yet the essential centre of self" (7). Her target here is the part behaviorist and part existentialist self espoused by the dominant strands of Anglo-American Utilitarianism and Kantianism of the 1960s. She is arguing for the ethical importance of what she calls "attention," a concept she derives from Simone Weil's *Notebooks*, which involves "the idea of a just and loving gaze directed upon an individual reality" (33). Murdoch invites her reader to consider "what the work of attention is like, how continuously it goes on, and how imperceptibly it builds up structures of value round about us, [so that] we shall not be surprised that at crucial moments of choice most of the business of choosing is already over" (36).

Murdoch's key point is that our freedom as agents does not exclusively consist of those moments of explicit deliberation, choice, and volition centered on the question, *what, in this case, is it right to do*? Rather, our continual efforts of moral "attention" to our world will build up around us "structures of value" that shape our deliberative thoughts and incline us to certain choices and actions rather than others. These structures of value include the things we hold to in our lives as "goods," the goods that give us a certain moral identity, that make us selves in moral space. As Murdoch points out, however, we are unlikely to make all our evaluative distinctions in such primary terms as "good," but rather this continual moral activity of attention will be mostly conducted through our use of "secondary moral words" such as "bumptious" or "gay" (22). In other words, the structures of value that shape explicit moral choices will be erected by means of the evaluative languages that we use to negotiate everyday life. Part of Murdoch's inquiry is to understand how we come to choose rightly, how we come to *be* good.

Part of her answer is through great art, which teaches us to attend to reality in a way that is "just and compassionate" (64), and which greatly enriches our languages of value. The intimate connection implied here between ethics and aesthetics is one I take up in chapter 4.[5]

Murdoch is of course not the only twentieth-century philosopher to mount a searching critique of prevailing strands of the ethics of right action by drawing on some aspect of the moral thought of antiquity. In her case, the key source is Plato, especially the Plato of the Allegory of the Cave. More common is the return to Aristotle and to what has come to be called "virtue ethics." The salient example is Alasdair MacIntyre's *After Virtue* (1981). His work is especially germane to a study of life writing since his notion of virtue depends on a concept of narrative selfhood. Questions of right action are addressed by a self constituted by stories: "I can only answer the question 'What am I to do?' if I can answer the prior question 'Of what story or stories do I find myself a part?'" (201). As with Murdoch, MacIntyre sees acts of moral deliberation and choice as meaningful only within an acquired structure of personal values—in his case the virtues, which sustain the self in a lifelong quest for the good. For both philosophers, the good is the more fundamental concept than the right.

As important as Murdoch and MacIntyre, among others,[6] are to the argument of this book, I do not make much explicit reference to them. The reason is that their work has been taken up by the study to which I am most profoundly indebted, Charles Taylor's *Sources of the Self: the Making of the Modern Identity* (1989). Taylor develops Murdoch's insights about the "structure of values" in which deliberation and moral choice take place into a theory about the embeddedness of the right within the good. He also takes her few remarks about the importance of "secondary moral words" and extends them into an elaborate account of self as constituted by "languages of moral and spiritual discernment" (35). In fact, we can see here one of the reasons why Taylor's work is generally so useful to contemporary thought about life writing:—it incorporates into its thinking a number of postmodern challenges. The concept of "languages of moral and spiritual discernment" plays a part analogous to that of "discourses" within contemporary literary theory, while retaining a crucial commitment to the agency of the self.[7] Similarly, Taylor anticipates the recent relational turn[8] in life writing studies with his important notion that we are selves within society's "webs of interlocution" (36). The various conversation partners who initiate us into languages of moral and spiritual discernment are part of who we are. In fact, Taylor's interlocutive self (my coinage) takes relationality in some important new directions.[9] At the same time, Taylor's account brings all these threads together with MacIntyre's notion of narrative selfhood into a systematic theory that he articulates in section 1 of *Sources of the Self* under the title of "Identity and the Good." The rest of the book consists of a searching and complex genealogy of the good in Western culture from classical antiquity to the present. The result is a philosophically powerful account of the Western self, which engages in highly strategic ways with the antihumanist self that is still so dominant in contemporary theories of life writing.[10] Taylor's account holds out the possibility of a wholly new and theoretically coherent humanist approach to life narrative.

It will be clear by now that I have avoided the word "ethics" in my title—though not elsewhere—because for many contemporary readers it is bound to arouse misleading expectations, as well as bring to mind an inadequate conception of moral selfhood. But then, it might be said, surely "the good" is bound to be at least as misleading, if indeed it calls to mind anything at all. Why then a book on the good and life narrative?

There are several reasons. The first is that, as I argue in chapter 1, the good is an inescapable framework for understanding any human agent and therefore for any writer of life narrative. Among the many notions of Taylor's that I draw on is his "best account" thesis, by which I argue that making the best sense of lives requires the use of "thick" evaluative languages of the good. I show what this claim involves by discussing the case of Wang Shih-min, who accounts for his life in overtly Confucian terms. Then I explore the limit case of Roland Barthes, whose self-account explicitly attempts to avoid the use of "thick" languages of the good. On analysis it turns out that even he cannot avoid such languages. Nor can Nietzsche, on whose work the whole relativizing project of postmodernity is claimed to depend. In fact, despite what neo-Nietzscheans claim about him, Nietzsche's own life writing is organized around quite an explicit view about what it is good to be. He himself is mostly quite clear-eyed about the fact that we all make sense of ourselves against horizons of value.

Not only is some conception of the good necessary to selfhood, but following the historical shifts in such conceptions can give us fresh ways of looking at the history of life writing right up the present. Taylor's genealogy of the modern Western self shows the key importance of clashes between rival goods, between Enlightenment and Romantic ideals, for example, as well as the role of those jealous "hypergoods" (63ff.) that require anyone recognizing them to give up older allegiances to the good. The history of life writing in the West roughly follows the course of a series of historical "supersessions" (65) when older conceptions of the good give way to new ones. Chapter 2, for example, focuses mainly on the clashes between Judeo-Christian other-regarding imperatives and a newer Romantic ethics of self-realization. Chapter 3 follows the clash between Enlightenment and Romantic ideals down to the present, where it manifests itself in the tension between universal and particular goods. I argue that this tension lies behind a current shift away from the politics of difference toward a greater emphasis on the ethics of commonality.

Another new perspective opened up by this focus on the good is the relationship between goods realized in autobiographical texts and the notion of "good" life narrative. In other words, we are enabled to see the intimate relationship between the ethics and aesthetics of life narrative—to explore the intuition of Wittgenstein, who held that the two are one.[11] An aesthetics of life narrative would be another book, of course, and potentially a very important one. In chapter 4 I have set down some preliminary thoughts about one direction such a project might take.

Another reason for a study of the good in autobiography is that it highlights one of the key values of life narrative:—readers are often drawn to the lives of others because they are searching to know how to live themselves. Through reading lives they can learn what it is good to be, and sometimes what it is right to do. In his *Autobiography*, John Stuart Mill reminds us of the importance for some of having heroes to admire and to imitate.[12] He describes how his needs were met at important moments by life writing:

> The same inspiring effect which so many of the benefactors of mankind have left on record that they had experienced from Plutarch's *Lives*, was produced on me by Plato's pictures of Socrates, and by some modern biographies, above all by Condorcet's *Life of Turgot*; a book well calculated to rouse the best sort of enthusiasm, since it contains one of the wisest and noblest of lives, delineated by one of the wisest and noblest of men. The heroic virtue of these glorious representatives of the opinions with which I sympathized, deeply affected me, and I perpetually recurred to them as others do to a favourite poet, when needing to be

carried up into the more elevated regions of feeling and thought. I may observe by the way that this book cured me of my sectarian follies. The two or three pages beginning "Il regardait toute secte comme nuisible," and explaining why Turgot always kept himself perfectly distinct from the Encyclopedists, sank deeply into my mind. I left off designating myself and others as Utilitarians, and by the pronoun "we," or any other collective designation, I ceased to *afficher* sectarianism. (99)

As we shall see in later chapters, life narrative is frequently structured around such moments of deepened moral insight, or in Taylor's terminology "epistemic gain" (72), when the autobiographical "I" lives through a transition in his moral experience. Such passages record processes of practical reasoning in which one way of being is discovered to be more admirable, more authentic, or in a certain respect better, than some other. For Mill, at this moment in his life, sectarianism does not embody the "wisest and noblest" way to be.

Also of importance is that Mill does not just simply happen to be reading Condorcet, but takes up the book because he feels the need of moral inspiration—"*needing* to be carried up into the more elevated regions of feeling and thought." The need is not simply to understand intellectually what is a better way to be, but to feel the conviction of it, if possible to *become* better. In his time of mental "crisis," Mill experiences a complete failure of feeling for the things that had previously moved him, a state he blames on his early over-analytical education. In describing this he uses some highly instructive metaphors: "I was thus, as I said to myself, left stranded at the commencement of my voyage, with a well equipped ship and a rudder, but no sail; without any real desire for the ends which I had been so carefully fitted out to work for: no delight in virtue or the general good, but also just as little in anything else" (115). It is in this state that Mill comes across a life narrative that breaks in on him like a light in the gloom:

> I was reading, accidentally, Marmontel's *Memoirs*, and came to the passage which relates his father's death, the distressed position of the family, and the sudden inspiration by which he, then a mere boy, felt and made them feel that he would be everything to them—would supply the place of all that they had lost. A vivid conception of the scene and its feelings came over me, and I was moved to tears. From this moment my burthen grew lighter. The oppression of the thought that all feeling was dead within me, was gone. I was no longer hopeless: I was not a stock or a stone. (116–17)

However we interpret this moment in psychobiographical terms,[13] it is clear that Marmontel's narrative speaks to Mill in some deeply transformative way. Not only is he drawn out of his depression, but his whole philosophical orientation begins to change. He is attracted to Carlyle's "anti-self-consciousness theory" which says that happiness only comes to those whose attention is fixed on some object other than their own happiness. Even more fundamentally, the importance he gives to feeling begins to change: "I, for the first time, gave its proper place, among the prime necessities of human well-being, to the internal culture of the individual. . . . The cultivation of the feelings became one of the cardinal points in my ethical and philosophical creed" (118). Mill is the site of a clash between Enlightenment ideals of detached rationality and a Romantic ethics of self-realization that gives centrality to authentic feeling.

What we see in Mill's memoir is another, but more fundamental, transition in his moral experience. Again, his new orientation in moral space is prompted by reading the life of another, which moves him to feel some new perspective on things and which in turn leads him to practical reasoning about "the prime necessities of human well-being." Mill, of course, is one of the philosophers whose work has been foundational in what has become the modern ethics of right action, but his autobiography, like that of so many others, is organized around a quest to discover what it is good to be. The quest is punctuated by his encounters with others, most significantly of course with the major people in his life, his father and Harriet Taylor, partner in "the most valuable friendship of [his] life" (145). But, as we have seen, he finds other partners in the lives he reads, who weave some of the most important "webs of interlocution" in which John Stuart Mill has his being. Another literary interlocutor is William Wordsworth, with whom Mill found a special affinity, especially in the autobiographical poem "Intimations of Immortality": "I found that he too had had similar experience to mine; that he also had felt that the first freshness of youthful enjoyment of life was not lasting; but that he had sought for compensation, and found it, in the way in which he was teaching me to find it. The result was that I gradually, but completely, emerged from my habitual depression, and was never again subject to it. I long continued to value Wordsworth less according to his intrinsic merits, than by the measure of what he had done for me" (122).

Important interlocutors such as Condorcet, Marmontel, and Wordsworth exercise their influence over Mill by expanding his repertoire of languages of the good. Such languages are resources for life. As we see with Mill's reading of Wordsworth, the poet shows him how to seek for "compensation"; he is a crucial teacher in Mill's quest to discover how to live. Mill was only in his early twenties when he encountered these life writers, the age of many contemporary undergraduates. Mill's example might remind us of one of the important roles of life writing in secondary and higher education, when many students, like Mill, are trying to work out for themselves how they should live and what it is good to be. Judging by the proliferation of such texts on school curricula, contemporary educators have some intuition of their appeal and value. The approach I take here clarifies several aspects of this appeal. Especially in what have become known as "relational auto/biographies," in which the autobiographer and some other, usually a parent, are co-subjects, we see the exploration of many "rite of passage" issues. One of these is the challenge of moving from seeing the parent as a reflex of psychic need to seeing her as an other, separate "centre of self, whence," as George Eliot puts it in *Middlemarch*, "the lights and shadows must always fall with a certain difference" (146).[14] This is one of the main themes of chapters 3, 4, and the conclusion, where I return to Iris Murdoch's notion of moral "attention" and to Plato's cave, which can be seen as an allegory of transcending the child's narcissism and coming to understand others with a fully adult empathic identification.

Life narrative is valuable, not simply because it identifies for us what Taylor calls "moral sources" (91ff.), but because, as we see in the case of Mill, it can bring these sources closer. As Mill's own metaphor indicates, life narrative can fill the drooping sails of moral feeling. It can open up fresh ethical possibilities, inspire change, empower the self to pursue new, life-enhancing ways to be.

To appreciate this power of life narrative fully, we need what Taylor calls "articulacy" about the good (91). Like Murdoch and MacIntyre, Taylor believes that modernity has erased certain essential features of our moral horizons—repressed the structures of value by which we nonetheless continue to make moral sense of our lives. His great achievement was to bring these sources of the modern Western self to articulation, showing the "full range of goods" we moderns actually live by (107). The first step in my argument here is therefore to follow Taylor in making explicit why we should view our moral being as constituted by "thick" languages of the good—in short why we should view human agents as selves in moral space.

CHAPTER ONE

Life Narrative and Languages of the Good

Good is sovereign, according to Iris Murdoch, in the sense that ethical decision-making emerges from "structures of value" built up around us by continuous processes of moral attention to the realities of everyday life. But how seriously can we take such a notion of the good? Ancient philosophers, notably Plato, believed that structures of value were metaphysical realities, inherent in the constitution of the cosmos,[1] but then this belief has taken a devastating battering from modern skepticism. In section 301 of *The Gay Science*, for example, Nietzsche tears away at precisely this "human, all too human" belief[2] that mankind has long lived by—namely, that its values are part of the frame of things: "Whatever has *value* in our world now does not have value in itself, according to its nature—nature is always value-less, but has been *given* value at some time, as a present—and it was *we* who gave and bestowed it. Only we have created the world *that concerns man!*—But precisely this knowledge we lack, and when we occasionally catch it for a fleeting moment we always forget it again immediately" (242). Such has been the power of natural science since Nietzsche's time that this view has lost its once corrosive bite. It is a familiar modern thought that values are not inherent in the universe *per se* but are imposed on it by us.[3] Less familiar perhaps is the thought that we are incapable of living with this bleak knowledge and that we immediately suppress it. In an earlier section, Nietzsche wrote that such illusions as this one about values are convenient "self-deceptions"—philosophical "errors" that have survived by natural selection because they have been found to be "life-preserving." In fact, Nietzsche sees the struggle between the austere "truth" and these "life-preserving errors" as the master-conflict of the coming age: "Compared to the significance of this fight, everything else is a matter of indifference: the ultimate question about the conditions of life has been posed here, and we confront the first attempt to answer this question by experiment. To what extent can truth endure incorporation? That is the question; that is the experiment" (170–71).

1. Making the Best Sense of Lives

Nietzsche's question is the one I wish to begin with here, in explicating the significance of Taylor's work for life writing. To what extent can what he calls the "truth" about values endure incorporation in everyday life? As we shall see, Nietzsche's notion of this question as entailing an "experiment," or what Taylor calls a "test" for the everyday viability of various theories of being, also strikes to the center of my argument. Nietzsche's question involves what Bernard Williams has called an "absolute conception" of universe,[4] shorn of all "anthropocentric" conceptions (Taylor, 56), such as values, which are thought of by Nietzsche as projections onto the natural world. In contemporary terms, Nietzsche is asking to what extent we can live by this "absolute conception" and explanatory theories and metaphysical views derived from it—that is, understand the human world, think and feel about it, in the clear-sighted belief that our values are no more than our own projections.

It is by no means clear that Nietzsche thought we could live in this way. Looking at *The Gay Science* itself we can observe his own thinking and feeling about the "world *that concerns man*." Three sections after the one with which we began (section 304), Nietzsche turns from metaphysics to ethics:

> *By doing we forego.*—At bottom I abhor those moralities which say: "Do not do this! Renounce! Overcome yourself!" But I am well disposed toward those moralities which goad me to do something and do it again, from morning till evening, and then to dream of it at night, and to think of nothing except doing this *well*, as well as *I* alone can do it. When one lives like that, one thing after another that simply does not belong to such a life drops off. Without hatred or aversion one sees this take its leave today and that tomorrow, like yellow leaves that any slight stirring of the air takes off a tree. He may not even notice that it takes its leave; for his eye is riveted to his goal—forward, not sideward, backward, downward.

What we do should determine what we forego; by doing we forego—that is how I like it, that is my *placitum*. But I do not wish to strive with open eyes for my own impoverishment; I do not like negative virtues—virtues whose very essence it is to negate and deny oneself something. (244)

This is Nietzsche the pitiless critic of Judeo-Christian morality, who will later expatiate on his antipathy toward servile self-renunciation in *The Genealogy of Morals*. The germ of all the later books is here, including his critique of Christian *ressentiment* (see section 305), which he opposes to the healthy ascesis of self-cultivation. Hard work, which strips one of all that is inessential "without hatred or aversion," is necessary for self-realization, for "doing this *well*, as well as *I* alone can do it." In an earlier epigrammatic section entitled "*What does your conscience say?*" he says, echoing Pindar: "You shall become the person you are" (219). This too points forward: the subtitle of his autobiography, *Ecce Homo*, is, "How One Becomes What One Is." As I argue at some length in a later chapter, Nietzsche's attack on Christian morality is not in the service of nihilism. His revolutionary program is the "revaluation of all values," not the dis-valuation. Becoming the person you are through the healthy ascesis of doing what you alone can do is presented as a significantly better way to be than following the self-hating path of slave-morality.

To return then to the Nietzschean question of "to what extent can truth endure incorporation?" what we observe from Nietzsche's own practice is the uprooting of one morality in the service of another. Certainly, the thought that all values are our subjective projections helps immeasurably to loosen up the soil for this process, but is this really thoroughgoing "incorporation"? Radical incorporation would seem to entail the belief that there is nothing in becoming the person one is that makes it any better than resentful self-renunciation, except that Nietzsche himself had chosen it to be so. But this case would hardly lead him to be "well disposed" toward the one and to "abhor" the other. In other words, there are clearly *reasons* behind his moral feelings and intuitions in section 304—reasons of the kind he sets out fully in later works.[5] This is to say that Nietzsche's own practice seems to suggest that he himself does not feel, think, and choose according to the "absolute conception" he outlines in section 301.

But this is purely an *ad hominem* argument, showing only that Nietzsche does not seem to incorporate his metaphysical skepticism into his own thinking, judging, and feeling about the human world, not that he *could* not. Taylor wants to go further and argue for the impossibility of living in this way. In *Sources of the Self*, Taylor argues against all forms of value antirealism, including Nietzsche's kind, in the following way: "Our value terms purport to give us insight into what it is to live in the universe as a human being, and this is a quite different matter from that which physical science claims to reveal and explain. This reality is, of course, dependent on us, in the sense that a condition for its existence is our existence. But once granted that we exist, it is no more a subjective projection than what physics deals with" (59). This line of argument is value-realism, which would say that moral feeling of Nietzsche's kind is a response to something real, revealed to him in the light of value-terms such as "impoverishment," "the person you are," and "doing this *well*." Such terms entail what Taylor calls "strongly valued goods." The argument for value-realism is outlined as follows:

1. You cannot help having recourse to these strongly valued goods for the purposes of life: deliberating, judging situations, deciding how you feel about people, and the like. The "cannot help" here . . . means . . . that you need these terms to make the best sense of what you're doing. By the same token these terms are indispensable to the kind of explanation and understanding of self and others that is interwoven with these life uses: assessing his conduct, grasping her motivation, coming to see what you were really about all these years, etc.

2. What is real is what you have to deal with, what won't go away just because it doesn't fit with your prejudices. By this token, what you can't help having recourse to in life is real, or as near to reality as you can get a grasp of at present. Your general metaphysical picture of "values" and their place in "reality" ought to be based on what you find real in this way. . . .

The force of this argument is obscurely felt even by non-realists. It comes in the confused sense that espousing the projection view ought to have a devastating effect on first-order morality. This is the sense that everyone has before they are got to by philosophical rationalization, that what they count with as they live—goods and the demands they make— is flatly incompatible with a projection view. To go along with this sense, a projectivist would have to reject morality altogether, as this is usually understood, i.e., as a domain of strong evaluation. But most non-realists are reluctant to make this choice. They themselves are committed to some morality, and they also have some distant sense of my point that one *couldn't* operate this way. . . .

If non-realism can't be *supported* by moral experience, then there are *no* good grounds to believe it at all. (59–60)

Some concepts here need to be unpacked before we can proceed to tease out the implications of Taylor's argument.

"Strongly valued goods" and "strong evaluation" are key Taylorian terms. An evaluation may be "weak" in that I simply desire, prefer, or choose something, for example, a Mercedes rather than a BMW; or it may be "strong," as when I don't buy a car at all on the grounds that private car ownership contributes to global warming. In the latter case, there is a discrimination of one choice being higher or lower, better or worse, right or wrong, which is not rendered valid by the choice itself, but offers standards by which the choice can be judged (4ff.). "Strong evaluation" involves the possibility that some desires, choices or preferences may be judged as base, ignoble, trivial, superficial, destructive, unworthy and so on.[6] In terms of the above example, a weakly valued good might be the superior comfort of a Mercedes; but a concern for the environment that encourages me to use public transport involves a strongly valued good. Returning to Nietzsche and morality in section 304, note that he sometimes tends to use the language of weak evaluation to describe his choice of self-realization over self-abnegation, saying that he "likes" one rather than the other, is more "well disposed" to it. But the word "abhor" already has overtones of the contempt he will express in later works for Judeo-Christian slave-morality. Becoming who you are is a strongly valued good—it is part of what he will later call *amor fati*, courageous yes-saying to life, living "without [self-]hatred or aversion," all of which for Nietzsche is most decidedly a matter of "conscience."

What Taylor aims to show is that humans cannot help having recourse to strongly valued goods such as these. His argument is that being a person of relative normality involves knowing where you stand in relation to a range of questions you cannot help facing, about what is good or bad, admirable or contemptible, what is worth doing and what not, what has meaning and importance for you and what is trivial and secondary. Your answers to these questions define who you are and inevitably involve strongly valued goods—what you see as important, significant, or meaningful in your life. For Taylor, identity is bound up in how you are oriented, toward which strongly valued goods. To know who you are is to be oriented in what he calls "moral space"—the space of questions outlined above about where you stand, about what important goods or values constitute your horizons of meaning and significance (25ff.).

Taylor depends on us recognizing the force in this phenomenological account of identity. For example, we need to recognize that the usual account of identity, involving self-definition in terms of group-membership, often leaves out the fact that only some groups we belong to are meaningful or important to us; as well as the fact that many of our identity-defining values—for example our admiration for political courage—may have nothing directly to do with group membership at all. Taylor also asks us to consider, as a thought-experiment, what a person with no orientation toward any strongly valued goods would be like. She would be completely unable to answer for herself about what is worth doing and what not, what is good or bad, what is important or trivial and secondary. Such a person would not merely be shallow, unprincipled or morally insouciant; such a person would be in the grip of a truly devastating "identity-crisis," deeply psychically disoriented, pathological, outside the range of what we would see as "normal." A person of relative normality must be to some extent oriented in moral space: "the horizons in which we live *must* include strong qualitative discriminations" (32). Without such horizons a human being would be barely recognizable as a "person" or a "self" at all.

It follows from this that human persons or selves have certain "constitutive concerns." "We are selves only in that certain issues matter for us. What I am as a self, my identity, is essentially defined by the way things have significance for me" (34). These concerns, orienting horizons, frameworks of significance, that constitute us as selves are by no means inborn. We are inducted into them by conversation partners or "interlocutors" (35). According to Taylor, a "self exists only within" what he calls "'webs of interlocution'" (36). This aspect of Taylor's thesis is reminiscent in some ways of the work of Mikhail Bakhtin. Beginning with our first caregivers and continuing throughout our lives we are initiated into various "languages of moral and spiritual discernment" which are equally "languages of self-understanding" or "self-definition" (35–36). These crucially involve value-words such as "love," "honesty," "courage," and "brutality" in which, as Bernard Williams has argued, the descriptive and the evaluative point are inseparable.[7]

These are the sorts of words I need to be able to use in order to "discern" critical qualities in myself and others, to judge situations and people, articulate feelings, to assess conduct, understand motivation, and so on. Drawing on the work of Gilbert Ryle and Clifford Geertz,[8] Williams has called these "thick ethical concepts,"[9] that is, concepts that are internal to the codes of signification that operate within a given culture or "web of interlocution." The languages of the good these concepts constitute therefore vary from culture to culture, from period to period, and a complex culture, such as the culture of Western modernity, is made up of many such languages.

Returning to the question we began with about whether I can live by some "absolute conception" of things, Taylor is arguing that I need some "thick" anthropocentric languages of value in order to "make sense" of my life. "Thin" theoretical languages of explanation in terms of some "absolute conception" of things cannot on their own give me the understanding of my life that I need.

> What are the requirements of "making sense" of our lives? These
> requirements are not yet met if we have some theoretical language
> which purports to explain behaviour from the observer's standpoint but
> is of no use to the agent in making sense of his own thinking, feeling,
> and acting. Proponents of a reductive theory may congratulate them-
> selves on explanations which do without these or those terms current in
> ordinary life, e.g., "freedom" and "dignity," or the various virtue terms
> mentioned before which resist splitting into "factual" and "evaluative"
> components of meaning. But even if their third-person explanations
> were more plausible than they are, what would be the significance of this
> if the terms prove ineradicable in first-person, non-explanatory uses?
> Suppose I can convince myself that I can explain people's behaviour as
> an observer without using a term like "dignity". What does this prove if
> I can't do without it as a term in my deliberations about what to do, how
> to behave, how to treat people, my questions about whom I admire, with
> whom I feel affinity, and the like? (57)

Thick anthropocentric languages are "ineradicable" from my life because I, as an agent in the human world, need them for a range of
unavoidable first-person uses. For this reason they are necessary for
"making sense" of my life, when I judge, think, feel, and, as we shall
see, when I come to write about it.

But Taylor wants to go even further: I need these languages of spiritual and moral discernment for making the *best* sense of my life. Here Taylor engages directly with "thin" theoretical languages that purport to "interpret" and "explain" my life from some kind of third-person perspective quite outside the significance that I myself see in it. In doing so, he raises the question, "What ought to trump the language in which I actually live my life?" To answer it, he develops what he calls a "best account" (BA) principle:

> The terms we select have to make sense across the whole range of both explanatory and life uses. The terms indispensable for the latter are part of the story that makes best sense of us, unless and until we can replace them with more clairvoyant substitutes. The result of this search for clairvoyance yields the best account we can give at any given time, and no epistemological or metaphysical considerations of a more general kind about science or nature can justify setting this aside. The best account in the above sense is trumps. Let me call this the BA principle. (58)

One test for the "BA principle" is whether or not any language can enable me to understand, explain or to articulate my moral feelings and intuitions about myself and others, about what is good and right, and so on; if it cannot, it falls foul of this principle. Thin theoretical languages derived from epistemology or metaphysics that demand that I set aside the meanings that things in the human domain intuitively have for me are proposals to "change the subject."

Changing the subject, a notion that Taylor derives from Donald Davidson,[10] is a useful concept. Taylor uses it to point to the naturalistic reduction in ethics that demands that all moral philosophizing start outside the meanings things have for us—in some absolute scientific conception of the universe. But this concept is equally useful to analyze some thin reductive accounts of the human domain that still have wide currency in literary studies. As we shall see, the concept is also useful in relation to accounts which require that analytic accounts begin with language systems, that we see all moral intuitions and feelings and anthropocentric meanings as mediated by a differential play of linguistic signs in which meaning is endlessly deferred. Demands that we begin with discursive systems, practices of signification, or with differential power relations in society, may be demands to change the subject—the preferred subject being "theory."

In fact the question of whether post-Saussurean or neo-Nietzschean theories can satisfy the BA principle in relation to life writing is closely connected to the question we began with, the question of whether Nietzschean value antirealism can be incorporated into everyday living. As we know, it is easily possible to conceptualize the "subject" in thin theoretical space. Literary scholars do it all the time. This involves abstracting ourselves in thought from our constitutive first-person concerns with what is important and significant to us and imagining ourselves from a third-person standpoint as being part of, and to some extent determined by, a larger system—of linguistic signs perhaps, discursive practices, or power-relations. The key BA question is the extent to which we "can actually *assume* that standpoint and live it." Taylor is "very sceptical whether contemporary neo-Nietzschean doctrines of overcoming the self or the 'subject' can meet this test" (526–27).

What follows, in fact, is partly an attempt to throw light on precisely this issue by exploring two related questions: whether it is possible to write my life intelligibly, and then to understand life writing satisfactorily, without recourse to thick anthropocentric languages of moral and spiritual discernment. In this regard, I will focus on some autobiographies that purportedly deny, or otherwise seem to contradict, the case that I am making here. Most importantly, I will begin with the "anti-autobiography" *Roland Barthes by Roland Barthes*, which I treat as a limit case about the possibility or otherwise of writing a life in the thin languages of post-Saussurean theory. Before I do that, however, I need to illustrate the argument I am making by examining a life that shows clearly the key Taylorian concepts in practice. Since Taylor's argument, as explicated so far, is about necessary frameworks, about the transcendental conditions of being a self and living a life, then it is not specific to Western culture. I have therefore chosen to begin strategically with an example from a non-Western civilization.

2. Wang Shih-min's "Self-Account": An Exemplary Life

The "Self-Account" of Wang Shih-min (1592–1680) is given as an eight-page appendix to Wu Pei-yi's ground-breaking book *The Confucian's Progress: Autobiographical Writings in Traditional China*. Wang was a scion of a wealthy and well-known family. His grandfather, Wang Hsi-chüeh, had been a grand secretary (1585–1594) in the late Ming administration and was well known as an upright scholar-gentleman and man of letters. Wang himself was a renowned painter, one of the so-called "Four Wangs" of the seventeenth century (187–93).

Wang explains at the end of his "Self-Account" that he wrote it to be kept in the family temple for the benefit of his "descendants in future generations. . . . Through the document they will trace everything back to the family instructions of my father and grandfather. They must strive to emulate former ways and do nothing to diminish the fame of the family. Perhaps someday they will restore the glory of the family by having several members simultaneously serving the government in high offices" (262). In fact, Wang's wish was at least partly realized: Wang's grandson rose to the same elevated position in the Qing bureaucracy as his great, great grandfather (Wang's grandfather) had occupied in the late Ming period. Wang himself was a Ming loyalist who lived through the traumatic change of dynasty. It is hard to say how much the "Self-Account" is shaped by the prudence of an astute official who was able to negotiate dynastic change successfully on behalf of the family and how much by the self-justification that tends to color the memoirs of all retired officials. All one can say is the obvious, that the "Self-Account" is no naïve outpouring of autobiographical sincerity, but the product of a highly evolved moral and political culture. Like all autobiography, it raises many mostly unanswerable questions of authenticity, fictionality, and referential truth, which I shall simply set aside. My focus will be on Wang as narrated in the autobiographical text.

As we have seen, a Taylorian approach to identity involves the notion that we all exist in a space of questions posed by our various interlocutors. In Wang's case, these include his contemporaries and superiors, his ancestors and descendants, the sages and posterity itself. The questions are about who Wang Shih-min is or was. Wang answers them in terms of certain concerns that arise from strongly valued goods. He describes his early life as being marked by two "calamities," the deaths of his father and grandfather, which left him, at the age of nineteen, not merely "forlorn" but in "mortal peril."

> All the burdens of the household fell on my shoulders, for I was the only man left in the family. I had to manage all the internal affairs as well as to deal with the outside world. Furthermore, the snobbery of the world was such that the family could be saved from tumbling down further only by

some member's acquisition of rank and office. It just happened that in recognition of my grandfather's service to the country I was offered the post of an assistant director in the Office of Imperial Seals. (253)

Wang makes sense of this critical point in his life in terms of what mattered supremely to him, namely, the "honor" of the family. This is the key good in his whole account, which forms the horizon of significance against which all his narrated actions are implicitly evaluated. Survival and prosperity are subsidiary goods and no doubt partly entailed in "honor," but to place "survival above honor" is unworthy and shameful (261–62). In an obvious way, the self inscribed in this narrative is oriented in relation to strongly valued goods.

Another Confucian good shaping the narrative here and at most points is self-deprecating filiality: almost every achievement of his is described as in some way traceable back to his father's and grandfather's good counsel, influence, or example. Wang reports how as a child he has observed their exemplary conduct and heard it praised everywhere, how he took note of his grandfather's sayings and how he admired their learned conversations about subjects such as calligraphy and the literary classics (257–61). These immediate forefathers are among his chief interlocutors and their words and example constitute one of the major "webs of interlocution" in which he exists very much as a relational self. Quite explicitly, their words shape his later conduct. As a child, he often heard his grandfather "remarking that a scholar-official out of office and residing in his hometown should consider as his primary duties the early payment of taxes and the diligent performance of good deeds. I made a mental note of this saying and never forgot it day or night." He goes on to describe how in retirement he himself has given to the poor and has always tried to pay taxes early (256).

What we see here in this somewhat quaint explicit example no doubt applied to Wang's whole approach to administration while he himself was in office: the boy who slept in his grandfather's room and waited on him night and day was being groomed for success in the world that mattered. A key part of this was clearly being inducted into the Confucian languages of moral discernment. When he gets his post in the office of Official Seals at the age of nineteen, Wang knows exactly how to behave. He acts according to the highest standards of propriety ("*li*") and rectitude, discharging all duties with "caution and diligence."

Against his immediate self-interest, he leaves court for long periods, volunteering for missions that involve long and arduous journeys. Hyperconscious that he owes his post to imperial favor rather than merit as established through the examinations system, he feels a need to "ward off the ridicule that [he] occupied an idle sinecure" (253–54). While on his missions he refuses gifts and trims expenses to such an extent that when he presents his travel tally his colleagues "laughed at [his] obtuseness." "Even the bureau director was politely derisive. But I only knew how to obey the law" (254). Yet he also shows that what seems like naïve dutifulness to these minor functionaries wins the trust and approbation of men of renown in the higher levels of the civil service. The narrative of his career ends with an account of routine merit evaluations conducted by an ancient enemy of his family. He is subjected to much scrutiny and faultfinding, but in the end they can find nothing against him (255–56). Such incidents make it clear that the stringent values he lives by enable him to survive and indeed flourish in the competitive and often hostile world of bureaucratic power.

So far Wang has appeared as a relational self, defined in terms of his proper performance of roles, as the only man in the family, as well as son, grandson, and official, in the fully charted moral space of Confucian values. He is, however, not fully defined by such roles. He describes how sad he was that his eldest brother, who had died when Wang was fourteen, has no son to perform sacrifices for him. He comes up with an unorthodox solution: "According to the rites, bachelors could not have sons adopted posthumously. However, I thought that the rites originated in what was right, so I prepared a statement and delivered it to the family temple, thereby making my third son Chuan the heir to my deceased brother, who would thus always enjoy sacrifices and libations" (258). The sentiments he expresses here about the rites and what is right are in the spirit of the Master, who held that "the gentleman considers the whole rather than the parts. The small man considers the parts rather than the whole."[11] At the same time, Wang's language here—"However, I thought . . . I prepared"—seems to imply degrees of individual autonomy and agency in his thinking and acting that may seem surprising in the light of some stereotypical views of Confucian culture. As William Theodore de Bary says in *Self and Society in Ming Thought*, a Confucian finds the Way in the web of reciprocal moral relations, but these do not totally define him.

"His interior self exists at the center of this web and there enjoys its own freedom."[12] The neo-Confucian self-cultivation De Bary writes about assumes individual agency, freedom, and self-responsibility. Wang certainly writes about himself in these terms. In talking about how he will not wrangle with perfidious money-lenders he describes his moral stance and his actions: "For I have always believed, during the last several decades, that I would let others take advantage of me rather than that I should take advantage of them and that I would rather suffer losses than pocket improper gains. I swore that I would never deviate from this practice. Everybody in my hometown can testify to this" (257). The self narrated here is an agent, what Ambrose King and Michael Bond call an "active and reflexive entity,"[13] defining himself as an individual in terms of a moral decision freely made and unswervingly acted upon.

Part of the writer's answer to the question of who Wang Shih-min was is that he was a man who swore to behave properly and honorably and did so. In other words, he presents his life in terms of thick description. Strong value terms such as "honor" and "propriety" are fundamental to his self-understanding. In the most explicit way, he defines himself by locating his stance in moral space. Looking back over his life at the end of his narrative, he notes: "I have never in all my life transgressed Confucian morality." At the same time, defining himself partly entails giving an "account" of his worth against standards that are embodied by others. Despite his Confucian virtues, he regrets his early "timidity and vigilance," expending too much in meeting obligations: "Therefore I failed to match the glories of my forefathers by mastering one canonical classic, nor did I achieve fame and excel among my contemporaries through the practice of one art" (261). Clearly, Wang interprets and evaluates his life as a whole within a temporal framework that is larger than his own lifetime.

For all its late Ming "individualism," Wang Shih-min's "Self-Account" is not just the narrative of an individual life. As we saw at the beginning, the story has its eye on posterity. Succeeding generations who read this self-account of Wang Shih-min in the family temple are being asked quite explicitly to "strive to emulate former ways and do nothing to diminish the fame of the family" (262). To this extent, Wang's life is exemplary, literally, the values he lives by being part of the family's "fame" that descendants must do nothing to diminish. Wang is intent to pass on these values of propriety, honesty, and rectitude that he inherited from his forefathers in the belief that the family's "fame" also depends on their perpetuation. His narrative has shown the ways in which they were important to him, enabling him to survive and even flourish amid hostility and resentment. To return to Nietzsche's evolutionary imagery, Wang knows from experience that such values are "life-preserving," especially in the civil service milieu in which a family's glory may be lost or won. Caring for the honor of the family makes it critically important to try to pass them on.

There is, of course, no shadow in Wang's narrative of the rest of Nietzsche's thought, namely, that all values such as the Confucian ones are philosophical "errors," self-deluding projections. Nor, *a fortiori*, is there any hint of the neo-Nietzschean thought, which we can hardly suppress in reading the "Self-Account," that such values were ideological, not only occluding the women and servants that made the whole traditional scholar-gentleman system workable, but also legitimizing their oppression. As we shall see in the chapters that follow, however "true" such thoughts may be, they too entail values and strongly valued goods—such as equality of respect. Incorporating them into lives involves the same processes of deliberating, judging, assessing people and conduct that Wang faced, or anybody must face. In order to do these things and make sense of our lives we need thick languages of value and the good. As the case of *Roland Barthes by Roland Barthes* shows, the attempt to do away with such languages makes lives opaque—and life narrative impossible to tell.

3. *Roland Barthes by Roland Barthes* and the Limits of Life Narrative

Nietzsche thought that the question of whether his skeptical "truth" about values could be "incorporated" into everyday living was an empirical matter, answerable by "experiment." In a similar vein Taylor, skeptical of neo-Nietzschean and post-Saussurean theories, expresses doubt about whether they can meet the "test" of incorporation, about whether one could assume their non-anthropocentric viewpoints and live them. In fact we can say that modern imaginative literature from Dostoyevsky onwards constitutes the experiment that Nietzsche was calling for. In the case of Taylor's challenge, one test is provided by avant-garde autobiography, where writers have attempted to write their lives in the languages of contemporary theories. No attempt to do this has been more thoroughgoing than *Roland Barthes by Roland Barthes*. Barthes' attack on authorship, the self, the referentiality of language and so on have been discussed fully by previous scholars. In *Touching the World* (1992) John Eakin shows that this "anti-autobiography" actually embodies many of the features of language and narrative it is committed to denying: it is a referential work despite itself.[14] Similarly, in *Threads of Life* (2001) Richard Freadman explores the self-contradictory stance of Barthes' text in relation to the will.[15] In fact both scholars use *Roland Barthes by Roland Barthes* as a limit case in order to demonstrate the necessity in autobiography of constituent features that Barthes explicitly jettisons: in one case, reference in life narrative, in the other, agency. I take a similar trajectory here but focus instead on the necessity of being a self in moral space. Here too *Roland Barthes* is a limit case, showing that his stance on values cannot altogether do away with strongly valued goods, nor with the need that such goods enable and entail of making sense of his life as an unfolding story. At key moments, the thin antihumanistic language of Barthes' theoretical stance keeps evaporating before the need to locate himself in moral space. At these moments, he reverts to thicker languages of self-understanding, along with an implicit biographical framework, which surfaces despite his best efforts to suppress it.

Roland Barthes describes itself as equivocal on the question of values. On the one hand it is "a whole long text on value, on a continuous affect of evaluation—which involves an activity at once ethical and semantic." On the other hand, it spends "an equal energy in dreaming of an 'abolition without leftovers of the reign of values'" (154). Equivocations of this kind are programmatic in RB's text, part of its dialectical mode of inquiry. Yet this particular equivocation has a special importance in *Roland Barthes*: in the table of RB's career "phases," the book's "genre" is given as "morality" and its "intertext" as Nietzsche (145). RB says that he was steeped in Nietzsche when he wrote it, so an activity at once ethical and semantic is not surprising here, embodied in often tersely epigrammatic entries such as the above one on the "Abolition of the reign of values." Equally unsurprising, given Nietzsche's role as chief interlocutor, is the text's mixture of deep ethical skepticism and innovative reflection. In an entry entitled "Between

Salamanca and Valladolid" he outlines a new moral philosophy he calls "preferentialism":

> One summer day (1970) driving and daydreaming between Sala-
> manca and Valladolid, he diverted himself by imagining a kind of new
> philosophy which he forthwith baptized "preferentialism," heedless,
> there in the car, whether it was frivolous or guilty: against a materialist
> background (a cliff?) in which the world is seen as no more than a fabric,
> a text unrolling the revolution of languages, the war of systems, and in
> which the subject—scattered, deconstructed—can grasp himself only by
> means of an image-repertoire, the (political, ethical) choice of this appar-
> ent subject has no establishing value: *such a choice is not important*; what-
> ever the style—pompous or violent—in which it is declared, it is never
> anything but an *inclination*: in the presence of the world's *fragments*, I am
> entitled only to *preference*. (158)

For the dispersed subject of postmodernism, in whom there is no centered self at home within but—a nice Barthesian pun—literally "*per-
sonne*" (120), there can be no founding choice to give him existential
being. However important Sartre may have once been to Barthes, his
thought is part of what has since been "deconstructed" into warring
linguistic "systems." At the same time, Sartrean thought remains important throughout *Roland Barthes*, for Barthes still assumes that without radical ethical or political choice there is no "establishing value" for
the "apparent subject": there is only *le néant*, nothingness. Philosophically, the world and the subject are nothing but "fragments," intelligible only within the great text of language systems. Like the coherent
self, existential choice is an illusion, part of the Lacanian imaginary, by
which it is bodied forth in this text as "image-repertoire"—to be put in
inverted commas or attributed to a third person, a "him," no more real
than a character in a novel.

In other words, without existential choice to "establish" self with
being and the world with value there is only "preference." Barthes
clearly senses what is at stake here: the decentered self can have no
enduring value-commitments, no commitments that make some preferences more admirable than others, only "inclinations" or patterns of
"likes" and "dislikes" as in the lists he gives in "I like, I don't like" (116–
17). In Taylor's terms, this is precisely saying that there can only be weak
evaluations, there being nothing to endow the preferences, inclinations

and likes of the postmodern subject with more value, meaning, importance, or significance than the dislikes and the things not preferred. In a playful section that comments on Barthesian "preferentialism," he asks a series of examination-type questions about it, one of them being "Cite the philosophies to which 'preferentialism' might be opposed" (158). If one of them is existentialism, another is Taylor's moral philosophy, which is based on the unavoidable necessity of strong evaluation. Again, the Taylorian challenge is posed as an empirical test: preferentialism can be easily stated as a theory, but can it be lived?

Since we have no unmediated access to Barthes' life, we cannot directly put him to this test. But what we can do is to examine the language in which he writes, or refuses to write, his life. Such an examination will reveal the extent to which it is possible to write plausibly about himself and his life in nothing but the language of weak evaluation. As I have said, Barthes senses what is at stake. He knows that what we are calling strong evaluation undermines the explicit theoretical case to which he is committed. This is why he is at such pains to avoid the language of existential choice. Thus in the entry "Sed contra" (162) he describes the dialectical process of his inquiry in *Roland Barthes* in terms that are resistant to such language. He starts, he says, with some stereotype or banal opinion he detects within himself. Then he turns against it, not because it is any worse, less meaningful, than anything else: "it is because he does not want that stereotype (by some aesthetic or individualist reflex) that he looks for something else; habitually, being soon wearied, he halts at the mere contrary opinion, at paradox, at what mechanically denies the prejudice." As we see, the language is somewhat artfully insistent—note the clarifying parenthesis—on the weak nature of the evaluation: banal opinions are not "wanted" either because they are not aesthetically desirable or because of some individualist whim, he cannot quite say which. In any case, the preference for the antithesis is itself a mere "reflex," a "mechanical" denial of the stereotype. The dialectical movement of his thought is all systemic, in other words, at one level happening in the brain, at another in the text of clashing languages, which the disengaged subject apprehends merely as a vaguely tiresome process, interesting only as "a kind of intellectual 'sport.'" Or like a cook, making "sure that language does not thicken, that it doesn't *stick*." This is a "pure language tactic, which is deployed *in the air*, without any strategic horizon." Then at this point, something else happens in his prose. The logic so far is that stereotypes are to be pursued to their contraries purely as a mechanical "tactic." But he ends by asking: "what is to be done if the stereotype *goes left*?" Presumably this would require his thought to veer by reflex to the right. This should make no difference, however, if one writes with only aesthetic preference and no strategic horizon. But this is not how Barthes writes of it: "The risk is that since the stereotype shifts historically, politically, it must be followed wherever it goes." The question is, why, on his account so far, should there be any "risk"? In other words, why should his reflex response to such an eventuality *matter*?

Barthes is canny enough—he has been one step ahead of my sort of analysis all the way—to know that this sort of equivocation amounts to an *aporia*[16] in his text. And the best thing about Barthes is that, for all his insistent if stylish theoretical commitments, a side of him is genuinely open to the aporetic and its implications. In short, he is open at moments to letting himself and us see that something does matter. We see this more clearly in the entry "The natural," which is an "illusion" that he has "constantly denounced" in his earlier work as the "alibi paraded by a social majority" (130). Then all of a sudden he becomes, in his elaborately anti-autobiographical way, autobiographical:

> We might see the origin of such a critique in the minority situation
> of R.B. himself; he has always belonged to some minority, to some
> margin—of society, of language, of desire, of profession, and even of
> religion (it was not a matter of indifference to be a Protestant in a class
> of Catholic children); in no way a severe situation, but one which some-
> what marks the whole of social existence: who does not feel how *natural*
> it is, in France, to be Catholic, married, and properly accredited with
> the right degrees? The slightest deficiency introduced into this array of
> public conformities forms a kind of tenuous wrinkle in what might be
> called the social litter. (131)

This account is at once hedged around with the usual Barthesian disclaimers: it is third-personal, the experience of "R.B.," like the rest of the text, "as if spoken by a character in a novel" (unpaged). Novel or not, I am not the first reader to find that the accent here is decidedly autobiographical.[17] His critique of "the natural" speculatively originates in the experience of marginality, which he felt as a child and continues to feel is "not a matter of indifference" in Catholic bourgeois France. We sense that he continues to feel it in the rhetorical question "who does not feel how *natural* it is, in France . . . ?" All his adult life he has resisted this collective attribution of social norms to an illusory "nature" and denounced the arbitrariness of it. There is something more than aesthetic inclination and mere "preference" here, something more like moral feeling. The natural is not simply arbitrary; it institutionalizes prejudice. Resisting it by "transgressive avant-garde action" is not just a matter of transitory "mood," as he will later suggest, but of career-long commitment. Barthes cannot name it as such, but this work is animated by a sense of justice, a demand for equality of respect, which is the strongly valued good entailed in this entry and much of the text.

It is part of Taylor's argument that what he calls the "naturalistic bewitchment" of modernity prevents modern Westerners—unlike late Ming scholar-gentlemen—from identifying and naming the goods they live by. As we shall see in later chapters, the relevant strongly valued goods entailed in the autobiographical text have to be brought to light by something like a form of deconstructive analysis, teasing out the ethical import of aporetic moments. This sometimes involves reading against the grain, as in the present case of Barthes' "preferentialism." The key analytical question is the plausibility of claims that he can either relish a sense of social belonging or denounce it, depending on his inclination, as in the sentences on which he concludes "the natural": "But he seems to remain strangely at the intersection of these two rejections; he has complicities of transgression and individualist moods. This produces a philosophy of the anti-Nature which remains rational, and the *Sign* is an ideal object for such a philosophy: for it is possible to denounce and/or celebrate its arbitrariness; it is possible to enjoy the codes even while nostalgically imagining that someday they will be abolished: like an intermittent *outsider*, I can enter into or emerge from the burdensome sociality, depending on my mood—of insertion or of distance." The logic is, of course, more sinuous than I have suggested so far: "celebrating" the arbitrariness of the Sign is not quite the same as enjoying the codes, nor these the same as entering into the burdensome sociality. But the notion of slipping between "insertion" and "distance" depending on mood, of being an *intermittent* outsider, reads to me like a deft preferentialist covering of his tracks. In one sense, every word may be "true." It is quite plausible to think that he may swing back and forth in feeling in the manner described. But it is less plausible to believe that, beneath such fluctuations, there is no persistent identity, or pattern of moral feeling, organized around a career-long resistance to "the natural" and a lifelong sense of himself as an "outsider." Around such recurrent and strongly felt concerns, the narrated "R.B." reads like a self in moral space.

I am not the first to sense the resonance between the entry on "the natural" and the one called "A memory of childhood:"[18]

> When I was a child, we lived in a neighborhood called Marrac; this neighborhood was full of houses being built, and the children played in the building sites; huge holes had been dug in the loamy soil for the foundations of the houses, and one day when we had been playing in one of these, all the children climbed out except me—I couldn't make it. From the brink up above, they teased me: lost! alone! spied on! excluded! (to be excluded is not to be outside, it is to be *alone in the hole*, imprisoned under the open sky: *precluded*); then I saw my mother running up; she pulled me out of there and took me far away from the children—against them. (121–22)

Apart from the photographs, this is one of the very few entries in *Roland Barthes* that is autobiographical in the sense that there is not the usual diffraction of discourse through pronominal shifts or the nominally semi-fictional "R.B." Nor is there a preferentialist meta-discourse to camouflage the anguished helplessness evoked by the words "lost! alone! spied on! excluded!" For all the antinarrative form of the text as a whole, there is at very least a strong thread connecting this incident with Barthes' feeling of exclusion in Catholic bourgeois heterosexual France. We do not need to suggest any teleological connection to see that both incidents involve significantly similar oppositions: aloneness versus the group, exclusion as against belonging, difference against sameness. There is also a nascent realization of the oppressive power of conformity, of what he will characteristically call "the Doxa," the orthodox. Insofar as we can consider this incident a fragment of identity narrative, the child in the hole is most decidedly experiencing himself as an "outsider," an identity more or less confirmed by his mother as she rescues him and takes him far away from his mockers, significantly "against them."[19]

What *Roland Barthes* refuses as narrative, it gives as a kind of mosaic of fragments, an "image-repertoire," which projects identity via patterns of response and reflection—as well as disruptions to them.

The trapped child, protesting against the oppressive conformity of the group, resonates with the adult speaker meditating on many topics, including "the natural" and the "three arrogances" from which he suffers: "that of Science, that of the *Doxa*, that of the Militant." The *Doxa*, he explains, is "Public Opinion, the mind of the majority, petit bourgeois Consensus, the Voice of Nature, the Violence of Prejudice" (47). "Arrogance" is a term of thick ethical description, at once descriptive and evaluative, used by Barthes to articulate his response to all victorious discourses, which entail "the humiliation of others" (46). At the same time, such thick evaluative terms locate Barthes in moral space. Through his stance on arrogance and humiliated others he reveals who he takes himself to be. He is one who opposes militant discourse of any kind, even that of the political left, because it cannot help bullying somebody. It shares with science and all orthodoxies the arrogant need to have, or to be, the last word on everything—including on language itself. Here Barthes also defines himself through his distance from some of his own former chief interlocutors, Marx, Brecht, and Sartre, when he complains of leftist "politics qualifying itself as the fundamental science of the real" and becoming endowed "with a final power: that of checkmating language, reducing any utterance to its residue of reality." Barthes turns the tables by considering such politics purely as language, language that monotonously repeats itself as pure "Prattle," becoming an "exhausting cortège of motionless phrases" (53).

Barthes locates himself morally in relation to two sorts of power invested in language. He is against any deadening discourse that claims "final power" over others and in favor of the ecstatic power unleashed in "the thrill of meaning."[20] The latter is what he calls the "morality of the sign," which makes itself felt at the moment when "the (abhorred) illusion of the *self-evident* chips, cracks, the machine of languages starts up" and when "meaning, before collapsing into in-significance, shudders still: *there is meaning*, but this meaning does not permit itself to be 'caught'; it remains fluid, shuddering with a faint ebullition" (97–98). The sign is "moral" before it collapses into the reifications of orthodoxy, or is pitilessly recuperated by repetition into the "solid meaning" of militant discourse. This is a post-Romantic expressivist version of what it is good to be, which values the stripping away of films of familiar thought, the cracking open of encrusted limits to meaning, the breaking through to the "*freshness* of language" (89). At the same time, it is Romantic morality with a Lacanian inflection: the familiar limits constitute the imaginary, the ego-ideal from which *jouissance* and the thrill of meaning promise escape. There is a good deal, then, invested in the morality of the sign.

It is more than a matter of mere momentary inclination or preference that makes the thrill of meaning better than stagnant reiterations of the illusory fixities of orthodoxy. The prospect of losing creative power is associated with fear. In "The image-system of solitude" he tells how in the past he always "worked successively under the aegis of a great system (Marx, Sartre, Brecht, semiology, the Text)," but today works more independently. Then comes a confession:

> He says this . . . to account to himself for the feeling of insecurity which possesses him today and, still more perhaps, the vague torment of a *recession* toward the minor thing, the old thing he is when "left to himself."
> —So you make a declaration of humility; you still don't escape the image-system for all that, and the worst kind of one: the psychological image-system. It is true that in doing so, by a reversal you had not foreseen and which you would readily overlook, you attest to the accuracy of your diagnostic: indeed, you *retrogress.*—But in saying as much, I escape . . . etc. (the ladder continues). (102)

Here we have the full pronominal procession: "he" confesses to experiencing "torment" at the thought that he has "recessed" toward the "minor thing" he produced before he worked within the framework of great systems; "you" comments self-reflexively on this declaration that not only there is no escape from the imaginary in such acts of "humility," they manifest the very "retrogression" they diagnose; so it is left to "I" to point out that this very act of diagnosis amounts to the kind of transcendent insight that is incompatible with retrogression. The "ladder" of thought thus continues to move dialectically upwards. There is of course something in the movement unfolded here that suggests an infinite process—hence the force of the "etc."—while there is also a movement "inwards" from third-personal reflection to first-personal. Given Barthes' position on subjective interiority, one cannot put too much weight on this latter point. And yet there is a sense of thought moving forward, which makes the word "dialectic" appropriate.

If this is so, two things stand out. First, the passage manifests a concern about where he is in his life. He begins with a "feeling of insecurity" and a "vague torment" about how he presently measures up to the man he has been. Then he moves to the reassurance that he must be in some sense moving upward. It is clear that the discovery that he has retrogressed would matter to him significantly. As I have said, there is more at stake here than mere preference. There is something higher and lower to be and to become; there is "major" work and "minor." Hedged around, distanced by pronominal play as it may be, this is the language of strong evaluation. There is a sixty-year-old man here revealing his "constitutive concerns"—trying to locate himself in the space of values that really matter to him. In the interstices of his stylish preferentialist meta-discourse, we catch a glimpse of the self in moral space. Once again, the glimpse is aporetic.

The second thing that emerges from this aporetic passage is that Barthes thinks of his life as having a direction. The "I's" "escape" from retrogression is an act of encompassing insight that is a progressive movement in thought: he is relieved from "torment" by the reflection that he is in some sense moving forward. The moment is aporetic because the whole text is premised on the notion that it is a "circle of fragments" in which each is a "beginning" but none is an ending: "(but he doesn't like the ends: the risk of the rhetorical clausule is too great: the fear of not being able to resist the *last word*)." Beginnings, of course, are redolent with the morality of the sign, the freshness of language; endings give closure; they bully by insisting on being the last word. As he has said, "incoherence is preferable to a distorting order" (92–94). This is the deeper reason why he eschews autobiographical narrative: because it implies that the older narrating self has some explanatory advantage over the younger narrated self, an advantage that is illusory because always open to further "interpretation."

> This book is not a book of "confessions"; not that it is insincere, but because we have a different knowledge today than yesterday; such knowledge can be summarized as follows: What I write about myself is never *the last word*: the more "sincere" I am, the more interpretable I am, under the eye of other examples than those of the old authors, who believed that they were required to submit themselves to but one law: *authenticity*. Such examples are History, Ideology, the Unconscious. Open (and how could they be otherwise?) to these different futures, my texts are disjointed, no one of them caps the other; the latter is nothing but a *further* text, the last of the series, not the ultimate in meaning: *text upon text*, which never illuminates anything.

What right does my present have to speak of my past? Has my present some advantage over my past? What "grace" might have enlightened me? except that of passing time, or of a good cause, encountered on my way? (120–21)

Barthes consciously distances himself from the autobiographical tradition of Augustine and Rousseau by laying out a standard postmodernist objection: life narrative, however "authentic" to his experience the writing subject may try to be, is always open to explanatory analysis in terms of determinisms of history, language or systems of power of which he may be unaware. Barthes is not saying that such analysis is right or true: his point is rather that it tells another story, and who is to say which should have the final word?

This is where we might profitably invoke Taylor's "best account" principle again and ask why first-person narrative ought to be sidelined simply because it is possible to generate any number of alternative third-person explanations. The reason for posing this question is that, as Barthes' example itself shows, such explanations cannot meet the subject's need to try to understand her life as a first-person story. Barthes as theorist of the sign may ask about the "right" of his present to interrogate his past and assert the last word over it. But Barthes, the sixty-year-old man, still has a need to think about where and how his life is going, about where he stands in relation to his more youthful self. Such questions can only be answered by an autobiographical narrative, which, as Taylor says, is necessary to myself as a being who grows and becomes: "I can only know myself through the history of my maturations and regressions, overcomings and defeats. My self-understanding necessarily has temporal depth and incorporates narrative" (50). If this is so, the present only has "privilege" in life narrative as the vantage point that I cannot help occupying as I try to understand myself now in relation to what I was and how I came to be as I am. As I argue in a later chapter, from my own vantage point—though others might deny it—I cannot but believe that I have a fuller understanding of myself than I did, since my self-understanding now encompasses what I was. As Barthes points out, a retrogression understood as such implies a certain kind of transcendence of retrogression, which is why the "ladder continues"—as it must.

It *must* because, as Taylor argues, I can only understand my life as an unfolding narrative. Barthes characteristically denies this because his semiological view is of a "dispersed" subject, who is but "a patchwork of reactions" in which there is nothing "*primary*." "Everything" a person can be passes by in dizzying procession, because "you pass through all the fringes of the phantom, the specter." He cites Diderot to the effect that "Everything has happened in us because we are ourselves, always ourselves, and never one minute the same" (143–44). Be all this as it may, as I have argued there still remains something observable as "primary" in *Roland Barthes*. When he is not being deliberately paradoxical, Barthes will never side with "the natural," the "Doxa," or the "normal" as against the transgressions of the outsider. He will never value militant reification over the thrill of meaning and never prefer the "last word" over fresh beginnings, all of which amounts to saying that he will never transgress the "morality of the sign." In other words, there is observable persistence of moral feeling in this text along certain axes of meaning and significance. This is why, when he writes of the "phases" of his writing career, of working successively under the aegis of Gide, Sartre, Marx, Brecht, Saussure, Sollers, Kristeva, Derrida, Lacan, and finally of Nietzsche, it is implausible to see this procession—as he presents it—as mechanically "reactive," just as "one nail drives out another." Of course, Barthes does not want a narrative of "phases of development," as this will make him "*intelligible*," which would constitute a sort of "imaginary operation" in the Lacanian sense (145). At another point, however, he writes of his work as "evolving" from "an ethic of commitment to an ethic of the signifier" (106). This implies a supersessive development that resonates throughout the whole text. Repeatedly he looks back on past "phases"—such as the existentialist or the Marxist (as seen in his attitudes to the "authentic" and the "militant")—with a sense of having outgrown them. At these revealing moments, we see that Barthes understands his life, as we all do, as an unfolding narrative, not just the story of arbitrary mechanistic "reactions," but of meaningful intellectual actions too—the actions of thinking through the significance of his successive interlocutors and intellectual allegiances, observing their limitations and passing on to fresh ones.

At some level, the author of *Roland Barthes* is aware of the force of the sort of argument I am making here. He admits that the intentions of his mosaic text do not finally succeed; the meta-commentary is a mere rhetorical insistence on something he cannot ultimately achieve:

> I have the illusion to suppose that by breaking up my discourse I cease to discourse in terms of the imaginary about myself, attenuating the risk of transcendence; but since the fragment (haiku, maxim, *pensée*, journal entry) is *finally* a rhetorical genre and since rhetoric is that layer of language which best presents itself to interpretation, by supposing I disperse myself I merely return, quite docilely, to the bed of the imaginary. (95)

The fragmentary mosaic achieves only the illusion that the subject is *"merely an effect of language"* (79) "dispersed" among its multifarious textual iterations. What it fails to obliterate is narrated identity, self understood as unfolding in time. For Barthes, of course, the anthropocentric notions of "identity" and "self" I am invoking here are part of an "imaginary" picture, the subject made intelligible through repression of its linguistic constructedness. In fact, we are back where we began with something very much like Nietzsche's point when he says that the "truth" about the "world that concerns man" is not one he can live with; man must live with "self-deceptions," must repress what he can only momentarily "glimpse." Of course, we can also invoke Taylor and ask why the Nietzschean or Lacanian accounts of the human should be thought to trump the language of "self" and "identity" Barthes needs, like all of us, to make sense of his life. Why, in other words, should an account that makes "language" the ultimate framework of meaning be thought to be more "true" than one that involves an intuitive self-understanding in time that proves ineradicable from the account of Roland Barthes by Roland Barthes? Certainly, such a self-understanding involves notions of "transcendence," giving the present privilege over the past, but even a vigilant Barthes has to admit to the necessity of a "return" to such "imaginary" conceptions, which prove as ineluctable as our "return" to any "bed."

This admission represents an advance on the *ad hominem* argument I applied to Nietzsche when I pointed out that his own practice shows merely that he does not incorporate his metaphysical skepticism into his thinking and feeling about the human world—not that he cannot. Barthes is very close here to saying that he *cannot* "disperse" into language effects when he comes to write about himself; he cannot escape the imaginary. Which is tantamount to saying what Taylor argues, namely, that we cannot escape the need for thick anthropocentric languages when we come to making sense of our lives. Put in another way, the thin third person languages of post-Saussurean theory are inadequate for many first person life purposes. Here again, Barthes at times shows that he is aware of this limitation of theoretical language. When writing about "Theory blackmailed" he complains about avant-garde texts whose "obvious quality is of an intentional order: they are concerned to serve theory." Since they serve in this way, they demand approval from people such as Barthes:

> . . . love me, keep me, defend me, since I conform to the theory you call for; do I not do what Artaud, Cage, etc., have done?—But Artaud is not just "avant-garde"; he is a kind of writing *as well*; Cage has a certain charm *as well* . . . —But those are *precisely* the attributes which are not recognized by theory, which are sometimes even execrated by theory. At least make your taste and your ideas match, etc. (54)

This entry is revealing because it shows the necessity for Barthes to use thick descriptive terms in coming to grips with his experience of works of art. The "charm" of Cage is not only "not recognized by theory," it is sometimes even "execrated" by it. "Charm" is part of a language of spiritual discernment that allows Barthes to discriminate qualitative values; it is simultaneously descriptive and evaluative, the sort of term needed for the articulation of "taste" and critical judgment. The thin languages of avant-garde "ideas" are inadequate to recognize and discern such qualities in art—and such qualities in his experience of it.

Such moments are aporetic in that Barthes' own text is also the work of his "ideas," rather than one in which he applies thick description to his own life. Like the avant-garde texts he attacks above, his own is above all a construction of theoretical intention. As we see everywhere, this amounts to a determination not to speak about himself autobiographically, not to reveal himself by confessional narrative. At one point he says, "*I am He who does not speak about himself*," rather like the Brechtian actor who thinks "out his entire role in the third person" (168–69). Yet, as we have noted, aporetic entries can be seen to subvert his anti-autobiographical intention in several respects. Barthes' intention to inscribe "R.B." exclusively in the weak evaluative space of "preferentialism" cannot hold out moments in which he identifies himself as marginal and resistant throughout his career to the "natural" and the mindless orthodoxies in his society. Along this axis there is a clear pattern of moral feeling, sign of a self defined in terms of strong evaluation. In his resistance to the deadening "arrogance" of triumphant languages, whether those of orthodoxy, science, or militant politics, we find a consistent commitment to an expressivist morality of the sign. In this sense, "R.B." is a self in moral space. We also see that, despite a clear intention to eschew narrativity, Barthes is one who intuitively grasps his life as a narrative in time—as a history of his progressions and retrogressions. Finally, we see that Barthes cannot do without thick evaluative terms such as "arrogance" and "charm," terms that allow him to discern and to express what matters to him—terms, in other words, that define him in the nontheoretical languages of his constitutive concerns.

In these respects, *Roland Barthes* is helpful in defining some constitutive features of thinking and feeling about one's self and one's life— things that cannot be done away with in any meaningful self-account. For Wang Shih-min, such features are manifested openly and unproblematically, because such was the nature of a culture powerfully shaped by Confucian ethics and much else. Late modern or postmodern Western culture is diametrically different. The strongly valued goods that shape selves have to be rescued from centuries of "repression"—as Taylor terms it—by a process very much like deconstruction in which we discern the constitutive features of life writing as manifesting themselves through the aporias of theoretical intention. These aporias are signs of a failed "experiment"—to revert to Nietzsche's term—suggesting the impossibility of incorporating value antirealism into everyday life. More particularly, they suggest that neo-Nietzschean and post-Saussurean theoretical languages cannot meet the Taylorian "test" of doing away with the richer languages of value that autobiographers need in order to live—and then to write—their lives.

4. Nietzsche's *Ecce Homo:* Inescapable Frameworks of the Good

Roland Barthes shows the force of the claim that strongly valued goods and thick languages of the good are fundamental to being a self and therefore to life narrative. Such a claim is very far from being recognized, or even intelligible, in contemporary Anglo-American studies of life writing where the prevailing paradigm for the past thirty years has been the postmodern politics of difference, founded on post-Saussurean and neo-Nietzschean theories. As we see with *Roland Barthes*, these theories involve thin reductive accounts of value that obscure the mostly implicit conceptions of the good[21] even post-modernists live by and access when they write life narrative. Apart from Barthes, the "political turn" in literary studies in the 1970s and '80s drew on Jacques Derrida's deconstruction of Western metaphysics, Michel Foucault's genealogies of the discursive networks of power and control, and Jean François Lyotard's critique of the meta-narratives of modernity.[22] All of these stressed what they saw as the binaries of domination and exclusion deeply embedded in Western language and culture—in universal thinking, in most important institutions and forms of knowledge, even in narratives of liberation.[23] It is true that some of these thinkers turned explicitly to ethical themes in their later work,[24] and followers have presented them—in a sense correctly—as always concerned with ethics.[25] Yet one of the main legacies of their work in Anglo-American literary studies has been the deconstruction of ethical and aesthetic interests into issues of cultural, class and gender politics.[26] Late twentieth-century literary theory has managed to change the subject in such a fundamental way that, some notable exceptions aside,[27] talk of the good now comes from far out of left field.

This has been the result of explicit attack, for example on the role of ethics in literary studies, as we see in Fredric Jameson's book *The Political Unconscious* (1981).[28] Jameson attributes to ethics the same insidious hierarchies as Derrida sees in metaphysics:

> To move from Derrida to Nietzsche is to glimpse the possibility of a rather different interpretation of the binary opposition, according to which its positive and negative terms are ultimately assimilated by the mind as a distinction between good and evil. Not metaphysics but ethics is the informing ideology of the binary opposition; and we have forgotten the thrust of Nietzsche's thought and lost everything scandalous and virulent about it if we cannot understand how it is ethics itself which is the ideological vehicle and the legitimation of concrete structures of power and domination. (114)

> . . . the concept of good and evil is a positional one that coincides with categories of Otherness. Evil thus, as Nietzsche taught us, continues to characterize whatever is radically different from me, whatever by virtue

of precisely that difference seems to constitute a real and urgent threat to my existence. So from the earliest times, the stranger from another tribe, the "barbarian" who speaks in an incomprehensible language and follows "outlandish" customs, but also the woman, whose biological difference stimulates fantasies of castration and devoration, or in our own time, the avenger of accumulated resentments from some oppressed class or race, or else that alien being, Jew or Communist . . . these are some of the archetypal figures of the Other, about whom the essential point to be made is not so much that he is feared because he is evil; rather he is evil *because* he is Other, alien, different, strange, unclean, and unfamiliar. (115)

Nietzsche's analysis, which unmasks the concepts of ethics as the sedimented or fossilized trace of the concrete praxis of situations of domination, gives us a significant methodological precedent. He demonstrated, indeed, that what is really meant by "the good" is simply my own position as an unassailable power center, in terms of which the position of the Other, or of the weak, is repudiated and marginalized in practices which are then ultimately themselves formalized in the concept of evil. The Christian reversal of this situation, the revolt of the weak and the slaves against the strong, and the "production" of the secretly castrating ideals of charity, resignation and abnegation, are, according to the Nietzschean theory of *ressentiment*, no less locked into the initial power relationship than the aristocratic system of which they are the inversion. (117)

I have quoted at length to illustrate a couple of key points. For a start, ethics is presented as false consciousness, an ideological way of representing realities that are *actually* political, part of a system of domination in which "the good" is "*simply*" my own power-legitimating position, as opposed to that of marginalized Others, who figure as "evil." Ethics is thus deconstructed into a master-code of the politics of difference, becoming a mere symptom of processes of social oppression and exclusion enshrined in language and culture. In this sense, the ethical criticism of literary texts obscures their political unconscious, where the repressed but real work of social domination and marginalization is perpetuated, unless it can be drawn to consciousness and exposed for what it really is by political analysis. The possibility that "the good" could be anything other than false consciousness in relation to underlying political realities is not entertained. According to this account, ethics is a purely dispensable social formation, mere sediment of the primitive prehistory of human consciousness and ripe to be superseded by Marxist analysis.

What such deconstructions inevitably obscure is the sense in which, as Taylor says, the analyst's own position is "powered by a vision of the good" (100). In this case, the concern with class oppression, domination, and marginalization draws on the "hypergood" underlying most postmodern theory, which is that of universal and equal respect. As we shall see in the following chapter, thinking that is moved by a hypergood tends to be hostile to rival visions of the good, especially to goods such as those recognized by humanist literary studies that are internal to established practices like literary criticism. Critiques driven by modern and postmodern hypergoods characteristically fail to recognize that their attacks on one vision of the good are in the service of another.

Another consistent feature of Jameson's account is its appeal to the example and authority of Nietzsche. Nietzsche is only once directly quoted, and only one direct reference is made to a work of his. For Jameson, the lesson and meaning of Nietzsche's work are presumably settled and obvious. The source he quotes is *The Genealogy of Morals*, and the early pages in particular, in which Nietzsche gives a historicizing account of morality that bears some resemblance to Jameson's. As we have seen already, there are grounds for doubting whether Nietzsche as a whole is so skeptical and reductive toward ethics as Jameson suggests. In fact, Nietzsche scholarship in the past ten years has questioned whether it is right to see Nietzsche simply as what Peter Berkowitz (1995) calls the revered "founding father of postmodernism, a ground-breaking critic of the underlying moral and metaphysical assumptions of the Western tradition, a seminal figure in the elaboration of the politics of identity, difference and self-making" (ix). According to Berkowitz, such readings as Jameson's and Foucault's focus in a highly selective fashion on Nietzsche's perspectivism, immoralism, and nihilism and his genealogical attacks on religion, morality, and reason, but they altogether occlude the more "traditional" appeal to the ethical and rational values that actually underpin his celebrated attacks and without which they would be meaningless. Nietzsche's critique of Christian *"ressentiment"* can be seen to entail a clear notion of what it is good and not so good to be, but this is ever filtered out of the Nietzsche appropriated by such writers as Jameson, who give accounts that are "aspect blind,"[29] evidence of what Taylor calls the "cramped postures of suppression" of the good (107), which are characteristic of modern and postmodern consciousness.

In fact the title of Berkowitz's book, *Nietzsche: The Ethics of an Immoralist*, nicely underlines the new understanding of Nietzsche's position in relation to ethics and morality. In a collection of essays entitled *Nietzsche's Postmoralism: Essays on Nietzsche's Prelude to Philosophy's Future* (Schacht, 2001), Maudemarie Clark outlines Bernard Williams's debt to Nietzsche. She points out how Nietzsche's "immoralism" is parallel to Williams's important distinction, made in *Ethics and the Limits of Philosophy*, between "morality" and "ethics." Like Nietzsche, Williams is opposed to morality, understood as a system of moral thought centering on blame, obligation, and volition, in which the notion of responsibility goes all the way down, such that, as a moral agent, I am responsible not only for my actions but also for my character (105). For Williams, this system not only threatens to dominate human life in various harmful ways, it is also nihilistic because it devalues every motive that is not driven by voluntary obligation, which it pictures as mere natural inclination. In other words, his position is that the morality system is ethically reprehensible. To say this is to say that ethics is the whole domain of normative thinking about action, character, and feeling, while morality is a distinct sphere within that domain (103–4). This is a helpful distinction that has become available to philosophy since Williams's book, and it is one that I once aspired to use more or less consistently in the present book.[30] It enables us to see Nietzsche's attack on morality, like Williams's, as one that is not merely within the domain of ethics, but actually ethically driven. This is Berkowitz's position, as it is fundamentally mine: "[Nietzsche's] criticism of morality is . . . ethical."[31] If this is so, the historicist reading of Nietzsche runs into trouble: as Berkowitz says, Nietzsche's deconstructive genealogies are ultimately about comparing "the value of rival forms of life," in order "to reveal the character of human excellence" (27–28).

It is certainly true that in the early pages of Nietzsche's *Genealogy of Morals* we can find the sources of Jameson's neo-Nietzschean notion of ethics as having its origins in social difference. Nietzsche locates the roots of ethics in pre-Christian societies in which the aristocrats felt that they themselves were high-minded, powerful, noble, and therefore "good," as opposed to the plebeians, who were low-minded and common and therefore epitomized all that was "bad" (26). (Not "evil," *pace* Jameson.) But Nietzsche soon parts company from his deconstructive followers in realizing that it is impossible to historicize away all values. For him, it simply does not follow from such an historical account that "good" and "bad" are *nothing but* sedimented traces of situations of social dominance. As soon as he moves to compare resentful slave morality, with its submerged hatred and impotent vengefulness, to the ethos of the nobles, there is a clear preference for the latter. Needing a hostile external world, slave morality is fundamentally reactive: "The reverse is the case with the noble mode of valuation: it acts and grows spontaneously, it seeks its opposite only so as to affirm itself more gratefully and triumphantly—its negative concept 'low', 'common', 'bad' is only a subsequently-invented pale, contrasting image in relation to its positive basic concept—filled with life and passion through and through—'we noble ones, we good, beautiful, happy ones!'" (37). While it is true that the "noble" ethos can have its vicious and destructive side, the main thrust of Nietzsche's account is to show it as spiritually healthier, more in line with how a human being should live. It is clearly better to value things spontaneously, gratefully, and triumphantly than reactively and with a heart secretly simmering with vengeful hatred. At certain points, Nietzsche makes this preference quite explicit:

> One may be quite justified in continuing to fear the blond beast at the core of all noble races and in being on one's guard against it: but who would not a hundred times sooner fear where one can also admire than *not* fear but be permanently condemned to the repellent sight of the ill-constituted, dwarfed, atrophied, and poisoned? And is that not *our* fate? What today constitutes *our* antipathy to "man"?—for we *suffer* from man, beyond doubt.
>
> *Not* fear: rather that we no longer have anything left to fear in man; that the maggot "man" is swarming in the foreground; that the "tame man," the hopelessly mediocre and insipid man, has already learned to feel himself as the goal and zenith, as the meaning of history, as "higher man"—that he has indeed a certain right to feel thus, insofar as he feels himself elevated above the surfeit of ill-constituted, sickly, weary and exhausted people of which Europe is beginning to stink today, as something at least relatively well-constituted, at least still capable of living, at least affirming life. (43)

What dominates the *Genealogy* is not the unmasking of moral values as political structures of domination, but the revaluation of all values—not the devaluation, nor, as I have said before, the dis-valuation, but the *"revaluation."* Surrounded by a nineteenth-century Christian bourgeois populace that saw itself as the endpoint of epochs of human evolution, Nietzsche is entering a plea for a radically new way for such men to see themselves—as tame, hopelessly mediocre, and insipid. To be able to inspire admiration, awe, even fear, as the noble man can, is not merely preferable to this bourgeois spiritual atrophy, it is humanly higher. To be courageous, honest, "well-constituted," as opposed to "ill-constituted" and insatiably thirsting for revenge like the man of *ressentiment,* is clearly a strongly valued good. This is the kind of good a person lives by and which helps to shape all of his or her deliberations and choices from below. This notion of the good is part of the larger realm of the ethical as it was construed by the Greeks, and it is fundamental to the broader picture of ethics put forward by recent Anglo-American moral philosophers such as Taylor, Williams, and Martha Nussbaum.

From this perspective Jameson's rather limited understanding of Nietzsche's project in relation to ethics and morality emerges clearly. After quoting the early pages of the *Genealogy,* he says: "Nietzsche's whole vision of history, his historical master narrative, is organized around this proposition, which diagnoses *ethics in general* and the Judeo-Christian tradition in particular as a revenge of the slaves upon the masters and an ideological ruse whereby the former infect the latter with a slave mentality" (201, my italics). No question, Nietzsche is scathing about the Judeo-Christian tradition and this certainly does involve slaves infecting their masters with a slave mentality. As we have seen, however, the idea that this diagnosis involves *ethics in general* is deeply mistaken. And this really is an error that invalidates Jameson's whole understanding of Nietzschean ethics, unless Judeo-Christian morality is seen to occupy the whole ethical domain, which would be ironical, since this was more or less the state of affairs at the time Nietzsche was writing, even if we include Kantian ethics, as Nietzsche himself would, as a variant of the Judeo-Christian tradition. But it is precisely the notion that this ubiquitous morality of selflessness was the whole of morality that he was raising his lone voice against in such vigorous complaint. As he says in *Ecce Homo*: "The decisive symptom that shows how the priest (including those *crypto*-priests, the philosophers) has become master quite generally and not only within a certain religious community, and that the morality of decadence, the will to the end has become accepted as morality itself, is the fact that what is unegoistic is everywhere assigned absolute value while what is egoistic is met with hostility. Whoever is at odds with me about that is to my mind *infected*.—But all the world is at odds with me" (291).

Most decidedly Nietzsche is not equating Judeo-Christian morality with "morality itself." For him, "what is egoistic" is also part of morality, but an altogether more capacious understanding of morality, such as that possessed by the Greeks, whose work he knew and respected so highly. For them, ethics was the whole domain of normative thinking about action, feeling, and character that organizes itself around the broad inclusive question, *How should a human being live*? Let us again revert to Williams's terminology and call this larger understanding "ethics," of which Judeo-Christian and Kantian "morality" occupies a part. As we see repeatedly in this book, the (anti-Nietzschean) incapacity to distinguish between Christian morality and *ethics in general* is part of a wider tendency that still exists, despite the supposedly pervasive influence of Nietzsche himself, to think of morality—and it is often simply given the name "ethics"—as simply equivalent to the obligations we have *to others* in the sphere of decision and action. Almost ubiquitously, ethics is seen as the sphere of the question, *What is it right to do*? Whereas, as Williams and Taylor and others insist, ethics must also include the wider question, *What is it good to be*? Including this question restores a pre-Christian breadth to the field of the ethical that enables it to include what Nietzsche calls "the egoistic" impulses within it—and to see that there are also self-regarding goods such as care of the self, including the Nietzschean ethical imperative *to become what one is*. These possibilities mean that there is room for literary scholars to look again at the question of ethics and literature, and certainly to look beyond the flawed and reductive version of the ethical held by Jameson and others working within the master-narratives of the politics of difference.

⤷

As I have been arguing from the beginning of this chapter, Nietzsche's adherence to a version of "the good" is not merely an interesting fact about him but helps us to see what Taylor means when he talks about "inescapable frameworks" of the good.[32] This will be especially the case when we look at Nietzsche's autobiography, *Ecce Homo*, which illustrates as clearly as any life narrative the close and necessary relationship between identity and the good. Even the most famous "immoralist" takes only a few pages to start framing himself in moral space.

Nietzsche's arrestingly paradoxical subtitle, *How One Becomes What One Is*, resonates throughout the text of *Ecce Homo*. At first the focus is on "what one is"—that is, as he says, the focus is on the demanding but "indispensable" task of trying to say "*who I am*" (217). As Nietzsche keeps pointing out, this task is next to impossible because of the place and age in which he writes. Nineteenth-century bourgeois Germany is everywhere steeped in the ethos, moral framework, and language of Judeo-Christianity and has no language in which to understand someone who would openly "prefer to be even a satyr to being a saint" (217). It might be said that Nietzsche has courted misunderstanding by his very title—a reference to Pontius Pilate's words before handing Jesus over to the Jews to be crucified (John, 19:5): "Behold the man!" In fact, as Walter Kaufmann points out in his introduction to *Ecce Homo*, Nietzsche's strategy is to focus attention, by this very device, on what is decidedly *un*-Christian about himself. Behold *this* man, he is saying, not a Christ or any sort of traditional sage, but a new *sort* of man, quite unlike anyone who has so far been revered by mankind—in fact a *modern* man (204). On the other hand, part of the force of the title is that Nietzsche half-expects to be revered by posterity—quite presciently as it turns out. This is why he ends his first paragraph saying: "*Hear me! For I am such and such a person. Above all, do not mistake me for someone else*" (217). What he fears above all is that he will be held up precisely *as* a traditional sage. This is why he is at such pains to insist that he is not a "moralistic monster": "I am actually the very opposite of the type of man who so far has been revered as virtuous" (217).[33]

So far the focus is on what he is *not*, on the possibility of being mistaken for the traditional sort of man of virtue. Within a couple of pages, he gets launched on the quest of saying who he is. He begins by talking about his philosophy, its icy mountainousness, its "wanderings *in what is forbidden*." Suddenly, he cuts to the center:

> How much truth does a spirit *endure*, how much truth does it *dare*? More and more that became for me the real measure of value. Error (faith in the ideal) is not blindness, error is *cowardice*.
>
> Every attainment, every step forward in knowledge, *follows* from courage, from hardness against oneself, from cleanliness in relation to oneself.
>
> I do not refute ideals, I merely put on gloves before them. (218)

All at once the complex layers of sardonic buffoonery and mordant satire fall away as Nietzsche reveals the difficult struggles in which the philosopher realizes himself in pushing forward to the truth. In the process, he must eschew weakness. *Becoming what one is* means above all transcending the intellectual cowardice that would accept the known and already-defined world. It means having the daring and hardness of spirit to resist the ubiquitous "faith in the ideal." For Nietzsche, truth comes not just from clear thinking but from character and integrity—in short, from *authentic being*. Here we see clearly that the pathway to saying *who I am* leads Nietzsche straight to what he values, what he thinks most important, what he considers "the real measure of value": the quest for truth and true "knowledge." And these can only be attained by "courage," "hardness against oneself," disciplined "cleanliness." For Nietzsche, then, expressing his identity involves articulating his key beliefs and values; saying who he is involves saying what qualities of being he holds most important—in other words, saying *what it is good to be.*

Values may be, in an absolute sense, as he says in *The Gay Science*, projections, but in making sense of who he is and accounting for his life Nietzsche, like anybody else, has to think within a thick anthropocentric language of the good. The narrator and protagonist of *Ecce Homo* consistently presents himself in terms of what it is good, and not good, to be. The details of the life of Friedrich Nietzsche the private man as we might find them in a modern biography are subordinated to a discussion of the thinker, the author of the books. The life is a series of moments in which the values espoused in the books are in the process of formation and discovery in the life of the author. Between Nietzsche's preface and his first chapter, "Why I Am So Wise," comes a passage that stands alone for emphasis in a way that is meant to introduce the whole life narrative:

> On this perfect day, when everything is ripening and not only the grape
> turns brown, the eye of the sun just fell upon my life: I looked back,
> I looked forward, and never saw so many and such good things at once.
> It was not for nothing that I buried my forty-fourth year today; I had
> the *right* to bury it; whatever was life in it has been saved, is immortal.
> The first book of the *Revaluation of All Values*, the *Songs of Zarathustra*,
> the *Twilight of the Idols*, my attempt to philosophize with a hammer—all

presents of this year, indeed of its last quarter! *How could I fail to be grateful to my whole life?*—and so I tell my life to myself. (221)

This seems to be a particular day: the perfect sunny weather, the grape turning brown, do not seem to be mere metaphors. It is his forty-fourth birthday, the end of a year he has just "buried." In this word we have a clear hint that much in this year has been far from sunny, but at this moment all the pains and troubles seem negligible because of what they have given rise to. For when he reviews his whole life at this moment he can see that "life," with all its transitoriness and sufferings, has been transformed into his immortal books. Looked at from this perspective, his life is full of the greatest riches. Even the pains and sorrows have been "saved" as the "good things" for which he must be grateful. Having not killed him, they have made him stronger, being gathered up into the creative flourishing of the last quarter of the year. The sense that all is "good" is not merely a transitory mood of spontaneous joy. It is a highly deliberate philosophical choice about what to be, a courageous decision about how to respond to life. It is the choice of *amor fati*, love of one's fate—which is the yes-saying at the core of Nietzsche's ethics.

The positioning of this paragraph, as an epigraph to all that follows, makes it clear that the life he is about to tell to himself is going to be shaped by an ethics of affirmation. The wisdom referred to in the heading of the first chapter, "Why I am So Wise," is *la gaya scienza*, the joyful wisdom. But the joy, as ever, gets its meaning from a background of suffering. He tells of a long illness in which he refused to be looked after, taking himself in hand, making himself healthy again. The episode is the occasion of a spiritual discovery:

> For a typically healthy person . . . being sick can even become an energetic *stimulus* for life, for living *more*. This, in fact, is how that long period of sickness appears to me *now*: as it were, I discovered life anew, including myself; I tasted all good and even little things, as others cannot easily taste them—I turned my will to health, to *life*, into a philosophy.
>
> For it should be noted: it was during the years of my lowest vitality that I *ceased* to be a pessimist; the instinct of self-restoration *forbade* me a philosophy of poverty and discouragement.
>
> What is it, fundamentally, that allows us to recognize *who has turned out well*? That a well-turned-out person pleases our senses, that he is carved

from wood that is hard, delicate, and at the same time smells good. He has a taste only for what is good for him; his pleasure, his delight cease where the measure of what is good for him is transgressed. He guesses what remedies avail against what is harmful; he exploits bad accidents to his advantage; what does not kill him makes him stronger. Instinctively, he collects from everything he sees, hears, lives through, *his* sum: he is a principle of selection, he discards much. He is always in his own company, whether he associates with books, human beings, or landscapes: he honors by *choosing*, by *admitting*, by *trusting*. He reacts slowly to all kinds of stimuli, with that slowness which long caution and deliberate pride have bred in him: he examines the stimulus that approaches him, he is far from meeting it halfway. He believes neither in "misfortune" nor in "guilt": he comes to terms with himself, with others; he knows how to *forget*—he is strong enough; hence everything *must* turn out for his best.

Well then, I am the *opposite* of a decadent, for I have just described *myself*. (224–25)

Here again we have a biographical moment recollected not in detail but in terms of its spiritual contours. The key is the discovery in himself of a basic "instinct" for health that allows him to mobilize his will in the service of "life." By "life" here he does not mean mere physical existence, but living *more*, more intensely, gratefully, and joyfully. But that sort of life is not achieved without deliberation, choice, or, if you are a Nietzsche, without a philosophy—in this case, a philosophy of affirmation. The choice of life is a choice, not merely against the insipid idealist, but against the Romantic pessimist in himself. Against the glamour of suicidal despair he counterposes the more classical ideal of the "well-turned-out-person," achieved by a neo-Hellenic ethic of *care for self* of the kind that appealed to the later Foucault.[34] Kaufmann is certainly right in pointing to the Aristotelian roots of Nietzsche's thought here. Behind the passage above lies Aristotle's portrait of the "great-souled man" in *The Nicomachean Ethics*, who, for example, "does not nurse resentment."[35] Certainly there is a form of virtue ethics in Nietzsche's work that becomes quite evident here: for Nietzsche the "well-turned-out-person" is admirable in character. He exemplifies *what it is good to be*. But in place of the Aristotelian *via media* we have the virtue of not bearing a grudge turned into a fundamental principle, that of *amor fati*—deliberately choosing all that makes for abundant life, having the strength to forget all that negates it. With such an orientation in moral space, the well-turned-out person comes to terms with life. For him, all *must* turn out for the best.

How does Nietzsche know all this? Where does this joyful wisdom come from? As he says, from himself, from his own life. The prototype of the Nietzschean well-turned-out person is himself. Nietzsche the protagonist of *Ecce Homo* is an *exemplum* of what it is good to be. The element of exemplification is after all what explains the grammatical form of Nietzsche's subtitle—not How I Became What I Am but *How One Becomes What One Is*. Throughout *Ecce Homo*, the protagonist, the narrated "I," keeps something of the exemplary force of the generalized "one." This makes itself felt as a discernible gap between the exemplary character of the protagonist of *Ecce Homo* and the narrator's often human, all-too-human, negotiations with the world. As we see in the passage above, the protagonist is claimed to be a triumph of *amor fati*, but that hardly seems to be borne out in certain of the narrating "I's" attacks on his German contemporaries and his former friend and mentor, Richard Wagner. There is certainly room to ask whether there really is no remaining *ressentiment* toward Wagner, toward Germans, or toward his former idealist self. Clearly there may be a gap between the ethics in the text and the realized ethics *of* the text, to which we will return when we take up the ethico-aesthetic questions raised by life narrative. For the moment it suffices to note that the protagonist of Nietzsche's autobiography may be partly an ideal self, a Yeatsian anti-self, as Alexander Nehamas has more or less argued in distinguishing between the private Nietzsche and "Nietzsche," the hero of his books.[36]

These distinctions are important to an understanding of how, according to Nietzsche, one becomes what one is—which is reflected in the story of how the protagonist of *Ecce Homo* became what he was. The passage about his illness discussed above is a forerunner to a section that describes the turning point in his life. That moment is the writing of *Human, All-Too-Human*, which is "the monument of a crisis. It is subtitled 'A Book for *Free* Spirits': almost every sentence marks some victory—here I liberated myself from what in my nature did not belong to me. Idealism, for example; the title means: 'where *you* see ideal things, *I* see what is—human, alas, all-too-human!'—I know man better" (283). A very important distinction is made here between what was in his "nature" and what "belonged" to him. The former is his inherited self, which has been socialized into Judeo-Christian "idealism"; the latter is the self he chooses to be, in which he liberates himself from "idealism" and all that is human, all-too-human within himself. This appears to be a process then of self-overcoming and at the same time of self-fashioning, of constructing one's own character.

But there are deeper implications in the process too. He describes suddenly "waking up" in the midst of the Bayreuth Festival, with a sense of "profound alienation from everything that surrounded [him] there." He recognized almost nothing—not Wagner, nor the wonderful intimate past they shared. Wagner had become "Wagnerian," draped with German "virtues," idealized (284). Nietzsche came to a moment of profound realization:

> What reached a decision in me at that time was not a break with Wagner: I noted a total aberration of my instincts of which particular blunders, whether Wagner or the professorship at Basel, were mere symptoms. I was overcome by *impatience* with myself; I saw that it was high time for me to recall and reflect on myself. All at once it became clear to me in a terrifying way how much time I had already wasted—how useless and arbitrary my whole existence as a philologist appeared in relation to my task. I felt ashamed of this *false* modesty.
> Ten years lay behind me in which the nourishment of my spirit had really come to a stop: I had not learned anything new that was useful; I had forgotten an absurd amount for the sake of dusty scholarly gewgaws. Crawling scrupulously with bad eyes through ancient metrists— that's what I had come to:—It stirred my compassion to see myself utterly emaciated, utterly starved: my knowledge simply failed to include *realities*, and my "idealities" were not worth a damn. (286)

This is clearly not yet *amor fati* for the protagonist: the shame, the impatience with all that is false in himself, makes him see his past as wasted time rather than as necessary preparation for the task of his life. But it is a necessary step in becoming who he is, all the same, prompting him to get a glimpse of what did not really "belong" to him.

To understand what did or should "belong" to him, he needed to get in touch with deeper impulses in himself. He needed to follow "instinct" before he could experience *amor fati*.

> It was then that my instinct made its inexorable decision against any longer yielding, going along, and confounding myself. Any kind of life,

the most unfavorable conditions, sickness, poverty—anything seemed preferable to that unseemly "selflessness" into which I had got myself originally in ignorance and *youth* and in which I had got stuck later on from inertia and so-called "sense of duty."

. . . Sickness *detached me slowly*: it spared me any break, any violent and offensive step. Thus I did not lose any good will and actually gained not a little. My sickness also gave me the right to change all my habits completely; it permitted, it *commanded* me to forget; it bestowed on me the necessity of lying still, of leisure, of waiting and being patient.—But that means, of thinking.—My eyes alone put an end to all bookwormishness—in brief, philology: I was delivered from the "book"; for years I did not read a thing—the greatest benefit I ever conferred on myself.—That nethermost self which had, as it were, been buried and grown silent under the continual pressure of having to listen to other selves (and that is after all what reading means) awakened slowly, shyly, dubiously—but eventually it spoke again. Never have I felt happier with myself than in the sickest and most painful periods of my life: one only need look at *The Dawn* or perhaps *The Wanderer and His Shadow* to comprehend what this "return to myself" meant—a supreme kind of recovery.—The other kind merely followed from this. (287–88)

This important passage shows how the "instinct" at the heart of "that nethermost self" can be covered over by habitual "selflessness," by what he later calls "the morality that would unself man" (292). Here the metaphor is not of psychic castration, however, but of a deep sleep, or even entombment. The nethermost instinctive self can be put to sleep, buried, by all that is other-regarding—the sense of duty, obligation, work, reading, listening to other selves. Here Nietzsche was inventing something germane to Freud's whole enterprise, namely, a language to describe what we might call the repression of the instinctive id by the moralistic superego. But that now-formulaic language does not capture what was then a discovery almost as tentative as the "shy," "dubious" awakening of the nethermost self. Some of us in the age of the so-called "me-generation"[37] may need to take a leap of historical imagination to grasp why *becoming what he is* had to have such a shy and dubious beginning for Nietzsche. Once again, he would have us picture a world dominated by a conventional Christian bourgeois morality and its Kantian philosophical counterpart:—crowded out, overpowered, deafened, by the ubiquitous morality of the not-self, the instinctive self comes to consciousness with extreme lack of certainty in its right to be.

Part of the force of Nietzschean *amor fati* is the affirmation of the right to be of this nethermost self, taking its desires seriously, giving *ethical* weight to its sense of what conduces to self-fulfillment and self-realization. Part of Bernard Williams's case against the system of morality in which the notion of responsibility goes all the way down is precisely that it devalues every human impulse other than voluntary obligation, thus foreclosing on the possibility of any ethical significance being given to "the *I* of my desires."[38] The core of both *amor fati* and *becoming what one is* involves seeing "the *I* of my desires" as ethically important in that its leadings may indicate the direction of my ultimate spiritual health and well-being, indeed the path I am born to pursue. In Nietzsche's case, his creative flourishing, as described in *Ecce Homo*, comes with its sense of joyful fulfillment, which is partly justified because it realizes itself in the production of what Nietzsche knows to be works of philosophical genius. Part of the proof that it was ethically good for Nietzsche to follow the promptings of his nethermost self is that doing so produced *such good books*.

One of the most important chapter-headings in *Ecce Homo* is "Why I Write Such Good Books," a heading under which most of *Ecce Homo* falls. There is an intimate connection between this long chapter and "Why I Am So Wise." In fact the spirit of joyful wisdom in these books is the most telling sign that they are so good.

> The *Dawn* is a Yes-saying book, deep but bright and gracious. The same is true also and in the highest degree of the *gaya scienza*: in almost every sentence profundity and high spirits go tenderly hand in hand. Some verses that express my gratitude for the most wonderful month of January I ever experienced—this whole book was its present—reveals sufficiently from what depths this "science" emerged to gaiety. (293)

La gaya scienza has such "high spirits" because it emanates from the "depths" of his instinctive self. In this sense, like the *Dawn* it is a yes-saying book, a work of *amor fati*. The profundity of the thinking in these books and their gaiety go "hand in hand." They are very good books in a sense that is at once ethical and aesthetic—they realize in themselves the spirit of affirmation they were written to proclaim.

Being "bright and gracious" is both the moral message of the *Dawn* and its artistic achievement.

For Nietzsche, "yes-saying" makes a book good in a sense we can call "ethico-aesthetic": its aesthetic value lies at least in part in its realized ethical attitude, spirit, or stance before experience. For him, the spirit of *amor fati* is a kind of evaluative touchstone. What would follow from this is that *ressentiment* in a book is likely to constitute an ethico-aesthetic flaw. Walter Kaufmann shows that he thinks like this in his introduction when he defends the portrait of Wagner in *Ecce Homo* from the charge that is full of *ressentiment*: "On the contrary, the portrait is imbued with gratitude and love—with *amor fati*, love of fate. *There is no 'if only' in this autobiography, and there are no excuses*" (206). In fact, as I am going to argue in chapter 4, most of us are inclined to read and value, or disvalue, autobiographies partly in these "ethicist" terms. The great success of books like *Angela's Ashes* by Frank McCourt can be accounted for partly in this way—the "yes-saying" spirit in which the horrors of direst poverty are recollected, together with the virtual absence of "if onlys" and *ressentiment* toward those who, like the father, contributed to their impoverishment.

It follows from Taylor's work that we value such qualities in books, as in life, because we are oriented in certain ways in moral space. We inevitably refer experience, both in life and literature, to certain evaluative frameworks of the good. Even the great "immoralist" does so, who is held to license the overthrow of all ethical values in the name of history and politics. Granted, Nietzsche does so in a revolutionary way, in a program he calls "the revaluation of all values." As we have seen, however, revaluation is most decidedly not *dis-valuation* in a spirit of genealogical deconstruction of all values into binary structures of social difference. To cite Nietzsche as the authority for such a relativistic program is to misunderstand in a profound way what he was all about. As we shall see in the next chapter, Nietzschean ethics is an important part of what Taylor calls the ethics of authenticity. In this sense, *becoming what one is* can be seen as part of a Romantic-expressive ethic that begins in the late eighteenth century and becomes dominant in the twentieth. Nietzsche's "yes-saying" also illustrates another theme of the present book, namely, the close link between ethical and aesthetic values for those of us who have not been too heavily socialized into evaluative relativism by the postmodern politics of difference.

For such people, a "good book" will be one that answers to a serious interest in ethical questions—and especially in the question, *what is it good to be?* This is another implication of Taylor's thesis that all of us make sense of ourselves and our lives in relation to inescapable frameworks of the good.

CHAPTER TWO

The Full Range of Goods,
Judeo-Christian and Romantic

We have seen that *Roland Barthes* sketches the outline of a story of development, suggesting that, despite his resistance to the notion, Barthes cannot help seeing his life as an unfolding narrative. The narrative is one of intellectual "phases," as one group of interlocutors gives way to another. In fact, from the critical attitudes expressed in *Roland Barthes* toward authenticity and political militancy, we can infer that later intellectual affiliations do not merely succeed earlier ones but supersede them. His metaphor of one nail driving out another implies something like this. It also implies a clash of goods—or moral ideals—in which one kind gains ascendancy over others. In this respect too, *Roland Barthes* is a little like many classic autobiographies that dramatize the struggle between rival goods. Among them, as discussed earlier, is *Ecce Homo* in which Nietzsche strives to realize the life-affirming good of *amor fati* within a psyche deeply informed by what he sees as the life-denying ideals of Protestant Christianity.

As we see in the chapters that follow, tracing this struggle in moral space means seeing autobiographies in the thick evaluative languages of the writers' constitutive concerns, the languages of self-understanding in which they attempt to make best sense of their lives. At the level of analysis and interpretation, we too can make illuminating sense of their lives by reading for the key strongly valued goods and the tensions between them. In fact, following the often intricate—and partly unconscious—interplay, tension, and active battle between the various goods that autobiographers are moved by is very much the substance of the readings that follow in this chapter and the next. Even the texts that have had most scholarly attention, such as St Augustine's *Confessions* and William Wordsworth's *Prelude*, have something new to reveal when read in this way. At the same time, there is an added strategic value in approaching these founding texts yet once again, since they prefigure and summarize so much in the clashes between rival goods throughout the Western autobiographical tradition. In their different ways, Nietzsche's *Ecce Homo* and Edmund Gosse's *Father and Son*, for example, display the continuing power of Protestant moralities heavily inflected by Augustine's hand in the shaping of a Judeo-Christian hypergood. His struggles to transcend certain goods of everyday life in the Greco-Roman world curiously prefigure their struggles to revalidate them and to give them ethical force.

Taylor's *Sources of the Self* gives an intricate genealogy of the many strongly valued goods by which modern Westerners are likely to be moved—goods such as the belief in rational mastery, expressive fulfillment, the importance of family life, or protecting the environment. There will always be the possibility of tension between these goods, such that individuals find a need to rank those they live by, giving one or two priority over others. Sometimes one of these higher-order goods, such as the individual's relationship with God, or devotion to justice and equality, will command undivided allegiance. This good may assume such importance that, beside it, the goods of everyday life pale into insignificance and may even be sacrificed in its name. Such a good is what Taylor calls a "hypergood." There will be a clear qualitative discontinuity between this and any other goods the individual may continue to be moved by. Orientation to the hypergood will be the core of the person's identity: being rightly placed in relation to it will often give her a sense of wholeness, or profound self-worth, whereas being turned away from it may involve a devastating sense of unworthiness or loss of meaning (62–63).

By their nature, hypergoods tend to be sources of conflict. Taking them seriously, following their demands, may require devaluing other goods. Kantian morality involves one such hypergood. The categorical imperative demands that I put universalizable moral obligations before my happiness or any merely "prudential" considerations—which means many other "ordinary" goods such as the welfare of my family, my health, reputation or career.[1] For those that recognize them, hypergoods tend to take the moral high ground with their strenuous demands for consistency, seriousness, purity, rationality, impartiality, or altruism. In their shadow, individuals often need to struggle to believe that other goods really are such. In fact the conflictual nature of hypergoods is in part inherent in the way they have tended to arise historically, by superseding earlier higher-order goods. Thus Platonic rational self-mastery displaced the Homeric honor ethic; following Christ superseded pharisaic adherence to the Law; and Enlightenment principles of universal and equal respect replaced traditional values inherent in hierarchical views of society. Of course the historical reality is always much more complex than this. As Taylor says in *Sources of the Self*: "The older condemned goods remain; they resist; some seem ineradicable from the human heart. So that the struggle and tension continues" (65).

1. Narratives of Supersession: Augustine's *Confessions*

The struggle and tension that hypergoods give rise to present individuals with a choice. At one extreme they can try to affirm many goods, perhaps in the manner of Aristotle, who saw integral human flourishing in the balanced fulfillment of a range of human goods. Or at the other extreme they can yield to the hypergood's demands in a thoroughgoing way, following it to the ends that consistency requires. Those attracted to the first option often see the hypergood as demanding self-repression, or the oppression of others. Their life narratives center on the struggle to overthrow this jealous all-demanding good, sometimes in defense of the older goods that seem ineradicable from the human heart. The autobiographies of Nietzsche and Edmund Gosse take this form. At the other extreme are the conversion narratives, of which St Augustine's *Confessions* is paradigmatic. The vivid drama of his narrative is structured around his drawn-out surrender to the love of a supreme hypergood, the God of Abraham and St Paul—and the supersession of older loves that must be sacrificed in his name.

One of these was Augustine's love of wisdom, the true meaning of "philosophy," as he reminds us. As a young man he reads Aristotle and is inflamed by Cicero's *Hortensius* in its exhortation to study philosophy. But the older narrator is quick to point out the limitations of such study. He quotes the Holy Spirit's admonition in the words of St Paul: "Take care not to let anyone cheat you with his philosophizings, with empty fantasies drawn from human tradition, from worldly principles; they were never Christ's teaching. In Christ the whole plenitude

of Deity is embodied and dwells in him" (Col. 2:8–9). For various reasons, Augustine finds an abiding spiritual affinity with Paul's characteristic view of the "world" and "human tradition." Without redemp-
tion by the one thing needful, these are at best sources of vain delusion
and at worst of sin and error. For Paul, what is not "Christ's teaching" is against it. To say in this context that Christ embodies the whole
plenitude of Deity means among other things that he is the source of
all true wisdom and that nothing is wise and true that does not come
explicitly from him. This is far from the only possible understanding of
pre-Christian philosophy, as we see in the later medieval incorporation
of Aristotle into the broader synthesis of St Thomas Aquinas. By contrast, the Pauline emphasis defines the Christian faith as an extreme
hypergood that will have no strange goods before it—or incorporated
into it. And in a fateful meeting of minds and hearts, Augustine, with
his powerful philosophical intelligence, helped to inscribe the nar-
rower Pauline view within Western understanding and in a way that
has shaped both Catholic and Protestant traditions.

One of the worldly loves that causes Augustine most pain in recollecting it is the friendship he describes in book 4. He and his friend
had grown up together and were utterly devoted to each other; he
describes his friend in Horatian terms as "the half of his soul" (78).
So deep was their attachment that when the friend dies, Augustine
becomes tired of living. His life seems to lose its meaning. To say that
at this early stage of his life the friendship was important and valuable to him would be a great understatement. It was most certainly a
strongly valued good in terms that Aristotle articulates in book 8 of
the *Nicomachean Ethics*: "[S]uch love has somewhat the character of
a virtue, or at any rate involves virtue. Besides, it is one of the things
which life can least afford to be without. No one would choose a friend-
less existence on condition of having all the other good things in the
world." He concludes: "Friendship then, being a necessity of human
nature, is a good thing and a precious" (VIII, 1, 227–28). Friendship
for Aristotle is most certainly a requirement of human flourishing, of
a good life lived among others. Looking back, Augustine cannot see
his friendship in that way, but only in terms of its effect on their beliefs: "Yet ours was not the friendship which should be between true
friends, either when we were boys or at this later time. For though
they cling together, no friends are true friends unless you, my God,
bind them fast to one another through that love which is sown in our

hearts by the Holy Ghost, who is given to us. Yet there was sweetness in our friendship, mellowed by the interests we shared. As a boy he had never held firmly or deeply to the true faith and I had drawn him away from it to believe in the same superstitious, soul-destroying fallacies which brought my mother to tears over me. Now, as a man, he was my companion in error and I was utterly lost without him" (75). Augustine can no longer value this friendship as good, not because of any vicious or evil deeds that came of it, but because it was not founded on a shared faith. It could not have been good, because their false beliefs impeded their souls from turning to God.[2] The only love or friendship that can be good is infused by God's grace into the soul. Natural virtue of Aristotle's kind is no virtue at all: "The good things which you love are all from God, but they are good and sweet only as long as they are used to do his will" (82).

Such is Augustine's God, whose will is the supreme hypergood in relation to which other goods either derive their value or cease to be goods at all. The central drama of *The Confessions* is the process by which Augustine yields to that all-encompassing Love who commands the love of his whole heart, his whole mind, and whole soul. The many other good things he loved—his son, friends, profession, learning, literature, the theater—had to be "used to do his will" and, if they could not, had to be "torn" from his heart. There are few more affecting things in *The Confessions* than his separation from the woman with whom he lived, the mother of Adeodatus, "a blow which crushed [his] heart to bleeding, because [he] loved her dearly." The narrating self confesses how he takes another mistress straight away, he is such a "slave of lust," but the recollection of his love for his first mistress cannot be obliterated by his need to denigrate it in those terms. "Furthermore the wound that I had received when my first mistress was wrenched away showed no signs of healing. At first the pain was sharp and searing, but then the wound began to fester, and though the pain was duller there was all the less hope of a cure" (131). This was a love harder to give up than the "lust" that was cooled by his new mistress. Like the rich young man, he had possessed a rich earthly good that was almost impossible to "wrench" from his heart when the command came to sell all he had and follow the Lord. Even here, the recollected pain of loss is over-layered, as it had to be for the older narrating self, by imagery of a disease from which he can only be washed "clean" by the healing hand of divine grace (131). The psychodrama played out within the Bishop of Hippo as he confesses his youthful "lust" hints at the way in which older superseded goods may be not quite eradicable from the heart.[3]

Nor perhaps, as his dealings with neo-Platonism suggest, can they be uprooted entirely from the mind. As he recollects the history of his reading and thinking, Augustine recalls the "pleasure" he took in the "so-called liberal arts," unable to see "the real source of such true and certain facts as they contained. I had my back to the light and my face was turned towards the things which it illumined, so that my eyes, by which I saw the things which stood in the light, were themselves in darkness" (88). This passage shows the persistent grip on the narrator's imagination of Plato's famous allegory of the Cave in which the Sun is an image of the Form of Goodness. Once perceived, this Sun enables the cave-dweller to see "that, for all things, this [Form of Goodness] is the cause of whatever is right and good; in the visible world it gives birth to light and to the lord of light, while it is itself sovereign in the intelligible world and the parent of intelligence and truth. Without having had a vision of this Form no one can act with wisdom, either in his own life or in matters of state" (226). Like the Judeo-Christian God, the Platonic hypergood, the Form of Goodness, is conceived to be the source of all other goods. Having viewed the Form, the soul sees all things with the light of wisdom and sees them as they truly are.

It was Platonism, mediated to him via Plotinus, which enabled Augustine to see clearly for the first time the error of the Manichean teaching that the world is half made up of evil, waiting to invade the good. As he later tells it, reading Plotinus enabled him to understand the idea of an all-good God: "For you evil does not exist" (148). Neo-Platonism was proto-Christian for Augustine, which means that, instead of the Augustinian God simply superseding the Platonic Good (as we might expect), he partly incorporates it. In fact The Confessions performs the historic task of Platonizing Judaism by linking the goodness of all things seen by the light of the Form to God's action in Genesis of creating all things and seeing that they were "very good." At the same time, he Platonizes Christianity when he connects the light-source of all wisdom and goodness with the Johannine Word of God, the Light who came into the world. In reading the Platonists, he discovered that the "sense was the same" as the beginning of the Gospel of St John: "In him there was life, and that life was the light of men. And the light shines in darkness, a darkness which was not able to master it" (John 1:1–14).

In some sense, then, the Platonic Form of the Good continued to shape Augustine's thoughts, also informing those later manifestations of Christianity we call "Augustinian" with the imprint of neo-Platonism. At the same time, being from the "world," neo-Platonic thought also had to belong as much to "human tradition" as Aristotle's.

The next step in Augustine's conversion, after renouncing Manicheism, is his discovery within Christianity of goods with no counterpart in the neo-Platonic books that had carried him so far. These included, above all, the incarnate Good, the Word made flesh, who came into the world. They included the notion of love, not as a natural disposition of the soul, but as supernatural grace infused into the soul. Wisdom too is seen as a gift of God rather than something of one's achievement in which one can take personal pride. God makes use not of the wise and the strong but of those the world accounts foolish and weak. The accent, of course, is Paul's, Augustine's primary interlocutor.

The Confessions is a patchwork of Pauline quotations. (The synoptic gospels come fourth in terms of numbers of citations, behind the Psalmist and St John.)[4] From Paul, Augustine derived the overwhelming importance of the virtue of humility, the good of accounting oneself nothing before God, and the ever-present danger of pride, through which the devil gains power over the soul. He is able to do this because the soul turned toward God has two wills, one directed to obeying God's will and a perverse self-will, enchained still to the old goods, now re-described in Pauline terms as the world, the flesh, and the devil. This is a notion that made perfect sense of Augustine's moral experience: "From my own experience I now understood what I had read—that *the impulses of nature and the impulses of the spirit are at war with one another*" (164). The passage from Galatians may be seen as appealing at once to the vestigial Manichean in him, with its continuous "war" between good and evil, as well as to the vestigial Platonist, with its opposition between "nature" and "spirit." But the concepts are distinctively Pauline, "nature" being neither simply body nor passions, and "spirit" implying a whole theology of dependence and personal faith not at all present in the Platonic "soul."

Paul's dualistic language of inward struggle was able to articulate for Augustine the stasis he reached in his agony of indecision before conversion. What holds Augustine back from wholehearted conversion is his attachment precisely to those "lower instincts" Nietzsche strove to validate in *Ecce Homo* as the life-affirming impulses of his "nethermost self." For Augustine, these instincts survive in his heart as "unclean whispers," "sordid" and "shameful" remnants of past pleasures and loves—everyday goods of the pagan world that he will have to give up for eternity. Given the Pauline form of the battle going on within him, it is little wonder that the text upon which his eyes fall, when he follows the divine promptings of *Tolle lege*, should be so decisive. "Not in revelling and drunkenness, not in lust and wantonness, not in quarrels and rivalries. Rather, arm yourselves with the Lord Jesus Christ; spend no more thought on nature and nature's appetites" (Romans 13:13–14). Augustine's destiny is most decidedly to arm himself with the Lord Jesus Christ, to take up the sword not merely against sins of indulgence and enmity, but also against "nature" and "nature's appetites."

There is a revealing ambiguity in the Pauline admonition to put behind him all thought of "nature." While nature, unredeemed by grace, may overwhelm the soul with its "appetites," Augustine is also committed to the view that God is the Author of that nature, which may be "desecrated" by perversions such as sodomy (64–65). For this reason, human nature must be in some sense originally good, but it is also fallen—according to Augustine's own distinctive teaching of original sin.[5] In his account of his own self-willed childhood, it is the latter understanding of nature that predominates, prompting him to ask: "Can this be the innocence of childhood? Far from it, O Lord!" But here the children in the synoptic gospels present something of a stumbling block. As Augustine reminds us, when the disciples of Jesus try to move the children out of his way, he admonishes them, saying that "the kingdom of heaven belongs to such as these" (Matthew 19:14). The gospels go further in fact and make children the type of blessedness:—"Unless you change and become like little children you cannot enter the Kingdom of Heaven" (Matthew 18:3). Augustine's gloss on such passages is that Jesus used children to symbolize humility "simply because they are small" and think of themselves as of little account (40). Reading these passages in the gospels in the light of William Blake and the Romantics, it is hard not to see more in the blessedness of little children than humility, though no doubt humility is an element in Romantic notions of childhood "innocence." However we read these gospel ideals, it is clear that Augustinian and Romantic understandings of human nature and innocence mark out widely divergent notions of the good, which turn out to explain much about why life narrative takes the form it does, even today. As we shall see, Augustinian and Romantic languages of the good are some of the key strands in those webs of interlocution that constitute the modern Western self.

2. Narratives of Supersession: Wordsworth's *Prelude*

At the heart of the Judeo-Christian hypergood is the command to love God with one's whole heart, soul, and mind and to love one's neighbor as oneself. In book 3, Augustine takes up this command to explain what is wrong with sins against nature such as sodomy, explaining that such proscriptions are therefore universal, unlike offences against human codes, which may be culture specific. He does not, however, pursue this issue of universality in the way it is in the gospel of Luke, where the lawyer tests Jesus by asking the question, "And who is my neighbor?" In reply to this, Jesus tells the parable of the Good Samaritan. This is, of course, one of the fundamental stories of the Western ethical tradition, a key source of thinking about what it is right to do, as well as delineating a high ideal of what it is good to be. It is a founding story of what has come to be termed the ethics of care, an ethics built around the personal I-Thou response of one individual to another in need. The Samaritan has "compassion" on the robbed and beaten man, which is one of the central meanings of Judeo-Christian "love." What he shows is what it means to love another as oneself, which implicitly includes the capacity to put himself imaginatively in the other man's place in an act of empathic identification. How else can the Samaritan know what com-passion—literally feeling with—entails in this case, so that he knows how to treat the man with such perfectly judged and complete neighborly love? As we see in life writing down to the present time, the story of the Samaritan defines an ideal that has informed the way in which self-other relations continue to be felt and experienced, even in individuals who do not remotely claim any allegiance to Judeo-Christianity. In other words, it delineates an ideal within that wide range of goods modern Westerners continue to live by, whether they recognize it or not.

There is another aspect to the story of the Samaritan that has equally deep and far-reaching implications, which we need to attend to in our account of the divergence of Judeo-Christian and Romantic ethical traditions. It is implicit that the "man" in the story is a Jew and the priest and the Levite who pass by on the other side are his co-religionists, fellow members of the tribe of Abraham and of Jacob. The Samaritan by contrast is not merely not a member of the tribe, but a member of a tribe toward whom the Jews had long been hostile. The parable comes from that side of the Judaic tradition that is critical of tribal particularism, of the ethos in which God is called upon to smite the enemies of his chosen people. When the lawyer is forced to admit that the Samaritan rather than the priest and Levite behaved like a neighbor, he is saying that even enemies are neighbors. Which is a hyperbolic way of saying that, insofar as I act like a good Samaritan, everybody is my neighbor. On this level the story is a foundational one for Christian universalism, indicating that, if I am a Christian, everybody, irrespective of race, color, or creed, merits my neighborly love and concern.

According to Taylor's detailed historical account, the Enlightenment may have jettisoned the theistic underpinnings of the Judeo-Christian ideal of neighborly love but it was indebted to its universalism in evolving a secular ethics of universal justice. There is no point in trying to summarize the complex multistranded filiations of the genealogy by which Taylor traces Platonic idealism through Augustinian interiority to the Cartesian *cogito* and thence to the Enlightenment. It is enough to say that, in various ways, Taylor teaches us to see the Enlightenment as partly continuous with the Augustinian synthesis of Platonic and Judaic sources.

Certainly this seems to make sense of the intellectual trajectory of a post-Enlightenment figure such as William Godwin (b. 1756). Formerly a nonconformist minister, he read Rousseau, Holbach, and Helvétius and eventually lost his religious faith. His *Enquiry Concerning Political Justice* (1793) articulates a principled view of justice "of the utmost universality" (14). The implications of this phrase become clear in his well-known exposition of his utilitarian thought using the example of Fénelon, Archbishop of Combray and author of what Godwin calls the "immortal *Telemachus*." He asks his reader to suppose that his palace was in flames, *Telemachus* not yet being written, and that only one person could be saved, either Fénelon or his valet. Who should be saved? The answer is: "that life ought to be preferred which will be most conducive to the general good" (70). This clearly means that Fénelon's life should be preferred, since *Telemachus* has benefited so many thousands of people and the valet presumably only a few. But what of the valet, how should he see this choice? Godwin's answer is clear:

> Suppose I had been myself the valet; I ought to have chosen to die, rather than Fénelon should have died. The life of Fénelon was really preferable to that of the valet. But understanding is the faculty that perceives the truth of this and similar propositions; and justice is the principle that regulates my conduct accordingly. It would have been just in the valet to have preferred the archbishop to himself. To have done otherwise would have been a breach of justice.
>
> Suppose the valet had been my brother, my father or my benefactor. This would not alter the truth of the proposition. The life of Fénelon would still be more valuable than that of the valet; and justice, pure, un-adulterated justice, would still have preferred that which was most valu-able. Justice would have taught me to save the life of Fénelon at the ex-pense of the other. What magic is there in the pronoun "my," that should justify us in overturning the decisions of impartial truth? My brother or my father may be a fool or a profligate, malicious, lying or dishonest. If they be, of what consequence is it that they are mine? (70–71)

As this example makes clear, Godwinian justice is universal in that its dictates include everybody, including those nearest and dearest to me. Its perfect impartiality demands that I override any preference based on attachments of family feeling, personal relations or obligation, or even my own will to live. Godwin knows that these everyday goods commonly inspire very many of my actions, but the requirements of pure, unadulterated justice demand that, when I act morally, I neutralize such feelings. When set in the scale against justice, these attachments and preferences should not weigh as goods at all. In short, justice has become a hypergood, valorizing the "truth" of impartial rationality over sources of habitual moral feeling.

Godwin's case is that universal justice should supersede particularist goods of any kind, individual or collective. Within the framework of the Godwinian hypergood, the first person pronoun "my," expressing anything that is particular to my own feeling, interest, preference, or perspective, can make no claim on my allegiance as a good.

Reading *The Prelude*, it is not hard to see what in Godwin's ethics brought William Wordsworth to a mental crisis when he tried to live by its implications in the wake of his disillusionment with the French

Revolution. In what is clearly the turning point of his life narrative, Wordsworth describes how he was at that time open to "speculative schemes/ That promised to abstract the hopes of Man/ Out of his feelings, to be fixed thenceforth/ For ever in a purer element . . . " (11:224–27). The "purer element" was mainly the impartial rationality of Godwinian justice in its attempt to "fix" ethics in principle. He talks of "Dragging all precepts, judgments, maxims, creeds,/ Like culprits to the bar," until he sinks in the end into moral confusion:

> I lost
> All feeling of conviction, and, in fine,
> Sick, wearied out with contrarieties,
> Yielded up moral questions in despair.
> This was the crisis of that strong disease,
> This the soul's last and lowest ebb; I drooped
> Deeming our blessed Reason of least use
> Where wanted most.
>
> (11:294–95; 302–9)

Wordsworth associates this breakdown with over-reliance on rationality alone, which in the end cannot "fix" principles to live by but rather undermines them with ceaseless soul-wearing "contrarieties." All this was possible because the "reasonings false" in his case were "drawn/ Out of a heart that had been turned aside/ From Nature's way" (11:289–91). Looking back, he sees this self-alienation from the promptings of his heart as what brought him to his soul's last and lowest ebb:

> I warred against myself,
> A Bigot to a New Idolatory;
> Like a cowled Monk who hath forsworn the world,
> Zealously labour'd to cut off my heart
> From all the sources of her former strength;
>
> (12:76–80)

Following Augustine's conversion narrative (which must be one of the chief models for *The Prelude*), it is not insignificant that Wordsworth captures the dynamics of the Godwinian hypergood in the imagery of a religious zeal that asks him to forswear "the world" and labor to cut off the heart from former sources of the self. In

Wordsworth's case, the inner war to supersede his older loves with pure Reason is ultimately lost because he senses that cutting off the heart completely from all such loves will destroy him.

Writing in retrospect, Wordsworth makes his spiritual diagnosis in full knowledge of the cure. Restoration consists in putting the heart back in living touch with all the sources of her former strength. The key vehicle is memory, whose action in knitting back together a fragmented self is deeply therapeutic.

> There are in our existence spots of time,
> That with distinct pre-eminence retain
> A renovating virtue, whence, depressed
> By false opinion and contentious thought,
> Or aught of heavier or more deadly weight,
> In trivial occupations, and the round
> Of ordinary intercourse, our minds
> Are nourished and invisibly repaired.
>
> (12:208–15)

This is Wordsworth's own distinctive vision of the good, that of self-continuity through time. It is the good of that "natural piety" by which the Child is Father to the Man. Though the spots of time may be scattered throughout one's life, those located in childhood often have greatest restorative virtue. Remembered childhood experiences more readily open up "the hiding-places of Man's power." Power is a key word for Wordsworth. It refers to the elusive energies of the creative self, lodged in memory but deep below his conscious control. Approach them too frontally and they close up. Tapping into them is what it means for the poet of memory to be fanned, as he is at the beginning of the poem, by the "gentle Breeze" of Nature. So moved, he can, in Nietzsche's phrase, become what he is. But unlike Nietzsche's case, this means re-affirming his earliest self, while at the same time casting aside the "burthen" of his false "unnatural self." This is the burthen of living too much outside the deepest sources of his strength and it clearly refers, among other things, to his Godwinian period of monastic rationalist zeal.

There is, in other words, a supersession at the heart of *The Prelude*, a turning away from false goods to the authentic good of natural piety. Self-continuity in time can only be achieved at the price of a certain discontinuity with the "unnatural self" the young adult had become. In this sense, there is a resemblance with Augustine's narrative, not least because his conversion also reconnects him with his earliest self.[6] Augustine can find the way to God partly because Christ's name and its inner meaning have been inscribed in his heart as he fed at his mother's breast:

> But, O Light of my heart, you know that at that time, although Paul's words were not known to me, the only thing that pleased me in Cicero's book was his advice not simply to admire one or another of the schools of philosophy, but to love wisdom itself, whatever it might be, and to search for it, pursue it, hold it, and embrace it firmly. These were the words which excited me and set me burning with fire, and the only check to this blaze of enthusiasm was that they made no mention of the name of Christ. For by your mercy, Lord, from the time when my mother fed me at the breast my infant heart had been suckled dutifully on his name, the name of your Son, my Saviour. Deep inside my heart his name remained, and nothing could entirely captivate me, however learned, however neatly expressed, however true it might be, unless his name were in it. (59)

For Augustine too there is a sense in which conversion to true self-understanding is the culmination of a process that began at Monica's breast. The words of Christ she uttered then imprinted themselves indelibly in his memory and deeply informed his consciousness in such a way that only Christ could ultimately satisfy him. This is one way of explaining why, in the words that open his narrative, his heart is restless until it rests in God. For Wordsworth too the infant at the breast is being profoundly shaped while he "Drinks in the feelings of his Mother's eye" (2:238). In his own case, the Nurse's voice blends unforgettably with that of the River Derwent:

> And, from his alder shades and rocky falls,
> And from his fords and shallows, sent a voice
> That flowed along my dreams? For this didst Thou,
> O Derwent! winding among grassy holms
> Where I was looking on, a Babe in arms,
> Make ceaseless music, that composed my thoughts
> To more than infant softness, giving me,
> Amid the fretful dwellings of mankind,

> A foretaste, a dim earnest, of the calm
> That Nature breathes among the hills and groves?
>
> (1:272–81)

The "immortal Spirit" within his infant self is informed by the river's music, an "earnest" of the calm he is later to find in hills and groves. Finding Nature's calm as an adult is partly recapturing this infant connectedness with a world in which such sounds "compose" his thoughts. In a way analogous to Augustine's, Wordsworth's heart too is restless until it rests in Nature's calm—a calm at once so ancient and so new.

It is implicit in both narratives that although these celebrations of self-continuity center on particular selves, they have implications for others too. The very beginning of Augustine's autobiography is about Man's "instinct" to praise God. His exact words are: "The thought of you stirs him so deeply that he cannot be content unless he praises you, because you made us for yourself and our hearts find no peace until they rest in you" (21). Augustine's talk of "Man" here might remind us of the way in which his remarkable discovery of an individual autobiographical voice emerges from a theological framework in which the soul is formed like all others: you made "us" for yourself and "our" hearts can find no rest. . . . The first person singular is ever shadowed by the plural, even when his autobiographical poetry flames up from his individual feeling: "But, O Light of my heart. . . ." Individual memory, such as his experience at Monica's breast, is meaningful only because he can read it—or indeed anything at all—by the indwelling Light in his heart. This Light is also at the same time the Life that holds him in being—or indeed anyone in being. The divine "you" with whom Augustine speaks so intimately is there for us all, a Form of the Good without which we contingent creatures are inconceivable. The particular soul in other words has a universal form. Even those of us not so fortunate as to have been suckled by the holy Monica have access to the divine Light dwelling at the center of our being. By this Light, the thought of God stirs us so deeply that we cannot be truly content unless we praise him.

For Wordsworth too the individual "I" also keeps breaking into the universal "we." Infant blessedness is the "Great birth-right of our being." But not everybody inherits her birth-right. The "infant Babe" is "blest" to have "in one dear Presence . . . A virtue which irradiates and exalts/ Objects through widest intercourse of sense" (2:239–41).

But he immediately reminds us that many a Babe is without such a benign presiding Presence to model the benevolence of the world. "No outcast he, bewildered and depressed" (2:242). Such an "outcast" is no sinner willfully separated from the divine presence who is able to recover it by turning back to God. This outcast is cut off from the "The gravitation and the filial bond/ Of nature that connect him with the world" (2:244–45). Shadowing the picture of happy infant and childhood interfusion with the world is the psychic harm of an absence of which the individual is guiltless. Such was the experience a little later in life of the "Friend" to whom the poem is addressed, when he was sent after the death of his beloved father to board at Christ's Hospital. Both Coleridge and Wordsworth knew what it was to be "bewildered and depressed," and they thought about these experiences in a way that made the importance of infant and childhood experience primary. Framed, in other words, by a psychological rather than theological conception of a life and its narrative possibilities, the relations between particular contingencies and universal potentiality are repositioned in *The Prelude*. Spots of time and hiding places of power may be there for most of us, but they are lodged in memories that are highly particular to an individual. The restoration at the heart of *The Prelude* depends on summoning up these particular childhood memories that form "a part/ And that a needful part, in making up/ The calm existence that is mine when I/ Am worthy of myself!" (1:347–50).

3. Narrative of Authenticity: Edmund Gosse's *Father and Son*

Returning to Godwin's question about what "magic" there is in the pronoun "my" that would justify overturning the decisions of "impartial truth," we can see that there may be considerable magic in purely personal experiences that make up the calm existence that is mine when I am worthy of myself. To see what this magic is we need to shift from a post-Enlightenment language of the good based on detached and impartial rationality to a Romantic language based on the importance of individual feeling, experience, and memory. We need to shift, in other words, from a universalizing language of the good to a particularizing one, as indeed do several important autobiographers who follow the example of Wordsworth in trying to make sense of their lives. They do this, even though their own stories of childhood may be more those of outcasts, bewildered and depressed. Coleridge, spending much of his childhood away from his mother and his beloved Ottery, "pent 'mid cloisters dim,"[7] was one of these; John Stuart Mill, force-fed on the classics by a well-meaning but tyrannical father was another; Edmund Gosse, brought up in London by parents of religious devotion of an extreme Augustinian kind, was yet another. In all these cases, the Wordsworthian language of the good makes itself felt in the absence of childhood blessedness, in which the alienating city is mostly the setting for an upbringing or education driven by repressive hypergoods.

I have called Godwin's a post-Enlightenment language of the good, as it is, ultimately. But in the first instance Godwin was not raising the question of *what is it good to be?* His hypothetical situation is rather designed to answer the question: if faced with the choice about who to save in Fénelon's burning palace, *what is it right to do?* When Wordsworth says that "wearied out with contrarieties/ [he] Yielded up moral questions in despair," this is the sort of question he had in mind. For most users of the English language, then as now, "moral questions" are concerned with issues of conduct and right action. Much the same is now true of the word "ethics." As we have seen, for most professional philosophers and laymen alike, ethics is the domain of questions of right action. As we have also seen, this applies even in the field of life narrative studies in which ethical interests have mostly centered on the legitimate but limiting question, *what is it right for the life writer to do?* My concern, of course, is with a different question that can be found at work at the heart of all written lives: *what is it good to be?*

How are the right and the good related? Gosse's *Father and Son* enables us to explore this issue further, which we touched on in the introduction, as well as with regard to Nietzsche's ethics, namely, the relations between "thin" ethical languages of the right and "thicker" languages of the good. Gosse's practical reasoning about how to act in the face of his father's demands reveals the way in which the good is entailed in the right. At the end of the Epilogue, having quoted a painfully remonstrating and reproving letter of his father's at length, Gosse moves to his conclusion:

> All that I need further say is to point out that when such defiance is offered to the intelligence of a thoughtful and honest young man with the normal impulses of his twenty-one years, there are but two alternatives.

Either he must cease to think for himself; or his individualism must be instantly confirmed, and the necessity of religious independence must be emphasized.

No compromise, it is seen, was offered; no proposal of a truce would have been acceptable. It was a case of "Everything or Nothing"; and thus desperately challenged, the young man's conscience threw off once for all the yoke of his "dedication," and, as respectfully as he could, without parade or remonstrance, he took a human being's privilege to fashion his inner life for himself. (251)

Given its placing at the climax of the narrative, this is clearly meant to be a key moment in the moral experience of the autobiographical protagonist. The narrator describes this as a moment in which he exercises his "conscience" in a choice between "two alternatives": either he must yield to his father's point of view or have the courage to think and choose for himself. It is a moment of deliberation, of practical reasoning, though of course the discursive mode is not philosophical in any strict sense. We can, however, catch the shadow of philosophy—of a kind that would have been familiar to Godwin—in the way in which the individual Edmund Gosse gives way progressively to the more universalized figures of "a thoughtful and honest young man" and, finally, a "human being." The procedural shadow, if anyone's, is Kant's, though the focus on the "human being's *privilege* to fashion his inner life for himself" sounds more like Mill. Either way, the focus is on moral *action*: the key verbs are of *throwing off* a yoke and of *taking* a privilege, complementary assertions of moral autonomy.

What is implicit in this ending is that, through this culminating act of choice, the young protagonist is "confirm[ing] his individualism" and existentially *becoming* the self telling the whole story. This is what the whole story has been leading to. I put it like that to underline one of the ways in which ethics may be central, not simply to authorial performance, but to the complex interrelations between narrated and narrating selves: their ultimate identity may be one of moral choice. But this is only one of the ways in which ethics may be central: in the protagonist's deliberations and choices about such questions as whether to yield to the opinions of an authoritative other or to summon the courage to think for himself.

These questions still bear a broad similarity to the ethics of authorial performance in that they are within the space defined by the question, *what is it right to do?* They would be instantly recognized as important by moral philosophers from Kant and the Utilitarians to mainstream contemporary Anglo-Americans in the analytic tradition, whose work mostly gives constitutive centrality to moments of deliberation and choice. According to Taylor, however, we cannot understand these moments properly if we disembed them from the whole background of what he calls the "qualitative discriminations" that are woven into our language and into the texture of our thought. "Prearticulately," he says, "they function as an orienting sense of what is important, valuable, or commanding, which emerges in our particulate intuitions about how we should act, feel, respond on different occasions, and on which we draw when we deliberate about ethical matters" (77–78). According to Taylor's picture, conscious moral deliberation and choice are shaped from below by our mostly "prearticulate" but identity-orienting systems of value, commitment, and belief, which turn out themselves to be partly formed by practical reasoning of another kind. In our moral experience the question *what is it right to do?* is the merest tip of a volcano of moral feeling and intuition.

Father and Son makes this point of Taylor's quite clear. We can only understand Gosse's identity-defining choice at the end of the Epilogue against the background of values, commitments, and beliefs the young man progressively distils from his experience. Some of his key moral feelings and intuitions are those he has toward his father's religion.

> Let me speak plainly. After my long experience, after my patience
> and forbearance, I have surely the right to protest against the untruth
> (would that I could apply to it any other word!) that evangelical reli-
> gion, or any religion in a violent form, is a wholesome or valuable or
> desirable adjunct to human life. It divides heart from heart. It sets up
> a vain, chimerical ideal, in the barren pursuit of which all the tender,
> indulgent affections, all the genial play of life, all the exquisite pleasures
> and soft resignations of the body, all that enlarges and calms the soul
> are exchanged for what is harsh and void and negative. It encourages a
> stern and ignorant spirit of condemnation. (248)

I have called these feelings and intuitions "moral," but not in a sense that would have been recognized by Godwin or Kant. This example is deliberately provocative, because certain expressions here will remind us that Gosse is often seen in very different terms from the ones I have just used: I mean expressions such as "the tender, indulgent affections", "the genial play of life," and "the exquisite pleasures and soft resignations of the body." These surely place Gosse where the editor of the Penguin edition, Peter Abbs, squarely places him, alongside such figures as Wilde and Gide in the decadent *fin de siècle* in which art for art's sake defined itself explicitly *against* morality. Abbs talks about Gosse as a hedonist and an aesthete and quotes him saying that the criterion for judging art is aesthetic pleasure, leaving it without any basis for "sizing up of moral values."[8] This is why, Abbs says, such criticism was powerless to deal with the shock of the First World War.

There is truth in this conventional historical positioning of Gosse, but what it ignores is that aestheticism itself has its own typical commitments to what is valuable and significant. Gosse clearly believes, for example, that "all that enlarges and calms the soul" is more worthy than "a stern and ignorant spirit of condemnation." I put it that way to invoke once again Taylor's notion of strong evaluation, which involves not merely preference of one thing over another but the belief that one thing is in some sense of higher value, more worthy of respect. For Gosse, the engagement with books, poems, and works of art is not merely more pleasurable or desirable than the pursuit of evangelical religion, it is more admirable because it enlarges the soul. And so it is a strongly valued good, part of Gosse's sense of what makes a human life worthwhile. To put it another way, being large-souled in these terms is part of Gosse's answer to the question, *what is it good to be?* For Taylor, the question *what is it good to be?* is integral to ethics, not least because our sense of what is worthy of respect or admiration—and the reverse—plays into our conscious deliberations on the question *what is it right to do?*

In Gosse's case, his final choice "to fashion his inner life for himself" draws on lessons he has learned in growing up about what it is good, and not good, to be. In the final stages of this process, at about the age of 16, he begins to read voraciously, especially Shakespeare and the Romantics, and begins to experience the "extension of [his] intellectual powers." At the same time, he begins to estimate his father in a new light. "I began to perceive, without animosity, the strange narrowness of my Father's system, which seemed to take into consideration only a selected circle of persons, a group of disciples peculiarly illuminated,

and to have no message whatever for the wider Christian community"
(230). He also perceived this narrowness as a major moral flaw in his
father:

> He who was so tender-hearted that he could not bear to witness the pain
> or distress of any person, however disagreeable or undeserving, was
> quite acquiescent in believing that God would punish human beings, in
> millions, for ever, for a purely intellectual error of comprehension. My
> Father's inconsistencies of perception seem to me to have been the result
> of a curious irregularity of equipment. Taking for granted, as he did, the
> absolute integrity of the Scriptures, and applying to them his trained
> scientific spirit, he contrived to stifle, with a deplorable success, alike the
> function of the imagination, the sense of moral justice, and his own deep
> and instinctive tenderness of heart. (231–32)

It is clear that, for Gosse, his father's religious "system" can have pernicious effects on the human spirit: to have "imagination", "the sense
of moral justice," and the "instinctive tenderness of heart" all "stifled"
is not a good way to be. By contrast, literature, among other things,
has enlarged Gosse's own capacity for moral perception and reflection, enabling a new kind of practical reasoning about his father's
thinking and feeling. In introducing his new way of seeing his father,
Gosse says, "I began to perceive."

Like the autobiographies of Augustine, Wordsworth, and Nietzsche,
Gosse's is a narrative of what we have been calling "supersession." At
the heart of it is a shift to a new perspective on his life, lit up by a new
understanding of what it is important or valuable to be and expressed
in a new language of the good. It is time to consider more broadly
why supersession seems to be so fundamental to life narrative—such
that even Barthes, for all his rhetoric against narrative's compact with
the imaginary, admits that the "ladder" of ascending moral insight
has to "continue." For him too, one nail of self-understanding drives
out another. Only Wang Shih-min, discussed in chapter 1, and who
claims to have lived his whole life by Confucian morality, seems to be
an exception. Yet even he, in a less radical way, nonetheless reviews
his youthful experience in the light of deeper insight gained in the
course of his life. The older narrator comes to see that the young official "wasted months and even years in timidity and vigilance," and
therefore "failed to match the glories of [his] forefathers by mastering

one canonical classic" (261). Like the Western writers considered so far, the Ming scholar-gentleman understands his earlier experience by what he sees as a truer conception of what gives life meaning.

In the terms Taylor uses in *Sources of the Self*, all of these writers, including the younger Gosse, have "lived through" a "transition" in their moral experience. On Taylor's account, such transitions are at the heart of practical reasoning:

> Practical reasoning . . . is a reasoning in transitions. It aims to establish, not that some position is correct absolutely, but rather that some position is superior to some other. It is concerned, covertly or openly, implicitly or explicitly, with comparative propositions. We show one of these comparative claims to be well founded when we can show that the *move* from A to B constitutes a gain epistemically.

The notion of "epistemic gain" is central to Taylor's account. It means not simply gain in knowledge, but a move to a new way of seeing things that constitutes a gain over the previous one. Its application to life narrative soon becomes clear:

> This form of argument has its source in biographical narrative. We are convinced that a certain view is superior because we have lived a transition which we understand as error-reducing and hence as epistemic gain. I see that I was confused about the relation of resentment and love, or I see that there is a depth to love conferred by time, which I was quite insensitive to before. (72)

Taylor is of course primarily addressing his philosophical interlocutors here and is arguing for a different way of looking at practical reasoning from the procedural models used by the proponents of Kantian and Utilitarian ethical theories. As we have noted, for Taylor one constitutive aspect of us as moral beings is that we grasp our lives as narratives that have a certain direction. We see ourselves as beings who are "growing and becoming"—or the reverse, as backsliding and diminishing; we know ourselves "through the history of [our] maturations and regressions" (50).

By "narrative" Taylor does not in the first instance mean written or even spoken narrative, but rather the mostly implicit stories I have of where I am "at" in my life—in relation to my sense of what it is good to be. What he is saying in the above passages is that practical reasoning comes to focus in the moments wherein these understandings themselves change and grow. Part of my life narrative will be the history of these crucial "transitions" when I came to see things—in my own terms—more deeply or truly. It seems to be the case that these implicit stories, about where I am "at" in my life, of how I came to be there and how I came to understand myself in this way, will almost necessarily contribute to the shaping of my written life. In fact this seems to be true of the classic autobiographies to which scholars and critics have given most serious attention. They all tend to be stories of "epistemic gain." The reason why they are, and arguably have to be, is the quasi-logical one we noted in discussing Barthes. From my own perspective, I cannot but believe that I have a fuller understanding of myself than I did, since my self-understanding now encompasses what I was. To put that in another way: if, as Taylor argues, it is a condition of being a functioning self that I speak from a moral orientation I take to be right, I simply *cannot* narrate the story by which I came to ultimate epistemic loss. I can tell the story of my backslidings, and I may see some of my earlier changes of perspective as epistemic loss, but the final move to *that* perspective must be gain. This is why, for me, the ladder of moral insight continues upwards. Though of course others may see my history differently. All of this follows from Taylor's opening chapters in which he shows how we need to be rightly placed against a horizon of significance that gives our lives meaning and value.

Father and Son certainly supports this line of argument. It is a narrative marked by its protagonist's practical reasonings from the evidence of experience, which are transitions in the progressive history of its narrator's current orientation in moral space. Some of these transitions involve inductive scientific reasoning, such as the child's experiment with idolatry (66–7). But the epistemic gains that seem to me to be dominant in the story are those that involve the protagonist's initiations into distinctively post-Romantic insights about the importance of such qualities as imagination and "*instinctive* tenderness of heart." I have said Romantic "insights," but equally it is clear that the initiation is also into Romantic concepts and vocabulary. Epistemic gains, in other words, will take place only in an available language and may in fact depend on a shift from one vocabulary or language to another. This follows from the fact that a self only exists within language communities, or webs of interlocution, which include not merely the people we know but the interlocutors we read and who crucially seem to be able to read us. From them we are initiated into our "languages of moral and spiritual discernment." Taylor's term is important because the more familiar term "discourse" has become irrecoverably mired in a certain poststructuralist conception of power before which we are relatively helpless.[9] Talking of our languages of moral and spiritual discernment stresses the agential nature of the self and views language as empowering us to pick out qualitative realities of experience such as acts of "courage," and to make qualitative distinctions that constitute acts of understanding. Gosse simply cannot discern his father's stifled "imagination" and "*instinctive* tenderness of heart" within the language of his childhood religion. To become aware of them he must move to a new language. The epistemic gain he makes when he starts his voracious reading as a young man is enabled, in other words, by the acquisition of a Romantic language of discernment.

The notion that languages of the good enable moral discernment and epistemic gain is critical to my wider argument, which can be seen if we compare it with conceptions of language that have become more familiar in literary studies over recent decades. There is nothing especially new, for example, in simply noticing the clash of languages in *Father and Son*. In an article published ten years ago, Cynthia Northcutt Malone offers a Bakhtinian reading of the text in which she sees it as the site of a "polemical debate between the contesting voices and belief systems of Philip and Edmund Gosse" (16). She correctly points out that the debate is by no means that open-ended polyphonic contestation that Bakhtin so admired in Dostoyevsky, but more of an "internal polemic" of the kind found in confessions such as Rousseau's. Right from the opening of the narrative, the reader is maneuvered into siding with the son. Malone quotes the opening in which Gosse says that of "the two human beings here described, one [the father] was born to fly backward, the other could not help being carried forward" (35). She astutely analyzes the "double-voiced" irony here of the son's echoing of his father's letter, quoted in the epilogue, in which he talks of the son's "rapid progress towards evil" (250). She concludes: "The inscription of the epigraph over the narrative juxtaposes directional readings of the son's 'progress': as sinful backsliding, on the one hand, and as intellectual movement forward, on the other" (18).

Analyzing the subtle polemical rhetoric of the text in this way is certainly insightful, but it does not capture some things that are central for me. The first is that the "voices" of father and son are not simply those of the two distinct individuals, but they also correspond to inner languages within the overall narrative of the protagonist's *becoming* the narrator. As I have tried to suggest, the narrator's identity cannot but be invested in a progressive story of ultimate epistemic gain, which in Gosse's case includes initiations into scientific and, above all, Romantic languages—and the leaving behind of the language of the saints. This is why it is misleading to talk of *juxtaposed* "directional readings," "on the one hand" forward and "on the other" backward, as we might ideally hope for in the open thought-experiment of a Dostoyevsky novel. This is not to deny that the self may be complex and multiply constituted in various languages, but that complete de-centered openness is the wrong expectation in an auto/biography, as is the word "polemical," which implies that it would be better otherwise. Authorial neutrality over the matter of an autobiography's ultimate language(s) is not an available option. For all Gosse's scientistic talk of this memoir as a "record" or a "document," he writes it, as any autobiographer does, with a particular orientation in moral space, which means with a whole background of strong evaluative beliefs and commitments that are woven into his language(s).

⤿

As we have seen, Godwin's hypothetical about Fénelon embodies an ethics that privileges the right over the good, while Gosse's narrative reveals the force of Taylor's claim that conceptions of the good inevitably underpin an individual's understanding of what constitutes right choice and action. A second feature of Godwin's hypothetical is the other-directedness of the ethical claim it is advancing. The problematic case is not whether, if I were Fénelon, I should save myself, but rather whether, if I were the servant or the servant's relative, I should put my own interest above the wider benevolence that would follow from saving Fénelon. This is benevolence principally *for others*. Godwin is by no means eccentric here. For most people, then as now, "moral questions" or what we normally regard as ethical issues almost exclusively focus on individuals' conduct toward others. What is much less recognized is that when post-Enlightenment moral systems such as Godwin's, Bentham's, or Kant's promote hypergoods of right and just action, as they inherently do, the claims of self must often struggle for recognition against the claims of others. Much the same is true when obedience to God's word becomes a hypergood, as it does in the extreme form of biblical Puritanism practiced by Gosse's parents. According to Gosse's narrative, his mother was a talented writer but felt called upon to repress her gift because imaginative self-expression seemed to run counter to various injunctions about truth-telling in the Bible. She could see no good in it and focused her energies instead on raising her son and evangelizing others. For the Gosse parents, as with Augustine, what is not explicitly for God is against him. The tragedy of this for Gosse is his mother's repression of the imagination in herself and in the life of her family. They are loving parents, wanting only the best for their child, but they create for Edmund a bleak, lifeless, and in many ways deprived childhood—deprived in fact of some of the riches Augustine denied in his life, such as secular friendships, the theater, and imaginative literature. Before she dies, his mother lays on her son's conscience what he comes to see as an intolerable burden of dedication. It is a burden of *conscience* precisely because it is other-regarding; it centers on his obligations to her. To become what he is, Gosse feels that he must cast off this burden. Like Nietzsche, he has to search for a language to give expression to his intuitions and feelings, which enable him to see them precisely as *moral* intuitions and feelings that can count in the scale, as we shall see, against the powerful claims of other-regarding morality.

To understand the challenge facing Gosse, we need to extend the discussion to confront what must seem like the most common sense of all objections. What does all this talk of imagination, personal feelings, and intuitions—entailed in "becoming what one is"—have to do with *ethics?* Ethics is surely the discourse that deflects attention from such me-generation preoccupations to demands that we think about our obligations to *others*. This is both a common-sense objection that many educated users of the English language might feel and at the same time the objection of many mainstream Anglo-American moral philosophers. For example, Thomas Nagel in *The View from Nowhere* argues that neo-Aristotelian philosophers of Taylor's stripe are wrong "because moral requirements have their source in the claims of other persons, and the moral force of those claims cannot be strictly limited by their capacity to be accommodated within a good individual life" (195ff.). Nagel's point is that (eudaimonic) philosophies of the good, such as Aristotle's and Taylor's, take the aim of the ethical life to be the human flourishing that comes from the realization of a range of goods. The claims of others on us, however, may well frustrate and defeat the project of realizing this range of goods in our lives. For this reason such claims cannot be adequately accommodated within an ethics of the good. The key question is what ought to give way under circumstances of conflict between the claims of self and the claims of the other? For a Kantian there is no problem. The procedure of universalization allows the claims of both to be weighed rationally and impartially against each other. Specifically it is a procedure designed to neutralize the irrational prejudices of egoism, inclination and self-interest that ever predispose us to self-preference.

Thus (deontological) philosophies of the right as opposed to the good tend to place their priority, as Nagel does, on "moral requirements" that have their "source in the claims of other persons." But there are powerful objections against this emphasis. They begin with the question of why the claims of others should virtually constitute the moral domain instead of being simply one sort of claim among others. What of the claims of self? Many contemporaries who ultimately derive their thinking from the Greeks keep returning to this question. They range from Michel Foucault (207ff.), with his hedonistic ethics of care for self to neo-Thomists such as John Finnis (107) who argues that there is scope for reasonable self-preference, not because my own flourishing is of more value than that of others, but because it is *mine*, and it is only by taking its claims seriously that I can begin to realize any good in my own life. Otherwise, as we have seen in the case of Nietzsche, where the procedure of universalization dominates practical reason, it is not so easy to see how "the *I* of my desire" ever gets much mass in the moral scale against the omnipresent and arguably more weighty obligations I have to others. The heuristic of impartiality not only insists on the moral equivalence of selves, it gives no weight to my *particularity* as a self. It can find no magic in the pronoun "my." In a word, it can find no place in the equation for the moral significance of my *difference*.

This is where Taylor's work is again especially pertinent. In *The Ethics of Authenticity*, Taylor outlines what he calls the "moral ideal of authenticity" (22) in which he pictures the modern project of self-fulfillment (or self-realization) as embodying a serious moral claim, "that of being true to oneself" (15). His argument provocatively takes on not only Anglo-American moral philosophy but also some popular analyses of modern culture, such as Christopher Lasch's *The Culture of Narcissism* and Allan Bloom's *The Closing of the American Mind*. These tend to picture the modern emphasis on self-fulfillment as relativistic, self-indulgent, and as narrowing the scope of cultural attention to the private and away from the larger concerns that transcend self, such as religion, politics, and history. These popular analyses join with Kantian ethics in their assumption that the project of self-fulfillment will merely license irrational self-preference, self-interest, narcissism or egotism—not to mention self-absorption and insouciance toward the needs of others. And so, one would have to agree, in many cases it does. So whence self-fulfillment as a specifically "*moral* ideal"?

Taylor begins to answer this question by presenting self-fulfillment as a strongly valued good. Thus we moderns, he argues, tend to see a fulfilled life as higher, as more worthy of admiration, than an unfulfilled life. What lies behind this observation of modern anthropology is the whole historical analysis he outlines in *Sources of the Self*, and in particular his reading of the profound contribution of the Romantic movement to the shaping of Western modernity. Following Rousseau, we moderns tend to subscribe to the notion of "self-determining freedom. It is the idea that I am free when I decide for myself what concerns me, rather than being shaped by external influences" (*Ethics of Authenticity*, 27). But this notion gets part of its authority for us, he argues, from a slightly later one, Herder's notion that "each of us has an original way of being human":

> This idea has entered very deep into modern consciousness. It is also new. Before the late eighteenth century no one thought that the differences between human beings had this kind of moral significance. There is a certain way of being human that is *my* way. I am called upon to live my life in this way, and not in imitation of anyone else's. But this gives a new importance to being true to myself. If I am not, I miss the point of my life, I miss what being human is for *me*. (28–29)

It is implicit in this notion that there is a sense in which I have a responsibility to and for myself. It is a responsibility not to yield utterly to demands from beyond myself to conform to some universal human template but to attend to the claims of my own inner nature and to realize my own *particular* way of being human. What Taylor calls the ethics of authenticity is in short an ethics of difference, of becoming what one uniquely is, and it is ever called into being against the perceived oppressiveness of universalizing moralities both ancient and modern, be they Stoic, Judeo-Christian, Utilitarian or Kantian. The final dictum of Blake's Hell captures this perception with memorable force: "One Law for the Lion & Ox is Oppression."[10] All of this was of course one of the main themes of Nietzsche's *Genealogy of Morals*— that moralities centered on, and constituted by, "the claims of other persons" can become vehicles of oppression. Specifically they can become such when they afford no *moral* weight to the claims of self, particularity, or difference. Such claims can only be regarded as immoral, amoral, or merely sub-moral, and so they are rhetorically disempowered before other-regarding considerations.

I take this conflict between the moral claims of self and "the claims of other persons" to be the ethical center of *Father and Son*. The "intolerable . . . burden of Atlas" (81) laid on the conscience of the child by his mother's dying wish is intelligible as such within the framework of the ultimate moral language of the narration, which I have described provisionally as Romantic, but which we can now call the language of authenticity. What happens at the end of the narrative is that, faced with his father's potentially overwhelming reminders of his obligations to his parents and to God, the young man is empowered by discovering authenticity specifically as a *moral* language that can provide not only an adequate counterweight to the Puritan language of the father but an armory of terms in which to mount a critique of it. In fact the end is implicit in the famous beginning:

> This book is the record of a struggle between two temperaments, two consciences and almost two epochs. It ended, as was inevitable, in disruption. Of the two human beings here described, one was born to fly backward, the other could not help being carried forward. There came a time when neither spoke the same language as the other. (35)

Setting aside for the moment the importance of evolutionary language ("one . . . born to fly backward, the other . . . forward"), we can clearly see the whole trajectory of the narrative as contained in the significance and weight given here to the innate individual difference between the father and son ("two temperaments"). That formulation of difference indicates the presence from the start of the distinctive "language" of the narrating "I." It is a language the narrated "I" will only acquire at length, leaving behind the language he and his father once shared, when they also shared a commonly framed "conscience." The two terms are intimately related. The "consciences" of the two men come to differ radically precisely because they are constituted by different "languages"—which means, as we saw earlier, different vocabularies of moral choice embedded in very different background pictures of what is valuable and good to be. For this reason it is justifiable to talk of Gosse's two languages as "languages of moral and spiritual discernment" in Taylor's sense.

But the force of talking this way will not be obvious because authenticity in Taylor's sense is not a familiar part of ethics, nor the son's exercise of "conscience" at the end a familiar part of what we might call the spiritual life. A more usual way to read these things in *Father and Son* is provided by Linda H. Peterson's excellent chapter on Gosse in *Victorian Autobiography: The Tradition of Self-Interpretation*, in which the son's gradual throwing off of his father's religion is seen as parodic of traditions of spiritual autobiography. There is certainly rich insight in Peterson's account of Gosse's baptism as the dramatic climax of the autobiography, in which we see a "simulacrum of true change of heart" (177). What her account occludes, however, is that there is a "true change of heart" later on, but that it takes place in terms of a very different language of the good. For Peterson there is nothing counterpoised systematically against the father's Puritan language: the loss of religious "authority is not re-invested in a single, alternative system", but "dispersed to a variety of interpretive strategies, which are applied locally rather than comprehensively" (182). While I would agree that there is more than one language of interpretation other than the religious one—the presence of naturalistic evolutionary language is quite pervasive—there is certainly a predominant one, which is the one I am calling the Romantic language of authenticity. The extent to which it is "systematic" can be glimpsed in the fact that the climax of Gosse's account of the baptism is the revelation that during the service in the Room he has put out his tongue in mockery to the other little boys. What is underlined here is that he is after all still a child, and what shapes our way of seeing this is a familiar Romantic model of self as an organism that unfolds in its own way and at its own pace.

In fact, self as an organism following—or trying to follow—its own inner laws is one of the major organizing metaphors of the narrative. The terms in which the baptism is presented are prefigured by the visit to his Clifton relatives where Gosse discovers a "healthy" and "wholesome" warmth that allows him to sink back, after many months of strain, "into mere childhood again." Here he lives the life of an "ordinary little boy, relapsing . . . into childish thoughts and childish language" (84–85). The Clifton family understand that the soul has its times and its seasons and that childhood is not the time for the spiritual intensities and compulsions that have controlled and distorted his life at home. His home in south London is figured as a sub-Coleridgean prison "cell," the child with his cheek pressed against the window looking wistfully out at the grey world of the street. Two memorable passages make the organic metaphor underpinning all this quite explicit:

> This, then, was the scene in which the soul of a little child was planted, not as in an ordinary open flower-border or carefully tended social *parterre*, but as on a ledge, split in the granite of some mountain. The ledge was hung between night and the snows on one hand, and the dizzy depths of the world upon the other; was furnished with just soil enough for a gentian to struggle skywards and open its stiff azure stars; and offered no lodgement, no hope of salvation, to any rootlet which should stray beyond its inexorable limits. (44)

> At this time I was a mixture of childishness and priggishness, of curious knowledge and dense ignorance. Certain portions of my intellect were growing with unwholesome activity, while others were stunted, or had never stirred at all. I was like a plant on which a pot has been placed, with the effect that the centre is crushed and arrested, while shoots are straggling up to the light on all sides. My Father himself was aware of this, and in a spasmodic way he wished to regulate my thoughts. But all he did was to try to straighten the shoots without removing the pot which kept them resolutely down. (210–11)

The passages both portray self as distorted by the parental religious system, in the one case by being half starved and frozen in a place offering no generous tending to the soul and, in the other, being crushed by an alien weight. In both cases, the self longs for free and vigorous growth—to put out a straying rootlet or a straggling shoot—but this is rigidly repressed. The organic metaphor provides what Peterson would call a pattern of self-interpretation, but its function clearly goes beyond interpretation. These passages also show patterns of evaluation, of "qualitative discrimination," which is why I think it is more meaningful to see the Romantic imagery as a "language of moral and spiritual discernment." The imagery gives the narrating "I" a vocabulary in which to discern repression as well as its remedy: the metaphor of the pot implies an obligation to remove it. When the time comes, the image of the crushed plant will help to justify the narrated "I"'s decision and action precisely as *moral* decision and action.

In this Gosse illustrates, perhaps in extreme form, a key point I am adopting from Taylor. It is that life narrators (like the rest of us), in accounting for key identity-forming decisions and actions, feel a need to speak from a moral orientation they take to be right. Gosse's case is extreme in that he is overthrowing the beliefs of a beloved parent, beliefs that cannot but continue to make a powerful claim on him, especially when that parent uses all of his considerable rhetorical powers to try to keep him faithful to them. The whole narrative is a complex act of "othering" these beliefs, together with the claims of the father's "conscience" on him and the "language" that informed it. An incident around his sixth birthday illustrates this process of "othering." Gosse is naughty and his father gives him several cuts with the cane, justifying it by reference to Scripture: "Spare the rod and spoil the child." Gosse flames with a rage he cannot fully account for:

> My dear, excellent Father had beaten me, not very severely, without ill-temper, and with the most genuine desire to improve me. But he was not well-advised especially so far as the "dedication to the Lord's service" was concerned. This same "dedication" had ministered to my vanity, and there are some natures which are not improved by being humiliated. (65)

As is evident here, the narrating "I" is conscious of the "genuine" other-regarding love driving the father to keep the child faithful to his dedication, but this very conscientiousness and selfless care make an opposing *moral* language of his own all the more necessary. Where the father's scriptural justification is founded on a universalistic proverb, the narrator's account scrutinizes the punishment through the lens of individual difference. The impact of the rod on "some natures" makes the proverb's validity dubious, and the attempt to improve these "natures" by discipline a morally dubious enterprise. The biblical language is thus subtly othered by reference to its others, those individual "natures" oppressed by its all inclusiveness.

The narrated "I" comes to take his stand in moral space on that which is "innate" in him, his own "nature," which stands against the attempts to make him yield to the Puritan template of individual "election" and "dedication." Gosse discovers and holds to a different sort of individuality altogether, one that is ultimately hard and resistant:

> Through thick and thin I clung to a hard nut of individuality, deep down in my childish nature. To the pressure from without I resigned everything else, my thoughts, my words, my anticipations, my assurances, but there was something which I never resigned, my innate and persistent self. Meek as I seemed, and gently respondent, I was always conscious of that innermost quality which I had learned to recognize in my earlier days in Islington, that existence of two in the depths who could speak to one another in inviolable secrecy. (168)

The hard nut recapitulates the imagery of the plant, with its organic implications of innate individual possibilities incipient within it and ready to unfold and grow under its own impulsion and blueprint, manifesting its own unique way of being human. But authentic being cannot find realization without protection against religious "pressure" from "without" ever ready to force it into conformity. Hence the *moral* force of the nut's hardness, emblem of the self's need to be "persistent" in the face of the system that seeks to assimilate it.

What the passage also reminds us of is that the older child self can only cling to the hard nut of its individuality because the younger child self had first "recognized" it at a particular moment back in his "days in Islington." The trajectory of the whole narrative, as I have been arguing, is to chart the key "transitions" in the narrated self's progress toward the self-defining existential decision in the last paragraph. For Taylor, such "transitions" are achieved when, under the stimulus of new experiences, practical reasoning breaks through to epistemically superior insight. The Islington experiences conform to this pattern. They crystallize around the inference Gosse draws from two otherwise trivial incidents that his father is not omniscient. This inference provokes a true epistemic shift, from the mistaken belief that his father, among other things, could peer like God into his innermost heart to the knowledge that his inner life is opaque to him. The "thoughts" open up an altogether new "secret" space that "belonged" entirely to him and to an inner other who was also himself:

> There were two of us, and we could talk with one another. It is difficult to define impressions so rudimentary, but it is certain that it was in this dual form that the sense of my individuality now suddenly descended upon me, and it is equally certain that it was a great solace to me to find a sympathizer in my own breast. (58)

Here the narrated "I" discovers all at once the greatest possible boon to his individual self-realization: an existing self-conscious subjectivity that will both focus his difference and become the site of all future independent feeling and thinking.

What the narrated "I" supposedly finds ready-made, in fact, is nothing else but the Romantic "autonomous self," of which scholars of life writing have made us so properly skeptical. My own take on this is that while the "autonomous self" is ontologically dubious, autonomy makes sense as the goal of an ethical narrative, which I am calling here, after Taylor, the ethics of authenticity. The ethical goal of autonomy in *Father and Son* is clearly stated in the final sentence of this text: it is taking "a human being's privilege [I would add responsibility] to fashion his inner life for himself" (251). We scholars of life writing now have relational or dialogic rejoinders to all this which tell us that such self-fashioning is ontologically impossible: the sympathizing other of self-conscious subjectivity gets its force from real others, real interlocutors, who come to inform self-consciousness in all-pervasive ways.

In fact, future transitions in the protagonist's realization of moral autonomy are indeed more interlocutive, to borrow a term that will remind us of Taylor's emphatically dialogic ontology of the subject, cited above: "A self exists *only* within what I call 'webs of interlocution'" (36, my italics). The "other" within Gosse's self-consciousness is of course powerfully shaped by Puritan voices and texts, while the resistant sympathizing "other" of his individuality is also informed by real others such as the Clifton relatives and his stepmother. But some of the most significant interlocutors for Gosse are those found in the authors and heroes of the books he can manage to get hold of. An important turning point is the reading of *Tom Cringle's Log*, which he says "tinged my outlook on life":

> I must not define too clearly, nor endeavour too formally to insist on the blind movements of a childish mind. But of this I am quite sure, that the reading and re-reading of *Tom Cringle's Log* did more than anything else, in this critical eleventh year of my life, to give fortitude to my individuality, which was in great danger—as I now see—of succumbing to the pressure my Father brought to bear upon it from all sides. (171–72)

It is evident here that individuality isn't simply a hard nut, banging in a Darwinian contest of power against the individuality of the father, though that too is implied throughout the narrative. Individuality is also the fulfillment of "fortitude," of a struggle within that needs nourishment from without.

My reading has stressed the ethical dimension of Gosse's struggle against powerful moral pressure, to bring into being that necessary element of self-flourishing we can call moral autonomy. To achieve this, he has to throw off the oppressive weight of other-regarding claims implicit in his "dedication" and to take on the right and obligation of fashioning his inner life according to the self-responsible ethics of authenticity. In case this emphasis, for all my advocacy, still seems eccentric, it may be as well to remind ourselves of some of Gosse's own formulations regarding *Father and Son*. In the Preface Gosse says that book offers a "study of the development of moral and intellectual ideas during the progress of infancy" (33). It is, he says, "the narrative of a spiritual struggle" (34). In a letter to Sydney Holland he outlines what is at stake in the struggle:

> To tell you the truth, what I should like to think my book might be . . . is a call to people to face the fact that the old faith is now impossible to sincere and intelligent minds, and that we must consequently face the difficulty of following entirely different ideals in moving towards the higher life. But what ideals, or (what is more important) what discipline can we substitute for the splendid metallic vigour of an earlier age?[11]

The final question, I take it, is rhetorical. *Father and Son* has answered it by advancing the new "ideal" of authenticity, which, while never "substituting" for the claims on us of other-regarding morality, is a necessary complement to it.

4. Authenticity and Recognition in Carolyn Steedman's *Landscape for a Good Woman*

The chapters that follow focus largely on intergenerational auto/ biographies of the past twenty years. These constitute something of a new sub-genre, in which the writer and some other, usually a parent, are more or less co-subjects; and so the narrative is as much biography as autobiography—hence the slash. At the same time, we should not forget that there is a continuum between classic autobiographies and recent auto/biographies such as Carolyn Steedman's *Landscape for a Good Woman*: the autobiographer has almost always felt a need to tell not merely the story of self but what John Eakin has called "the story of the story" (*How Our Lives Become Stories*, 176), which has its origin in earlier generations. The story of Augustine entailed the story of Monica. None the less, the recent texts, such as Raimond Gaita's *Romulus, My Father,* Frank McCourt's *Angela's Ashes,* or James McBride's *The Color of Water,* really do seem to be distinctive in certain respects from an obvious precursor, such as Edmund Gosse's *Father and Son.* One important difference is that whereas Gosse's father was an eminent Victorian scientist, the parents and grandparents in the more recent texts tend to be obscure figures, brought to prominence only in and by the texts of their children or grandchildren, who are themselves typically much more highly educated and often even eminent in their own right.

A deeper difference is that whereas Gosse's narrative terminates in an act of moral dis-identification with his father, the recent texts typically discover significant sources of self in the figures of parents and grandparents. If in the earlier texts the immediate familial past is stifling the writer's individuality, the more recent texts tend to find in their forebears qualities that merit attention and respect, qualities that have shaped the narrating self in important ways. An archetypal example of the former is Stephen Dedalus, preparing to take flight as an artist by casting off the nets of family, Irish nationality, and religion. He discovers himself when he finds his true lineage, not through the earthly Simon Dedalus, but through the mythical "old father, older artificer" whom he invokes in the very last words of the novel, to stand him "now and ever in good stead" (253). If that is Stephen's writerly manifesto, if not Joyce's, I would contrast it with another manifesto, written fifty years later by an equally great Irish writer, which ends:

> . . . the curt cuts of an edge
> Through living roots awaken in my head.
> But I've no spade to follow men like them.
>
> Between my finger and my thumb
> The squat pen rests.
> I'll dig with it.
>
> (Seamus Heaney, "Digging" 1966)

As we shall see in a later chapter, the final line asserts poetic identity in terms of a continuity and an identification that the poem itself has made vividly real. The skill levering the bright edge of the spade with such precision as it drives down to the good turf is a true source of the poet's self.

If Gosse and Joyce typify what we have been calling a narrative of authenticity centered on a drive to individual moral autonomy, then Seamus Heaney and the more recent writers might be said to typify a narrative of recognition. The word "recognition," which is derived from Hegel, has been given currency by Taylor in his essay "The Politics of Recognition." In the past twenty years especially, a concern with recognition has transposed the concept of authenticity from the individual level to that of culture. Members of minority cultures particularly are said to suffer from the nonrecognition or misrecognition of their distinctive forms of life, especially in the post-Enlightenment universalizing languages of the modern state. Where in the narrative of authenticity it is the writer who tends to be marginal and the parent a figure of the cultural center, in the more recent narrative there is often an implication that the forebears embody specific values that have been unrecognized or misrecognized by the dominant narratives of the culture. These forebears have tended to slip through the interstices of the available conventional languages, and sometimes the writer's work, even life's work, can be seen as an attempt to find an adequate language in which to articulate what distinctively makes them, and part of the writers themselves, worthy of serious notice.

As we see in many recent auto/biographies, the drive for recognition almost always includes self-recognition, dialogically construed in terms that give due attention to the narrating self's first conversation-partners. In fact, the project of finding an adequate language is often closely related to the project of re-articulating the moral languages of these first interlocutors as constitutive languages of the self.

We need to make a qualification, however. As we see in Heaney's poetry, the narrative of recognition may well simply assume the narrative of authenticity as its starting-point, or else—as in the case I am exploring in this chapter—the two are tightly interwoven. The psychologist Jessica Benjamin suggests that the interweaving of these stories may be the expected pattern, since growth of self requires "the balance of assertion and recognition" (25). We see the force of this in another of Heaney's much-anthologized early poems, "Follower." After describing the child's bumbling and worshipful following of his heroic, Atlas-like father, the poem ends with an abrupt cut to the present.

> But today
> It is my father who keeps stumbling
> Behind me, and will not go away.

As many readers observe, in the final phrase "and will not go away" there are at least two things being said at once. The first is that the poet, now at the height of his powers, moves effortlessly in realms where his father can at best only stumble behind him. In these realms his ungainly closeness can only be inhibiting. The poetic life at once proclaims and requires a certain distance. In a certain sense, the poet needs him to "go away." At the same time, the rest of the poem, and indeed the volume, make it apparent that the father "*will* not go away" in the sense that he remains powerfully present within the poet. He remains precisely as the heroic figure whose skill in ploughing the poem itself reproduces in the shapely word-lines and turnings of well-crafted verses. And part of the poet's exquisite control of his medium can be seen in the way in which, at the end of "Follower," he brings the two narratives I am describing to a single and unsettling focus.

⌐

There is a similar intertwining of these narratives, and the effect is equally unsettling, in Carolyn Steedman's much-discussed memoir

Landscape for a Good Woman (1986). The book begins with a sort of Prologue entitled "Death of a Good Woman." The title refers to Steedman's mother, whose goodness is explored in a complex layering of perspectives. The first is the perspective of Steedman's childhood: "We'd known all our childhood that she was a good mother: she'd told us so: we'd never gone hungry; she went out to work for us; we had warm beds to lie in at night. She had conducted a small and ineffective war against the body's fate by eating brown bread, by not drinking, by giving up smoking years ago. To have cancer was the final unfairness in a life measured out by it. She'd been good; it hadn't worked" (1). As children, Steedman and her sister believed in their mother's goodness, but it is clear that the narrating self is now standing back from this belief. The sisters then believed she was a good mother mainly because they had been "told so" by her—a firm distancing marker. The narrative is detached, to say the least. The tone here is very much of a piece with the fact that is dropped right at the beginning: Steedman made her final visit two weeks before her mother died. It was her first in nine years. Her parent so stifled who she wanted to be as an adult that Steedman, like Gosse, had to keep her distance.

But then the narrative takes a more radical twist.

> Upstairs, a long time ago, she had cried, standing on the bare floorboards in the front bedroom just after we moved to this house in Streatham Hill in 1951, my baby sister in her carry-cot. We both watched the dumpy retreating figure of the health visitor through the curtainless windows. The woman had said: 'This house isn't fit for a baby.' And then she stopped crying, my mother, got by, the phrase that picks up after all difficulty (it says: it's like this; it shouldn't be like this; it's unfair; I'll manage). . . .
>
> And I? I will do everything and anything until the end of my days to stop anyone ever talking to me like that woman talked to my mother. It is in this place, this bare, curtainless bedroom that lies my secret and shameful defiance. I read a woman's book, meet such a woman at a party (a woman now, like me) and think quite deliberately as we talk: we are divided: a hundred years ago I'd have been cleaning your shoes. I know this and you don't. (1–2)

At first glance this episode might seem simply of a piece with what went before. In other words, it is a narrative of authenticity that turns on an act of dis-identification: where her mother found a kind of moral resilience in accepting the unfairness of her lot, the now confident déclassée academic and writer exercises moral autonomy in standing up to such women, showing them unremitting "defiance." As we shall see, the genealogy of Steedman's "defiance" turns out to be more complex than this episode might suggest. But at the same time the episode of the curtainless bedroom has become an indelible moment in Steedman's experience of class injustice—not primarily an injustice to her, but to her mother and foremothers. The act of writing is of course itself a defiance of a class-based dismissive disrespect, but more than that, it is a re-mapping of the landscape such that the lived meanings of the curtainless bedroom are more justly inscribed into social history. From this perspective, Steedman is drawn ineluctably into an identification with her mother and foremothers that is inseparable from her defining sense of responsibility, if not her sense of vocation. In this respect, the adult narrating self can be seen to move between and draw together the two sorts of intergenerational narrative I have been trying to distinguish. I shall also be arguing that these are each underpinned by a distinctive sense of responsibility, couched in a distinctive language of the good.

‿

Steedman's shuffling between narratives includes explicit denials that she subscribes in any simple way to those feminisms that ask her to "return Persephone-like" to her own mother and "find new histories of [her] strength" (16). She also distances herself from those working class boys that "grow up to write about their mother's flinty courage" (17). The genealogy that she traces is one of transmitted guilt and a crippling sense of duty. On the one hand, she breaks the female line in her own refusal to mother, which is a refusal to reproduce her own life (7) with its debilitating enmeshment in her mother's needs and desires. But even that casting off of the maternal net is itself a reproduction of her mother's desires: " 'Never have children dear,' she said; 'they ruin your life.' Shock moves swiftly across the faces of women to whom I tell this story. But it is *ordinary* not to want your children, I silently assert; normal to find them a nuisance" (17). This asks to be read as *defense* of her mother, an assertion of the normality of her mother's view in the face of those shocked and all-too-conventional women. But at another level there is a clear and unsettling implication in her mother's words that it is Steedman and her sister who have ruined *her* life. And what is never far away in Steedman's quoting of her words is the further implication that these very attitudes of her mother's are what have ruined *Steedman*'s life. Steedman's defense of her mother often reads like displaced resentment, re-directed at the figures of other women.

Steedman delineates a genealogy of resentful defiance passed on from one generation to the next in a serial narrative of authenticity. She presents her mother's system of "good mothering" as "partly a system of defiance, that she constructed out of . . . resentment, and by which she could demonstrate how unlike her own mother she was" (102–3). Where the grandmother likes men and drink, the mother defines herself over and against her as a "good mother," determined that her own children will be kept fed and warm. But this goodness in turn lays an intolerable burden on Steedman, the weight of the mother's ever-reproving self-sacrifice. What crushes Steedman's childhood is the burden of being "good": "She wasn't like my grandmother, didn't go out enjoying herself; and neither should I. In this way you come to know that you are not quite yourself, but someone else: someone else has paid the price for you, and you have to pay it back. You grow small, and quiet, and take up very little room. You take on the burden of being good, which is the burden of the capacity to know exactly how someone else is feeling" (105). Steedman's analysis of the pathology of this form of goodness is acute. What looks like the child's caring empathic identification with the mother is in fact underlit by a burning resentment toward her, a hatred in which the child is entrapped by the belief that she *was* her (55). In fact the dominant image of this childhood pathology is not of burning but of coldness. Like Kay in Hans Christian Andersen's "Snow Queen," she has a sliver of ice in her heart that will end up freezing her heart entirely.

At the time, the child experienced her childhood as a good one. The book's insights all came later, prompted by Steedman's reading of, among other things, Alice Miller's *The Drama of the Gifted Child and the Search for the True Self*. Miller presents the good child as "transparent, clear, reliable and easy to manipulate" (105). Steedman accepts this as an analysis of her own childhood, but parts company from Miller in one important respect. In Miller's gifted child, intelligence and feeling are supposed to be divided, which makes the achievement of the so-called "true self" extremely problematic. In her own case, she had resources to overcome this. As a teenager, she came to experience her resentment toward her mother's manipulations and especially at the unfairness of being called unfeeling. She came to see then the relevance of the "Snow Queen" image and that it was her mother who had turned her heart to ice. Out of this "explanatory device" came Steedman's own defiance of her mother, which took the form of a refusal to be manipulated, a refusal to *be* her mother. Indeed to be herself and not her mother required in the end that she more or less shut her mother out of her life (60).

Thus Steedman's own narrative of authenticity. But how do we square Taylor's talk of the strongly valued good with Steedman's analysis of goodness as neurotic passivity and pliability? Partly Freudian but mainly Marxist, this analysis tends to reduce the good to an economy of power:

> I was made good within specific class and social circumstances: to know how my mother felt meant acquaintance with all the ghostly army of good women, scrubbing the Lancashire doorsteps until they dropped, babies fed by the side wall of the mill, bringing the money home, getting the food to the table, never giving in. I carry with me the tattered remnants of this psychic structure: there is no way of not working hard, nothing but an endurance that allows you to absorb everything that comes by way of difficulty, *holding on* to the grave.
>
> This psychology must have served capitalism at least as well as a desire for the things of the market place, which the cultural critics condemn. At least the cut-out cardboard teenage figures of Seabrook's *Working Class Childhood* know, as they sit sniffing glue and planning how to knock off a video-recorder, that the world owes them something, that they have a right to the earth, an attitude at least as potentially subversive as the passivity that arises from not ever being given very much. (107)

Steedman is drawing a contrast here between working class women, including herself, who work until they drop within an exploitative capitalist system, and glue-sniffing teenagers sitting around and planning burglary. Conventional morality labels the first "good" and the second "bad," but Steedman's Marxist analysis unmasks the capitalist ideology underpinning such morality. To put it simply, her analysis exposes the "good" as service of the system and the "bad" as "potentially subversive" of it.

Without question, this sort of familiar late twentieth-century reduction of conventional morality into politics makes a powerful case for questioning the other-regarding servitude, dutifulness, and unremitting grit that are often presented as key constituents of goodness. As we have seen in our discussion of Fredric Jameson, it is this kind of political analysis that tends to make the word "good" equivocal to late twentieth century ears. And it is precisely this resonance that makes it hard initially to recuperate the broader philosophical sense of "good" and "the good" that are central to Taylor's work. The key to recuperation is to see that Steedman's critique of dutiful goodness is itself, as Taylor says of neo-Nietzschean theories in *Sources of the Self*, "powered by a vision of the good" (100). In fact, the good in question, that of equality of respect, has become a distinctive hypergood in the past thirty years, driving the postmodern politics of difference in such a way that other goods are devalued and suppressed—and can only be recovered by a kind of ethical reading against the grain. Such a reading starts by noting that in comparing the women and the teenagers Steedman is comparing two psychic structures, one compulsively dutiful and self-effacing, the other having the virtue of a certain kind of self-belief and sense of self-worth. The key point is that her comparison goes beyond the purely political point of what serves or subverts capitalism. It is a comparison of what we might call two states of being and the terms are far from evaluatively neutral. The contrast being drawn is by no means black and white, but alongside the grim self-denigration of dutiful endurance, the adolescents are "at least" in some sense taking themselves seriously, believing that they have a right to exist, "a right to the earth." This is no isolated example. Throughout this text Steedman makes it clear that it is important to have a robust sense of self-worth. The British Welfare State is praised because it taught her to believe that "I had a right to exist, was worth something" (122). When she says of her compulsive dutifulness, in the passage above, "I carry with me the tattered remnants of this psychic structure", she is clearly saying that in some ways this is not a good way to be.

Steedman, like all life writers, can be seen to have a certain orientation within moral space, a space of self-constituting concerns centering around the question of *what is it good to be?* In other words, in charting the course of her own life, and those of her foremothers, Steedman is taking her bearings from a certain picture of the good. According to

Taylor, some "sense of the good has to be woven into my understanding of my life as an unfolding story" (47); it is this that gives the story a direction, that allows me to see myself as becoming, growing, or maturing. In Steedman's case, the narrative of her life, from the repressed "good" child, to the resentful adolescent, to the adult who will not let herself be put down by middle-class women, can be seen to have a definite direction. It is a supersessive narrative of moral growth, and its direction is intelligible in relation to the good of self-worth, of taking herself seriously. At each stage, Steedman lived through certain transitions in her moral experience: the "good" child comes to feel her resentment and its implications, that it is "unfair" of her mother to call her unfeeling, when she herself has made her so. As we have seen, Taylor describes such moments as acts of practical reasoning (73–79) in which the person makes a definitive "error-reducing move" in her thinking. She comes to see that she is not, as the "good" child believed, to blame for everything; the way she is has been largely shaped by her mother. This is a clear epistemic gain, not just a new isolated insight, but a move to a new way of looking at things, a new understanding of the good, that constitutes a clear gain over the previous one. As we have seen, these transitions in the writer's moral experience inevitably tend to be important moments in autobiography, key steps in the story by which the narrated self becomes the narrating self. They are also moments at which a life-story tends to be re-cast.

Of course I am oversimplifying. The "unfolding story" of self is rarely so rational, progressive, and linear. The old psychic structures persist as "tattered remains," as compulsions to please, to empathize, and to bear injustice without complaint. In any case, moral space contains many rival goods, each with its powerful gravitational pull on both narrative and self. And what I have called the narrative of autonomy is only one self-constituting narrative. The unjust mother of that narrative, whom Steedman has to keep at a distance, is also the victim and protagonist in a story of historical injustice. In this second story, identification with the mother is no longer a childhood pathology but a highly theorized commitment that is, at the same time, an unearthing of sources of the adult self.

Within a page of the passage in which Steedman compares the wreckage of her dutiful childhood self with the glue-sniffing teenagers, she is writing of her mother, not as the wrecker of her childhood but as one who, like the teenagers, believed the world owed her something.

Now her very selfishness has a kind of exemplary force: "She was self-indulgent and selfish in a way that 'our mam' is not allowed to be, and she learned selfishness in the very landscape that is meant to have eradicated it in its children. She wanted things. Politics and cultural criticism can only find trivial the content of her desires, and the world certainly took no notice of them. It is one of the purposes of this book to admit her desire for the things of the earth to political reality and psychological validity" (108–9). In one way, the ethical orientation of this passage is aligned with what we have been looking at before. Steedman is calling for a moral and political transvaluation in which wanting things such as expensive New Look clothes and envying those that have them can be seen not merely as "proper" responses to deprivation, but as radical in their political implications. Believing that you have a right to the earth and its things calls inequality into question in a more rigorous way than moralizing about mindless greed. The trivial woman projected by working-class morality is actually the "good woman" of Steedman's title.

What is most significant in this passage is that Steedman's mother is exemplary of this form of radical working class desire. The book has been written not simply to gain recognition for materialistic desire per se but "to admit *her* desire ... to political reality and psychological validity." Steedman's claim is that conventional working-class morality has not simply condemned such desire among working class mothers, it has denied its very existence, airbrushed it out of the socio-political landscape. In order to understand her point, we have to see that the sentimentalized figure of "our mam" in classic working class histories and memoirs, such as Hoggart's and Seabrook's, has occluded important aspects of political and psychological reality. In order to grasp these we need to pay attention to Steedman's mother. The language Steedman uses is classic language of social theory of the past twenty-five years. Hoggart, Seabrook et al. have narrated a "central" working class story that depicts a social landscape of sameness. Steedman's mother is a figure out there on the margins of this story. In order to make her come into focus, Steedman must inscribe her difference, which is also Steedman's own, into social history. It is a story of a working mother in a working-class townscape in which mothers are not supposed to go out to work. It is also the story of a mother who was virtually a single parent and of a father who was not a patriarch. The landscape in the book's title, the landscape for a good woman, is a properly particularized and historicized landscape that at last includes such a woman, so that she and others like her can finally recognize themselves.

Recognition is the ethical raison d'être of this narrative. The point of historicizing and particularizing is not to present a revised sameness, nor to suggest a spurious uniqueness, but, in Steedman's words, "so that the people in exile, the inhabitants of the long streets, may start to use the autobiographical 'I', and tell the stories of their life" (16). By inscribing her particular "I" into the socio-political landscape, she empowers others like her to recognize themselves, and in a certain sense to have an autobiographical "I" for the first time. Steedman herself realized this truth when she read memoirs and histories such as *Jipping Street* where she recognized her life in the narrative of a mother who kept telling her daughter how hard it was to have her (16). Because it empowers others to achieve self-recognition, life writing of this kind can be viewed as a responsibility.

Many relational intergenerational narratives are driven by a complex sense of moral obligation that has something of the following form: unless I tell my story, and that of my forebears, the dominant story may prevail, along with misrecognition or nonrecognition of people like me. And it may well be that only I *can* tell the story, perhaps because the relevant memories, particularly of my forebears, are alive only in me. If I do not remember and tell, nobody else will. The ethical imperative is at once self-constituting—the memories of these forebears in a sense *are* me, their languages partly constitute my speaking position; but the imperative is also, at the same time, other-regarding: only I can prevent their potentially empowering voices and stories from vanishing forever. As the early Heaney poems show, in the same act by which the poet finds self-recognition in his forefathers, he holds them up for timeless recognition.

Steedman is never quite as upbeat about her project as this, but the similarities with Heaney's in this respect are worth noting. In an interesting passage, Steedman speaks ironically about her debts to the working-class tradition mediated to her by her mother: "'No one gives you anything,' said my mother, as if reading the part of 'our mam' handed to her by the tradition of working-class autobiography. 'If you want things, you have to go out and work for them.' But out of that tradition I can make the dislocation that the irony actually permits, and say: 'If no one will write my story, then I shall have to go out and write it myself'" (23). Behind all the ironies in this passage there remains a clear implication that in writing the book Steedman sees herself following in her mother's tradition of self-help. As with Heaney, there is also a strong sense of historical "dislocation" from her mother's kind of work, which is crystallized in much the same trope: when Steedman goes out to work for what she wants, it will not be with manicure scissors but with a pen. Nonetheless, the moral import of the mother's attitude has entered Steedman's soul in a self-constituting way. The quoted words, still alive in Steedman's memory, constitute one of her languages of moral discernment—for all the complex wariness produced by later, more sophisticated languages of self. We can see the wariness in Steedman's denial that this text makes a Persephone-like return to her mother as a source of strength, but as I have been suggesting all along, the text keeps edging toward such an implication. When Steedman is not on guard, so to speak, the implication is sometimes quite clear. We saw at the beginning that Steedman practices a "defiance" of such women as the health visitor that is contrasted with her mother's resigned acceptance of her unfairness. And yet there are moments in which her mother is herself quite exemplary in this respect. On one occasion as a manicurist, she flung a sixpence back at a titled lady who had given it as a tip. She says: "If you can't afford any more than that Madam, I suggest you keep it." Steedman comments: "Wonderful!—like tearing up the ration books" (37–38). As I said at the beginning, the project of finding an adequate language in which to articulate what makes the forebear worthy of attention is often closely related to the project of re-articulating the moral language of this first interlocutor as a constitutive language of self.

Part of what I am saying is that, in defiantly rejecting the meanness of titled ladies, the mother is a model of identity for her daughter. She is the exemplary good woman of the title who survives all the distancing, reduction, and ironization that the word "good" comes in for in this text. The text rescues her desire for the good things of the earth from moralization, holding it up for moral transvaluation and political recognition. She is also explicitly, in the sense made familiar by Winnicott, a "good enough" mother (107). But in the end we need to notice that the title refers not only to her, but to Steedman herself. Steedman is a good woman in the sense that, like all narrators of auto/biographies, she speaks from an orientation in moral space. As I have argued, Steedman's growth toward this orientation can be seen as a series of supersessive "transitions" between different understandings of what the good is. I've described the first as a move from the compulsively "good" child to the rebellious adolescent who can experience her resentment and its moral implications. It was this move, with its epistemic gain, that still drives the narrative of authenticity throughout this text. But the grown-up narrating self has made a further epistemic gain when she becomes aware of the injustice of the central working-class narratives that have marginalized her mother and her kind, including herself. This move marks the shift to a relational intergenerational narrative that is underpinned by an ethics of recognition. Just as these narratives coil around each other, so do the multiple senses in which Carolyn Steedman is a good woman.

There is yet another twist to this whole story that takes it more or less full circle. The picture I have presented of successive epistemic gains and successive re-castings of life narrative is ever complicated by the fact that the old transcended goods may be never fully superseded. They tend to remain and, as Taylor says, often seem ineradicable from the heart. In Steedman's case, deny her as she will, the compulsively "good" empathic child is a permanent part of the grown-up narrating self. Steedman wrestles explicitly with this fact:

> She [Steedman's mother] made me believe that I understood everything about her, she made me believe that I was her: her tiredness, the pain of having me, the bleeding, the terrible headaches. She made me good because I was a spell, a piece of possible good fortune, a part of herself that she exchanged for her future: a gamble. If you expect children to be self-sacrificing and to identify with the needs of others, then they often do so, and cannot restrict their identification to one other person. They may even find themselves much later, unknowingly, in their mirror image, in the little watercress girl, the good and helpful child, who eased her mother's life. Whenever I cry over that child, I think what a fool she would think me to waste my tears in this way. (141)

This interesting passage shows Steedman being empathically "good," not just as a child neurotically taking on the perspectives of the powerful, but also as an adult identifying with the needs of the most powerless, such as the little Victorian watercress girl she brings to life so movingly in *Landscape for a Good Woman*. She discovers the girl in Henry Mayhew's articles on the London poor of 1849/50, an eight year old who supports her family by buying and selling water-cress in the street. Prematurely responsible and alert to the economic realities of the world, she has not had a childhood in the familiar post-Romantic sense. Steedman quotes the girl, and we hear in her voice the unsentimental practicality that would certainly not have understood the tears that so overcome Steedman as she listens to her. There is no difficulty in recognizing the older anti-empathic self who so readily identifies with the watercress girl's unsentimental realism in seeing such tears as foolish. But the tears are a fact.

It would be all too easy, and not a little sentimental, to see the tears as evidence of a residually "good" Steedman, her heart made sensitive to the powerless by her own deprived childhood. This cannot be right in any simple sense as Steedman's heart, she has said, is all ice. In her last visit to her mother she finds herself "absent in [her] presence" and "outside any law of recognition: the mirror broken, a lump of ice for a heart" (142). The broken mirror is a key image. The mirror of empathic identification is broken. The sliver that transfixes her heart indicates that she is not, in any simple sense, capable of tears for anybody else. When she weeps for the Victorian girl, it is for her "mirror image," in other words, for herself. She weeps counter-transferentially for her own lost childhood, lost in taking responsibility for her "good" moth-er's suffering. But at the center there is ice: the cold, resentful anger of a child treated as a commodity, an object of exchange.

What I am calling the "further twist" in this story emerges here. The "selfish" woman Steedman rescues from socialist obloquy, the woman whose desire for "things" is to be recognized for its radical strenu-ousness, is the same woman whose calculating materialism produced a household ethos of emotional deprivation for her daughters. Once the mirror of compulsive identification is broken, Steedman sees the stark economy of investment and expected return in which she and her sister have been conceived (42). The precisely-costed, measured out nature of the food is an emblem not just of the mother's meanness, but of children treated rigorously *as* means—to the end of securing a marriage. As I have said, this analysis is brought to light by a moral autonomy that has broken the mirror of neurotic identification, under-lit by an icy resentment. Only later can Steedman see the force of her sister's point when she tells her to "recall a mother who never played with [them]" (46)—that is, a mother who never recognized them as ends in themselves.

Jessica Benjamin argues that mother-child relationships only flourish fully as two-way relationships of mutual recognition. One-way recognition, such as the "good" child anxiously offers the mother whose love is highly conditional, may end up turning the child's spontaneous heart to ice. The result may be "good enough" mothering, but there is clear recognition in Steedman's text that this is not as good as it can be. The mother may have "done her best" in her own terms, but these are shown to be severely deficient: children do not live by organic bread alone. Throughout Steedman's narrative, there is an implicit understanding that the child will not feel she has a right to the earth, a deep sense of self-worth, unless this is conferred by recognition of a significant other. Another word for recognition in Benjamin's terms might be empathy, the capacity to put oneself inter-subjectively in another's place—in the manner of the Good Samaritan. This is nothing short of the much-traduced other-regarding goodness—not the neurotic compulsion produced in the unrecognized child, nor goodness seen purely as pliability to the desires of the strong, but the un-ironized, un-reduced goodness of an ethics of care. This is an implicit good of Steedman's text, its "ethical unconscious,"[12] which is part of the narrating self's extremely complex orientation in moral space.

The fact that it is not an explicitly articulated good is not the point. Most of us, according to Taylor, do not recognize the full range of goods we actually live by (107). The self in moral space, as he articulates it, is a self constituted by more moral languages than it will easily articulate. These may range within a given individual from the neo-Nietzschean to the Judeo-Christian, from the Romantic to the post-Enlightenment, from the universal to the particular. Part of the point of the present project is to suggest what an approach to full articulacy might look like.

CHAPTER THREE

The Full Range of Goods, Universal and Particular

The life narratives of Wordsworth and Gosse show the first-person "magic" that is characteristically denied by post-Enlightenment and Augustinian moral systems when they become universalizing hypergoods. These narratives of individual authenticity counterpose against such systems the particularistic ethics of becoming what one is—which becomes the dominant ethical pattern of autobiography throughout the nineteenth and twentieth centuries up to the "relational turn" of the past twenty-five years. Relational auto/biographies introduce another twist to our story, which was also implicit in nineteenth-century Romanticism, when the ideal of authenticity shifts to the level of culture. The notion that there is a way of being human that is my way is transmuted into the idea that there is a way of being human that is distinctive to my culture—and by extension to my ethnicity, race, gender, class, or sexual preference. As a politics of recognition resisting the universalizing hypergoods of the modern state, this form of particularism has been a significant force of liberation underpinning, among other things, major new developments in autobiography and cultural theory.

Yet in some forms the postmodern politics of difference has itself become a hypergood. We have seen this tendency in Fredric Jameson's attack on ethics, when he presents good and evil as nothing but false consciousness, obscuring the ways in which these concepts originate as socially encoded differences in power. This form of analysis too emanated from the nineteenth century in Marx's writings, but it is given a distinctively postmodern inflection by its highly selective incorporation of Nietzsche's attack on Judeo-Christian ethics. The neo-Nietzschean tendency to reduce the good to a technology of domination is also present in *Landscape for a Good Woman*. For Steedman, to be "good" is to be a dupe of the powerful. But this cannot mean that Steedman is not herself morally moved by any goods. Her autobiography shows that she comes to understand her life, as most writers seem to, in a series of supersessive moves toward deeper and deeper moral insight. In her case, these are embodied in complicatedly interwoven narratives of authenticity and recognition—the particularistic master-narratives of her historical period.

And yet, as we have seen, beneath this highly self-reflexive text there is an implicit ethics of care, which goes quite against the grain of its conscious allegiances. Despite herself, Steedman laments the absence in her mother of the kind of love that would have regarded her as an end in herself. All this suggests the deep impression left on Western culture by the sort of ideal embodied by the story of the Good Samaritan in which "good" is understood not in the reductive sense of the politics of difference but in the sense of loving your neighbor as yourself. Historical supersession is never complete; as Taylor says, the older goods sometimes seem ineradicable from the heart. However important particularistic languages of the good may become in our period, the older "superseded" universal goods remain, ready to make a continuing claim on us.

It is for this reason that our identities, according to Taylor, are "complex and many-tiered."

> We are all framed by what we see as universally valid commitments (being a Catholic or an anarchist . . . [for example]) and also by what we understand as particular identifications (being an Armenian or a Québecois). We often declare our identity as defined by only one of these, because this is what is salient in our lives, or what is put in question. But in fact our identity is deeper and more many-sided than any of our possible articulations of it. (29)

When Taylor says "we are all" like this he is not referring to metaphysically-derived transcendental conditions that apply to all human beings. He means "we" in the contemporary West whose moral possibilities happen to be historically constituted by various Western philosophical and spiritual traditions. These emanate, as we see, from the universalistic bent of Greek and thence Christian thought, which form the background to the universalizing bent of the Enlightenment, and so on via modernity to the present. On the other hand, there is the post-Romantic heritage, with its emphasis on individual and cultural differences and self-discovery through self-expression, which form one sort of background to postmodernity. Through hundreds of pages of intellectual history, Taylor makes a compelling case to show that we have been shaped by both of these broad traditions and in more ways than we normally realize. This explains the otherwise strange-sounding claim that "our identity is deeper and more many-sided than any of our possible articulations of it." Any given articulation will tend to express one dimension of identity and suppress others.

Before I elaborate on the thinking behind this claim, I need to point out that the binary "universally valid commitments" and "particular identifications" is a complex and unstable one, perhaps more so than Taylor himself always realizes. To take one of his own examples, "being a Catholic" is cited as a universally valid commitment. And so it may be in most contexts. The content of the Church's faith and moral teaching are universalist. In this sense, being a Catholic is the same kind of commitment for anyone, anywhere. And yet on the streets of Belfast "being a Catholic" will mean something quite different from what it will mean in the corridors of the Vatican. In Belfast it will mean a highly "particular identification," much like being an Armenian in fact. It will be an identity to which one would have to be born, rather than one which could be embraced by anyone by consent. If we follow this thread, it is evident that "being a Catholic" anywhere will often entail a dimension of cultural particularity that may come from a particular ethnic heritage and attending certain sorts of schools, supporting certain unions or political parties, and so on.

This example illustrates Taylor's general point that identity is dependent on context, in which different dimensions become salient at different moments. How I decide where I stand in moral space depends to a great extent on the precise question being posed at that moment. The question of whether I am a feminist, for example, may sound different in the context of an English department in a university from the way it sounds in a redneck football crowd. In the heat of debate with militant colleagues about whether women writers should constitute 50% of the curriculum, I may not think of myself as particularly feminist. But confront me with sexist abuse or with a situation in which women's rights are systematically denied, I may discover the extent to which a feminist moral perspective is part of who I am. One might say that in the first situation my feminism is a suppressed side of my identity, one that may only rarely find the occasion to express itself with any clarity. The example shows how identity unfolds extensively so to speak in space and time. Which is one reason why an autobiography, in which the narrated self moves through varying contexts, will often give a fuller and more dialogic picture of identity than will question-and-answer surveys which are conducted in a given context, moment, and place. And yet even in autobiography we may not find the conscious expression of what Taylor calls "the full range of goods" any individual actually lives by (107). In fact, as we saw in the case of Carolyn Steedman, unacknowledged commitments sometimes emerge in autobiographical texts anyway, often as suggestive fissures in the grain of the author's explicit allegiances.

1. Difference and Its Discontents

The dominant paradigm in autobiography over the past twenty-five years, especially in multiculturalist milieux such as those of the United States and Australia, has been the configuring of identity around one or more (particularist) dimensions of difference—that is, of ethnicity, gender, class, race, sexual preference, and natural language. This chapter considers signs that in contemporary autobiography we may be starting to see the exhaustion of that paradigm. All the writers seem to be reacting against a multiculturalist ethos that they see operating as a repressive hypergood, one which resists recognizing communally shared goods that transcend boundaries of difference. At the same time, these writers may be reacting to a wider change. If globalization—broadly understood—has brought with it profound cultural transformations, then one of them may be a more universalist awareness that most of us now inhabit multiple dimensions of difference—in short, that difference is something we all share. The new emphasis tends to stress consent rather than descent in identity-construction and to draw on ethical vocabularies as well as those of cultural politics.

Of the four autobiographical texts I am going to look at in this section, two are American and two Australian. They are: (1) Eric Liu, *The Accidental Asian: Notes of a Native Speaker* (1998). Liu is the son of Taiwanese immigrants to the US. (2) James McBride, *The Color of Water* (1997). McBride has an African-American father, but the focus is on his Jewish-American mother whose own narrative is interleaved with his. (3) Andrew Riemer, *Inside Outside: Life Between Two Worlds* (1992); Riemer is a Jewish immigrant from Hungary who arrived in Australia in 1947. (4) Ien Ang, "On Not Speaking Chinese: Postmodern Ethnicity and the Politics of Diaspora" (1994). Ang is of Chinese descent, born in Indonesia, arriving in Australia via Holland in the past decade or so.

These texts are profoundly different from each other, and the languages they employ range from liberal humanist to evangelical Christian to postcolonialist. For all these differences, they exhibit certain common identity-themes that have become something of a trend in the past decade. As is already evident, all four belong to minority groups within polyethnic societies. Yet all four resist, or are at best ambivalent about, the particularist identifications you might have expected in their work. They suggest that such identifications, as they are often expressed in contemporary identity politics, are in various ways problematic for them. The models of identity that command their deepest moral respect tend to be of another kind.

Ien Ang illustrates this in one way when she says that in writing autobiographically as a Chinese she runs the risk of being "self-indulgent, of resorting to personal experience as a privileged source of authority, uncontrollable and therefore unamendable to others" (3). A striking example is cited by Andrew Riemer in *Inside Outside*. Riemer is expressing his moral "distaste" for the "emotional blackmail" sometimes visited on others by those who suffered from war-time atrocities: "In the mid-sixties, a middle-aged Viennese lady effectively disrupted a course on twentieth-century literature I was teaching by leaping to her feet at every opportunity to roll back her sleeve and display the tattoo number on her arm. 'What do you know about *The Waste Land?*' she would screech at a roomful of embarrassed young people. 'You know nothink until you know zis!'" (57). Riemer sees such claims to privileged insight as exercises in self-display and self-assertion. Werner Sollors in his book *Beyond Ethnicity* (1986) calls this phenomenon "insiderism."

Ang comes at this point from another direction in stressing the precariousness of an identity such as being Chinese. Adopting such an identity, she says, "always involves a distancing from oneself since one's subjectivity is never fully steeped in the modality of the speaking position one inhabits at any one moment" (4). Her point is closely related to what I was saying in explicating Taylor: a monologic identity-defining stand along the axis of difference may be a strategic political choice, but it will never be more than a partial and temporary positioning in moral space. Her tactic as an autobiographer is to write precisely about the difficulty of speaking as a Chinese and of "the *indeterminacy* of Chineseness as signifier for 'identity'" (4). Eric Liu asks, in a similar vein:

> Where does my Chineseness lie? In my looks, surely. In my culture, vestigially. In my behaviour, too? I have been told, in the years since my father died, that I have been the prototypical Confucian son, a textbook example of filial loyalty to my mother. But if that is true, is it because Chinese values seeped down into me? Or is it because I am the first child and only son of a widow, whom I love, who has become perhaps my closest friend? I find it difficult to separate out the part of my behaviour shaped by ethnicity and the part shaped by my situation. I also find it, after a while, pointless. . . . What is Chineseness? It is anything, everything, and ultimately nothing. (30–31)

In this passage we find Liu examining himself with the expectation of discovering a clear sign of his "difference" as a Chinese. Others recognize him as prototypically Confucian, and it would be easy for him to consent to that reading, were it not for a universalizing language that draws attention to the fact that *any* first child and son of a widow might behave in this way—and so the question is finally undecidable. In giving full dialogic expression to the issues, he can only opt for an anti-essentialist skepticism rather like Ang's. Both make the "return" to China and see it as something quite other than the sentimental epiphany scripted by cinematic narratives of ethnic "homecoming" (Liu, 132). Indeed all four authors visit ancestral first places with a mixture of disappointed expectation and a bemused sense of distance.

On the whole, they also tend to see the contemporary practice of ethnic or race identity as a divisive and sometimes coercive politics. Riemer talks about what he calls the "ghetto mentality" prevailing in Australian multiculturalism (13, 209) in which "Greek sticks with Greek, Vietnamese with Vietnamese, where Arabs are deeply suspicious of, sometimes hostile to non-Arab people taking courses in

Islamic studies" (165). While he is critical of the narrow-minded assimilationist politics of the 1950s, he sees the multiculturalist politics of the 70s and 80s as merely replacing "one rigid orthodoxy by another" (160).[1] Ang goes much further and talks about the pressure currently on diasporic peoples to know their heritage, language, and history, a pressure that comes not merely from within the minority group itself but also from the mainstream society. She is suspicious of this as "a ploy to keep non-white, non-western elements from fully entering, and therefore contaminating, the centre of white, western culture" (15). She sees this as playing into the hands of separatist neo-nationalisms around the world with their "ethnic absolutism" and variants of ethnic cleansing, which amount to a pressure for all diasporic peoples to "return 'home'" (15).

In the face of pressure to make particularist identifications, the authors I am looking at tend to locate the key goods by which they orient themselves not so much in cultural difference as in human commonality. Eric Liu begins his book with a moving memoir of his father, whom he sees as the moral foundation of his own life. His father, though born in Taiwan, spoke very good English, became a top executive in IBM and was a relatively highly assimilated American. Liu admires the way in which his father made his way in 1950s America, which was characterized, above all, by his dignity in not asking for concessions. "If there was one dominant theme in his life," Liu says, "it was that he didn't want to be treated differently—better or worse—just because he was different" (20–21). Riemer, surveying his life as an immigrant, is at pains to point out the extent to which his own sense of uprootedness is an experience "shared by many" (2). He and his parents were victims of persecution, war, and famine, but the last thing Riemer seems to wish for is to present himself *as* a victim, such as the "Viennese lady" with her concentration-camp tattoos. "The hardships and brutalities we suffered," Riemer says, were experienced "in common with millions of others from one end of Europe to the other" (56). This sense of commonality in fact is the reason why his own Holocaust experience is rigorously excluded from *Inside Outside*.

For several of these writers, the capacity to transcend "difference" tends to be a virtue, a good in itself. James McBride's mother, for example, is admirable precisely for a color-blindness that seems positively heroic in her black neighbourhood.

The image of her riding that bicycle typified her whole existence to me. Her oddness, her complete nonawareness of what the world thought of her, a nonchalance in the face of what I perceived to be imminent danger from blacks and whites who disliked her for being a white person in a black world. She saw none of it. She rode so slowly that if you looked at her from a distance it seemed as if she weren't moving, the image frozen, painted against the spring sky, a middle-aged white woman on an antique bicycle with black kids zipping past her on Sting-Ray bikes and skateboards, popping wheelies and throwing baseballs that whizzed past her head, tossing firecrackers that burst all around her. She ignored it all. (7–8)

Ruth McBride's apparent obliviousness of the tumult of race and danger exploding around her in the streets of Queens must not be confused with obliviousness pure and simple. When it comes to getting things done for her children, nobody is shrewder or more worldly-wise. In fact her resourcefulness and single-mindedness are among the key virtues celebrated by the text. She sees, but strenuously ignores, all "matters involving race and identity" (9). Her stand is principled. McBride, like Liu, locates the version of the good by which he aspires to live in his parent's principled difference-blindness. And their own accounts manifest these sources of self in presenting their parents primarily in terms of their common humanity. Liu ends his tribute to his father by attempting to strip away the particularizing filter of his Chineseness:

In the end, Chineseness does nothing to explain the courage my father summoned to endure fourteen years of dialysis, more years than the doctors had ever thought possible. . . . When your father, who was Chinese, has died, Chineseness seems an irrelevance: an inert container, just one among many, for holding the memories of shared experience. When your father has died, you realize this: it is the liquid of memory, not the cup we drink it from, that gives our lives content and reveals our humanity. (31)

The rhetorical insistence of this passage tells us that Liu knows he is being transgressive here, even though what he says is evidently true: courage is not in itself a culture-specific good; and death is a universal experience. Why, at such moments, must we be obsessed with their cultural forms? What makes us so uneasy about excluding them? Liu says that his instinct at times is to "sand away difference, to aspire to a hairless, skinless, bloodless universalism." But no sooner is the u-word out than Liu turns back on himself: "But it occurs to me . . . that nothing becomes universal unless it is first particular. And it occurs to me that I have never been grounded so: in a historical tradition, or a faith; in the rites of an ageless culture" (153). The uneasiness of Liu's rhetoric when he is universalizing lies here—in a sense of the dialogic claims of particularist language, a language that is not given adequate space by figuring culture as an "inert container" or a "cup" for the wine of universal experience.

The dialogue between particular and universal is different in *The Color of Water*, where the narrative of Ruth McBride's life includes her grounding in a particular "historical tradition." Partly for this reason the universalizing language of this text is more assured. When as a child James McBride asks his mother about the color of God, she tells him that God is a spirit. He then asks:

> "What color is God's spirit?"
> "It doesn't have a color," she said. "God is the color of water. Water doesn't have a color." (51)

The importance of this moment is of course underlined by the fact that it provides the title of McBride's memoir. Behind it lies the story of Ruth's exogamous marriage and the dramatic expulsion from her family, culture, and tradition with which the memoir begins:

> *I'm dead.*
> *You want to talk about my family and here I been dead to them for fifty years. . . .*
> *I was born an Orthodox Jew on April 1, 1921, April Fool's Day, in Poland. I don't remember the name of the town where I was born, but I do remember my Jewish name: Ruchel Dwajra Zylska. My parents got rid of that name when we came to America and changed it to Rachel Deborah Shilsky, and I got rid of that name when I was nineteen and never used it again after I left Virginia for good in 1941. Rachel Shilsky is dead as far as I'm concerned. She had to die in order for me, the rest of me, to live.*
> *My family mourned me when I married your father. They said kaddish and sat shiva.* (1–2)

The reborn Ruth McBride sees it as axiomatic that her "death" drama-tizes the moral limitations of this form of exclusive cultural particular-ism and that her rebirth as a protestant Christian is an opening up to a more inclusive morality in which tribal lineage is irrelevant. What matters in this new tradition, and what is identity-defining for her, is a choice, a decision—in short, to borrow Werner Sollors' key terms, it is a matter of consent rather than descent.

This is another common theme in the texts I'm looking at. Identity tends to be construed more in terms of life-choices than of origins, or, as Ien Ang puts it, more in terms of where the writer is "at" than where he or she is "from." Ang is referring to work of Paul Gilroy, who writes so illuminatingly about the "double consciousness" of being both black and European[2] and for whom it is "where you're at" rather than "where you're from" that provides the deepest "anchor-age" for self (10). "Where you're at" is of course both a geographical and a moral location, an orientation in moral space. This latter can take the form of a Kierkegaardian existential choice of yourself, of your own life-circumstances, determinations, and contingencies, in-cluding your own race, ethnicity, or culture of origin. Both Ang and Liu talk about *choosing* to be Chinese and both of them do it precisely in Sollors' terms. Ang ends her essay by saying: "if I am inescapably Chinese by *descent*, I am only sometimes Chinese by *consent*" (18). Liu argues that Chineseness depends on whether Chinese culture, history, and language are transmitted to the individual, which, for a Chinese of the diaspora, depends ultimately on consent: he says, Chineseness is "just a decision to act Chinese" (10).

That "just" of Liu's draws attention to the languages in which he articulates his position. Most tellingly, he calls himself an "identity lib-ertarian" who wishes for a "postethnic America" that "treats race as an option" (65).[3] This notion of self is one with a lineage that the word "libertarian" defines precisely. It is what Taylor calls the "punctual self" of John Locke, or the "unencumbered self" of Robert Nozick,[4] to which Liu in fact expresses his allegiance (84). It is a self in a kind of historical or cultural void supposedly free of all defining communi-ties. The stress is on the self's freedom to make identifications wher-ever it chooses. Liu's strongest impulse is to resist any implication that he is obliged to choose among Chinese or Asian models, which he calls the path of "ethnosclerosis" (65). He talks about the autobi-ographies that seem to articulate his own experience or which make him "feel connected to something." Some of these are Asian, but some of them are not. He lists among the most "resonant" for him Philip Roth's *Portnoy's Complaint*, Henry Louis Gates's *Colored People*, Richard Rodriguez's *Hunger of Memory*, and Norman Podhoretz's *Making It*. He concludes: "I define my identity, then, in the simplest way possible: according to those with whom I identify. And I identify with whoever moves me" (81). If we may transpose this into Taylor's communitarian terms, Liu is saying that some of his most essential interlocutors, those who are now important to his identity, are outside his ethnic culture of origin. In fact, in the acknowledgements, he talks about the book as the "product of many conversations." The list of conversation-partners is poly-ethnic, to say the least, including such figures as Kwame Anthony Appiah and Francis Fukuyama—and not least, Liu's Jewish-American wife (205–6).

The question is, what are we seeing in these texts? One possibility is that they represent a reactionary or nostalgic hankering for the assimilationist past. In the cases of Liu and McBride, it might be said that the admired parent's principled difference-blindness is nothing else but the assimilationist ideology of pre-multiculturalist America. And Ang and Riemer each grew up in a place and time in which such ideology was official state policy. Ang recalls that when she was a child in Sukarno's Indonesia, Chineseness seemed like an "imposed identity, one that [she] desperately wanted to get rid of" (9). Likewise Riemer as a child embraced assimilation (15) and found himself deeply at odds with what he saw as the "sentimental" and "grotesque" attempts of his parents' generation to maintain the culture of the homeland (134). However, these authors are also clear-eyed about the repressiveness of assimilationist cultural politics. Riemer, for example, may be scathing about multiculturalist "orthodoxy" but one of the main burdens of his memoir is to show the high price paid by his parents and himself for their attempt to fit into the "narrow, inward-looking" (3) society of postwar Australia. He himself had to unlearn his first language and culture, to "lock away in an inaccessible compartment of [his] personality . . . the whole network of influences, emotional and social legacies that define and in a sense create an individual" (88–89). As a result he experiences his early life as an "emotional vacuum" (89), while he himself comes to parrot and mimic the new language and culture around him in a way that wins him no more than a grudging acceptance. His life is one permanently on the margins, neither inside nor outside Australian society. Similarly, Liu compares himself to his father, for whom Chinese history, language, and culture seem to remain intact as a deep spiritual source, giving him "an endless reserve of inner strength and self-knowledge." Beside him, the wholly assimilated Liu experiences himself as having "but an echoing well." "To fill the hollow," he says, "I look sometimes to Chineseness" (30). These writers are at best ambivalent about assimilation. For this reason it is problematic to see their moral and political stances as simply reactionary or nostalgic.

The possibility I am drawn to ponder is that in the past twenty-five years the broad context of identity-formation has changed—as a product of the spectrum of things we call "globalization." Roland Robertson argues that "in a world which is increasingly compressed . . . and in which its most 'formidable' components—nationally constituted societies . . .—are increasingly subject to the internal, as well as external, constraints of multiculturality . . . the conditions of and for the identification of individual and collective selves . . . are becoming ever more complex" (98). One of the important things about this formulation is that globalization is reckoned to include the greater salience of experienced multiculturality within such societies as the US and Australia largely as a product of waves of immigration and intermarriage—as well as the imploding of multiculturality without, through rapid travel and the electronic media. Robertson is one of those who see globalization in this broader sense as entailing new dialogic relationships between universalism and particularism.

The greater "complexity" of multiculturality at the beginning of the twenty-first century, according to Liu, can be seen in the multiracial figure, Tiger Woods. Woods, he reminds us, is a mixture of African American, European, Thai, Native American, and Chinese. According to Liu, Woods is the "face of our intermingled future" (190). Liu is thinking partly of his own yet-unborn children, who will also be "intermingled." The question some of these texts raise is how does such a person orient his or her life in moral space? For some, a politics of difference will seem to be thrust upon them partly because of the way they are seen by others. For others this politics will be a deliberate moral choice. But for the multiply marginal such a choice may seem inherently conflictual or otherwise problematic. This is the case of James McBride, who grew up deeply attracted to the Black Panthers in Queens in the 1960s and yet who feared at the same time for his white mother. "I thought to myself, *These people will kill Mommy*" (27). How to assess such a reaction? On the one hand, McBride is clear about the possible ideological implications of feeling this way, namely, that he had internalized "the white man's fear" of the black man (26–27). However, he cannot help finding his mother's no-nonsense approach to these matters morally cogent. When he asks his mother whether or not he should think of himself as a mulatto, she replies, "You're a human being. . . . Educate yourself or you'll be a nobody" (92). I don't think there is any doubt that *The Color of Water* aims to vindicate her way of seeing things, with its final family parade of doctors, professors, and professional people, the triumphant outcome of her values. But what are her values? McBride makes it clear that they have been shaped by her Orthodox Jewish background and her immigrant experience (29). They begin, in other words, with the culture that McBride later sees as the other side of his double inheritance. At one stage, in a visit to the South, he explores the possibility of finding some point of connection with his family's Jewish past. But this proves even more problematic than black identity and provides even less anchorage in moral space. At one point he says: "My view of the world is not merely that of a black man but that of a black man with something of a Jewish soul" (103).[5] It is not hard to see how his mother's universalizing answer offers such a man one persuasive language for making sense of his life.

The case of McBride raises an interesting possibility: if the populations of countries such as the US and Australia are increasingly "intermingled" in the way Liu suggests, then this may be one reason why particularist and universalist languages of identity may be beginning to interrogate each other in new ways.[6] Intermarriage is involved in all of the texts I have been concerned with. Another reason may be the tendency, also evident in Liu, to make identifications outside the culture of origin. Orientation in moral space may be achieved via points of reference on the other side of the world. This tendency has long been part of education and indeed of religious belief—Greek and Semitic models and sites of identity have, after all, been held before non-Greeks and non-Jews for centuries. But with the spatial and temporal compression of the world we call "globalization," groups and individuals will increasingly face each other with what Bourricaud calls an "open ensemble of interlocutors and partners" (cited in Robertson, 101).[7] With the increase in world travel, migration, higher education and electronic media, some believe that we may be on the brink of what the anthropologist Gordon Mathews calls the "global cultural supermarket" in which the self can shop for identifications among a whole world of alternatives.[8] Certainly in the affluent West the discovery of meaning in non-Western religious systems has been familiar since the 60s, and it constitutes part of what was then called the "global village."

But this first conception of globalization hasn't always been evidently underpinned by universalism. Indeed, it might be argued that the notion of the "global village" took hold at the moment, par excellence, of cultural particularism. When burning Vietnamese villages appeared on TV screens in the West, it began to become clear to many that this was not simply a universal battle between communist and democratic political systems, but the attempted destruction of one culture by another. It suddenly seemed evident that all cultures have their own integrity, their own complex systems of meaning. They all merit respect. A whole range of interconnected things began to happen almost at once—anti-Vietnam war marches, the black power movement, and the beginnings of multiculturalism. Werner Sollors tells the story of how Afro-American culture provided models of self-discovery for other American ethic groups. This also happened globally. In *My Place* (1987) Australian writer Sally Morgan tells how her grandmother gradually began to own her own Aboriginality. A crucial part of the process was seeing black people around the world on television:

Slowly, over that year, Mum and I began to notice a change in Nan. Not a miraculous change, but a change just the same. Her interests began to extend beyond who was in the telephone box opposite our house, to world affairs. Nan had always watched the news every night on each channel if she could, but now, instead of just noting world disasters, she began to take an interest in news about black people.

If the story was sad, she'd put her hand to her mouth and say, "See, see what they do to black people." On the other hand, if black people were doing well for themselves, she'd complain, "Just look at them, showing off. Who do they think they are. They just black like me."

About this time, Nan's favourite word became Nyoongah. She'd heard it used on a television report and had taken an instant liking to it. To Nan, anyone dark was now Nyoongah. Africans, Burmese, American Negroes were all Nyoongahs. She identified with them. In a sense, they were her people, because they shared the common bond of blackness and the oppression that, for so long, that colour had brought. It was only a small change, but it was a beginning. (137–38)

Here we see the beginning of a reversal of many years of denial. The worldwide television images enable Nan to identify as an Aboriginal partly by enabling her to identify with the struggles of black people everywhere. It is a particular identification with her own specific cultural heritage, and yet at the same time it is inextricably bound up with a sense of the "common bond" shared by black people all over the world. African Americans are as much "her people" as Aborigines. They are all poor Nyoongah, oppressed by the white man.

What this passage suggests is the sense in which, especially in a globalized world, particularism tends to be shadowed by universalism. As Roland Robertson says, once the world gets more compressed and singular, it becomes more and more evident that the basis for identity-construction is widely "shared." Modes of difference tend to be constituted within the same basic paradigm. In "The Politics of Recognition," Taylor shows how both the politics of universalism and the politics of difference have evolved out of the same core contemporary notion, which he calls the "politics of equal recognition" (137). Whereas the first insists on the need for difference-blindness and the equalization of rights and entitlements, the second insists on the distinctiveness, the unique identity, of individuals and groups. But, as he argues, even this latter notion is founded on a form of universalism, in the sense that it depends on the idea that "*Everyone* should be recognised for his or her unique identity" (38). If this is so, then, after thirty years, it may be precisely the global sameness of difference[9] that is one of the "contradictions" under which various forms of particularism seem to be in danger of collapsing.[10]

There may be other reasons too. In a recent essay Guy Rundle laments the passing of what he calls "the political imagination" ("The Processes of Globalisation," 144). He argues that in a globalized society, especially with mass scientific and technical education, every aspect of life is drawn "towards the most socially-abstracted plane of constitution," by which he means "universal reflexive critique" and "instrumental rationality." The one "enables people to criticise particular and inherited conditions from the universal perspectives of humanity, justice, ethics, authenticity"; by means of the other, "they became universal subjects *via* universal media and understood themselves to be humans *per se* prior to being humans of a particular colour" (146). I think it is clear that the texts I have been examining on the whole support Rundle's contention.

The "universal perspectives"—of humanity and justice—produced by a new global consciousness can certainly be found in contemporary ethics. An important book by the moral philosopher Peter Singer, *One World: The Ethics of Globalization* (2002), provides a good example. Singer's argument is that, ethically speaking, physical distance and cultural difference between me and some other in need ought to be irrelevant:

> In 1971, at a time when several million Bengalis were on the edge of starvation, living in refugee camps in India so that they could escape from the massacres that the Pakistani army was carrying out in what was then East Pakistan, I used a different example to argue that we have an obligation to help strangers in distant lands. I asked the reader to imagine that on my way to give a lecture, I pass a shallow pond. As I do so, I see a small child fall into it and realize that she is in danger of drowning. I could easily wade in and pull her out, but that would get my shoes and trousers wet and muddy. I would need to go home and change, I'd have to cancel the lecture, and my shoes might never recover. Nevertheless, it would be grotesque to allow such minor considerations to outweigh the good of saving a child's life. Saving the child is what I ought to do, and if I walk on to the lecture, then no matter how clean, dry, and punctual I may be, I have done something seriously wrong.
>
> Generalizing from this situation, I then argued that we are all, with respect to the Bengali refugees, in the same situation as the person who, at small cost, can save a child's life. (156–57)

Singer concludes that "it makes no moral difference whether the person I help is a neighbor's child ten yards from me or a Bengali whose name I shall never know, ten thousand miles away" (157). He argues that equally there is no sound argument for giving moral preference to compatriots over foreigners, or to give overriding privilege to those "of our own kind" over those of other kinds, other communities. In other words, ethics requires an element of impartiality, or difference-blindness. According to Singer, without such impartiality there is a slippery slope to racism.[11]

Singer's argument is that in various special ways globalization is beginning to make the universalizing claims of ethics more and more inescapable. A host of transnational issues such as global warming, terrorism, systematic human rights abuses, genocidal wars, as well as vast and increasing economic inequalities between nations, all challenge those of us who live in the West to recognize that "we live in one world" (13). The same political priorities that allow first world drivers of SUVs to contribute to global warming also contribute to climatic changes that end up as flooding in low-lying countries such as Bangladesh. Equally, the exigencies of domestic politics in Australia result in the turning away of boatloads of refugees from places such as Afghanistan and Iraq and the forced detention of others. Richard Freadman's paper, "The Bonds of Civility Cut Asunder," shows another example of the way in which Western life writing has responded to such ethical issues. In Zable's work, Nazi death-camp survivors identify with the Asian and middle-Eastern "boat people" arrested in Australia's northern waters. Freadman is interested in the ways in which Zable moves in space and time beyond his own Melbourne Jewish community, pointing up the connections between the Holocaust survivors of his parents' generation and the asylum seekers of another generation, between the European nightmare and Australian multicultural experience. With such a vision, Zable calls on readers "to be citizens of a global moral community" (129). Here too the writers in my present study would no doubt find themselves in some sympathy.

And yet the issue is more complicated. Ien Ang ends her essay by reminding her readers of the point I was making at the beginning—that identity is context-dependent. For all her hybridized "liminality," there will be a moment when it will be right and necessary to stress her Chineseness, depending on the specific political question asked. Ang presents this as conscious strategy. Other writers in my group seem to be taken by surprise and discover particular identifications as it were by accident. It is partly in this sense that Liu writes of himself as an *Accidental Asian*. During the "Asian money" scandal, Liu, as a Clinton aide, is invited to be a "special guest" on TV. The issue is the allegedly racist cover of the *Nation Review*, which shows the Clinton camp as stereotypical Orientals. Liu at first finds himself merely playing a role, the Asian spokesman, until he is asked why he finds the cover so offensive when "normal people" are not offended. At this point he is outraged and finds himself merging with the role of the Asian American. The interesting thing is the element of surprise by which the identity overtakes him:

> What was curious to me . . . is how I managed, if even for a moment, to lose myself in [the role]. Here is where the sense of danger came into play. I may not have started out being terribly exercised about the perils of Yellow Peril stereotyping. But once I perceived the smarmy hypocrisy of this fellow—once I heard his intransigent insistence that the fault lay only with whiny, race-peddling Asians like me—I was chilled by the sense that maybe there *is* danger out there. Maybe it *is* true, as I was then asserting on camera, that what separates insulting caricatures from more troubling forms of anti-Asian sentiment is only a slippery slope. At that moment I began to comprehend the most basic rationale for pan-Asian solidarity: self-defense. (62–63)

Later he will return to himself, so to speak, and explain why he still finds the "Asian American" identity "contrived" and "unnecessary." But how can we explain Liu's notion that he "lost himself" momentarily in the role? What he had lost presumably was his habitual orientation in moral space, underpinned by his familiar universalizing take on race and ethnicity. What he discovers before the cameras is the extent to which, in the context of race-hostility, there is another side to himself, framed by another language of identity, in which "difference" is a key term. This particularizing language picks out the fact that people such as he have been historically abused, misunderstood, and misrecognized, and if this is to stop, such people have to speak out. Liu discovers by "accident," in other words, the full dialogic reality of his identity.

Something similar occurs in *Inside Outside*. Riemer not only refuses to speak of his Holocaust experience, but never once refers to himself, his family, or their friends as Jewish. He says that others had worse experiences, and no doubt this is true, but what is remarkable is the complete elision of the fact that the family only narrowly missed being transported to Auschwitz. Those who flaunt their Holocaust experiences, such as the "Viennese lady"—itself a curiously evasive circumlocution—who disrupted his classes, are subject to a mild form of ridicule. Why should this be so, unless Riemer is himself at some level uneasy about what he is avoiding? There is, however, one place in the text in which the suppressed emerges in any case. Riemer relates a ceremony to which he has been invited at the Hungarian Embassy in Canberra. Someone offers to translate from Hungarian for him, but he says that it is not necessary as he "was born there." He then anticipates the reply, "But you don't look Hungarian!" (204). He is reminded of how alien he is to Hungarians and suddenly of how completely he had forgotten the racism he had witnessed in his childhood:

> I now begin to search the faces of these people around me, most of them alive with emotion and patriotic pride, trying to work out how old they might be, wondering whether any of them, as very young men and women, could have spat and jeered at those lines of people, wrists tied to wrists with long strands of rope, as they were dragged off to be killed on the embankments of the Danube (205).

As with Liu, we sense the presence here of another sort of moral language in which a key binary is the "difference" between those spitting and jeering and those tied by the wrists. At this moment he is less aware of human commonality than a sense of the distinctive historical experience of the people being led off to death. If he does not quite identify them as *his* people, he nonetheless clearly identifies with their oppression by the most extreme form of racism. This is another side of Riemer's identity, occluded by his habitual universalist orientation in moral space, yet waiting, so to speak, for the moment to express itself. What both Liu and Riemer show is the force of Taylor's claim that "our identity is deeper and more many-sided than any of our possible articulations of it."

This insight takes us back to Carolyn Steedman and the implicit but unrecognized expectation of care that a good woman will offer her children. In this domain of her moral feeling, the good of other-regarding love is not ironized, placed in inverted commas, by neo-Nietzschean thoughts about how such conventional women are exploited by the powerful. Steedman cannot easily let herself see this, presumably because it runs counter to her habitual particularist orientation in moral space. With Liu and Riemer, it is the particularist side of their identity that is hard to recognize, and for similar reasons. We can now see that Taylor's notion of orientation in moral space will be misleading if we think of the good as a single bearing of the compass, as in a moral True North. As we see with Augustine and Gosse's parents, there may be some people whose identities are broadly framed in this way, people whose lives center around some single jealous hypergood. But even they, as we see with Augustine and with Gosse's father, are more complicatedly constituted, drawn to a wider range of goods than the hypergood perspective could strictly allow. This is why, especially those of us whose identities are invested in defense of a certain version of the good, there will be goods that move us in ways we cannot easily allow ourselves to recognize. This is one reason why the term "ethical unconscious" has usefulness in our analysis: in helping us to focus on and then to recover part of that wide range of goods we all tend to live by.

There is another reason why I use this term, which is illustrated by the case of Australian philosopher Raimond Gaita, though it is implicit in most if not all intergenerational auto/biography. It is that recognizing a particular other, especially a parent, often involves confronting habitual constructions of them, sometimes at points where powerful psychic defenses are massed. Recognition may require quite new perspectives, realized in new languages of the good.

2. Common Humanity and Its Limits in Raimond Gaita's *Romulus, My Father*

Like those life writers just considered, Raimond Gaita resists contemporary multiculturalism and emphasizes the abiding need for an ethics of common humanity. In fact, the title of one of his books of philosophical reflections on contemporary issues is *A Common Humanity* (1998). Throughout the book, Gaita gives an account of his own characteristic kind of universalist ethics, which, very like Iris Murdoch's (on which it is partly based),[12] emphasizes the qualities of moral attention we give to each other. He focuses on a few limit cases, such as that of a woman M who believes that a certain Vietnamese woman who loses a child can simply "have more." To believe that, M cannot be seeing the Vietnamese woman as, in Simone Weil's phrase, "another perspective on the world," that is, with a similar inner life and depth to her own. She is not, in short, responding to her with a sense of common humanity.

Gaita's elegiac memoir of his father, *Romulus, My Father,* was published in the year before the philosophical book and was widely acclaimed as a classic of Australian autobiographical literature. It began with the elegy Gaita gave at his father's funeral in 1996. Friends who heard it encouraged him to publish it, and the highly favourable response to that led Gaita to write the book. In some important ways the two books are very much of a piece. In *Romulus*, for example, Gaita praises his father's "unqualified sense of common humanity" (207), despite the characteristic severity of his moral judgments. Indeed, this phrase points to the nature of the tribute he is paying his father: Romulus, who had no more than a primary school education, is one major source of Gaita's whole philosophical life. Gaita learns much of what he is to become in "conversation" with his father, and perhaps above all, in the conversations between his father and his friend Hora:

> When Hora was at Frogmore he and my father often talked into the early hours of the morning, the kitchen filled with cigarette smoke and the smell of *slivovitz*. They talked to each other in Romanian, which I understood reasonably, but could not speak. To me they spoke in German until my teenage years when, to accommodate my foolish embarrassment, they spoke to me in English. Their individuality was inseparable from their talk—it was revealed in it and made by it, by its honesty. I learnt from them the connection between individuality and character and the connection between these and the possibility of "having something to say," of seeing another person as being fully and distinctively another perspective on the world. Which is to say that I learnt from them the connection between conversation and Otherness. (72–3)

Gaita's tribute to his father and friend is also explicit when he talks about the part "recollection" of them plays in his own moral and philosophical life:

> The philosopher Plato said that those who love and seek wisdom are clinging in recollection to things they once saw. On many occasions in my life I have had the need to say, and thankfully have been able to say: I know what a good workman is; I know what an honest man is; I know what friendship is; I know because I remember these things in the person of my father, in the person of his friend Hora, and in the example of their friendship. (74)

These memories of his father and Hora are for Gaita important sources of self and identity. As philo-sopher, literally lover of wisdom, he can draw in recollection on these examples of the goods he lives by. That the point is derived from Plato is important in another sense. The goods these men instantiate, and by which Gaita identifies himself, are not particular goods—that is, goods derived from or definitive of a particular national or ethnic culture with which Gaita is claiming continuity. There is no sense in which these goods are particularly Romanian or Yugoslav, though they are defined in terms of a broad and deep "European" culture, with which many Australians have lost contact. The goods they instantiate are rather universal: "a good workman," "an honest man," "friendship." To say that the goods are universalist is to say that these are goods that anyone may aspire to. It is my view of *Romulus, My Father* that the book itself, in its presentation of these men as opposed to those around them, is giving them an imaginative substance for readers such that they too may have the examples of such men to cling to in recollection.

The imaginative substance they are given does not ignore their cultural and historical particularity, or their cultural difference in relation to the Anglo-Celtic Australia in which they settled. They drink *slivovitz*, argue all night about philosophy, speak Romanian or German, and indeed their ability to move from one language to another is difference enough in Australia of the 1950s. And when Gaita introduces his father, he situates him in Yugoslavia of the 1920s and 30s, a world in which apprentice blacksmiths start work at 1 AM and work through to 4 PM or at the age of thirteen walk across Yugoslavia to look for work. This is another era and another world, in every sense Other to readers in Australia at the end of the twentieth century. Nor do we forget the particular forms of deprivation, of food and education, or the harshness of life that formed Romulus Gaita. Nourished by hard physical work and the reading of the Old Testament, his spirit becomes "strong," hard like the steel he tempers. He becomes, and here we come to a key word in this text, a man of "character."

But the primary focus at the beginning of the book is not on the otherness, or the cultural and historical particularities, of the world that produced Romulus. *Romulus, My Father* begins with a highly dramatic incident: "He stood behind the front door of his grandfather's house, with a pitchfork held tightly in both hands, knowing that he would probably kill his uncle if he forced his way into the room. To ensure that he would not do so he jumped through the window just before his uncle broke down the door, and he fled, to return only for a month five years later" (1). In the next paragraph, we discover that Romulus is thirteen years old and that his drunken uncle beats up his own father. Romulus flees, but not because he is afraid for himself. Rather he is afraid of his own righteous strength. His fear is *on behalf of his uncle*, who might suffer the consequences at his hands of his own drunken rages. This reason for Romulus jumping through the window is unexpected, to say the least. But it is highly deliberate. The courageous strength being delineated by Gaita here is not physical, but moral. It is the strength of self-denial for the sake of another, even another who may not seem to have much claim on his compassion. It is this same strength of character that will show itself in Romulus's self-denial for the sake of his infant son, by walking eighty kilometers for milk. But in this first scene, the self-denial is the denial of a mixture of justified self-protection and revenge. The scene sows a seed in our minds, one that only comes to full explicit expression in Gaita's elegy for his father at the very end. In referring to Romulus's "common humanity," he talks of his refusal to cause intentional suffering to anyone. Gaita concludes: "He was truly a man who would rather suffer evil than do it" (207). That is, at the heart of Gaita's conception of his father is not some particular cultural and historical ethos but a timeless and universalistic ethic that reaches back to the beginnings of Western moral thinking. The ethic, of course, is Plato's, and the tribute Gaita is bestowing on his father is nothing else but the philosopher's praise for the moral greatness of Socrates.

The terms of the son's tribute, however, only make sense against the background of the varying ways in which others have regarded him since his arrival in Australia. Most obvious is the "respect" in which Romulus is held by those who know him well. But, to my reading, there are undertones of something else even in Gaita's account of this. His wife, Christina, runs off with Hora's brother, Mitru. Yet, as is repeatedly made clear, all of them continue to hold the husband in much greater "respect" than the unhappy lover. Indeed Romulus continues to support his wife when the times are tough, as they so often are. He smoothes their quarrels with landlords. Mitru says to Gaita in his mother's hearing: "'Your father would know what to do. He would come with his shoes slap slap slapping, but he would sort things out.' He laughed as he said this. The reference to my father's shoes arose from the fact that, except for one good pair, he cut all his shoes down to the shape of slippers, and wore them like that even in winter. It amused Mitru (and others), and the reference conveyed the thought that though my father was at heart a peasant no one should draw the wrong inferences from that. It was an humiliated acknowledgment of my father's greater strength of character by the man who was living with his wife and had made her pregnant" (82). On the face of it there would seem to be two potential sources of humiliation for Gaita's father in this passage, and both of them are dismissed. Indeed, the main one, that his wife is pregnant by another man, is not even explicitly entertained as having that possible implication. So overwhelming is Romulus's "greater strength of character" that it is *Mitru* who is "humiliated." It is hard not to read this attribution of humiliation to Mitru, somewhat against the grain of Gaita's account, as at least partly defensive, as a way of displacing any implication that *his father* might have found his own humiliation in the situation. This is very much in the same spirit as the alacrity in Gaita's prose— the "thought" is attributed somehow to Mitru—to defend his father against unwelcome implications in the word "peasant." "No one," the passage says, "should draw the wrong inferences from that."

Gaita's understandable sensitivity to the "wrong inferences" that might be drawn from the word "peasant" emerges when he talks about the way in which his father is taken up, later in his life, by some middle-aged hippie neighbors. "They responded to my father with the delighted double-mindedness with which some Australians discovered multiculturalism. They responded to his charisma, admired his skills, and his peasant know-how, but their tone of voice and the ease with which they touched him and comported themselves in his home betrayed the qualification that it was, after all, *peasant* know-how" (182). This passage captures well the ambiguous spirit of some Australian multiculturalism. Cultural characteristics that were merely Other in the 1950s are now part of that greater richness that is "us," which we can now somewhat self-admiringly admire. But to Gaita's eye there is too much chummy intimacy in this and insufficient respect for personal boundaries. These people would not behave with such ease in the home of one they considered a true equal. In the end, their attitude is patronizing. In this the hippies are little different from Romulus's neighbors of the 1950s. "Those were the days before multiculturalism—immigrants were tolerated, but seldom accorded the respect they deserved. It occurred to few of the men and women of central Victoria that the foreigners in their midst might live their lives and judge their surroundings in the light of standards which were equal and sometimes superior to theirs. That is why it never seriously occurred to them to call my father by his name, Romulus. They called him Jack" (100). The name "Jack" seems to reflect a certain wary and perhaps even affectionate recognition on the part of the Anglo-Celtic neighbours, but the terms of the recognition are limitingly assimilative: they could recognize him only within their own constricted lexicon of proper names. "Romulus" certainly is not one of them, too much a marker of that Other world they do not believe it necessary even to try to engage with. Behind this lies the ready thought: become like us or go back to where you came from. The irony, of course, is that these Australians are also Europeans, and had they known anything of their own deeper roots, they would have known the name Romulus as part of the founding mythology of Europe. Gaita's focus is not on the irony of Australian self-ignorance, but on ensuring that his father and his kind finally get "the respect they deserved" from those who patronized them, first as "New Australians" and then, in the age of multiculturalism, as culturally rich and interesting "ethnics."

But what kind of respect do they deserve? What would an unpatronizing and justly respectful recognition of them look like? For Gaita such recognition has to begin with the sort of respect Romulus and Hora, in their conversations, show to others, the respect of "seeing another person as . . . fully and distinctively another perspective on the world" (73). Gaita's own philosophical writings unpack at length the meaning of this important phrase of Simone Weil's, which includes seeing others not simply *as* Other, but with the eyes of a "common humanity" which genuinely entertains the possibility that, in a sense that "goes deep," they are morally equivalent to ourselves. In the present case, Australians would have to understand the "equal and sometimes superior" standards of judgment these immigrants lived by, standards that derived from living contact with deeper European cultural roots. His father, Gaita says, "belonged to a long tradition of European thought which celebrated, as an essential constituent of a fulfilled human life, a community of equals, each worthy to rejoice in the virtues and achievements of the other" (100). Once again, Gaita's presentation of Romulus and Hora teaches us how to read them: the ethos of equality of respect in which they live is the spirit in which they deserve to be seen. The ethos is that of Plato's Athens, from which in one sense Gaita's deepest understanding of Romulus and

Hora derives. In other words, to respect these men as they deserve is to strip away the short-term cultural and historical Otherness of such terms as "immigrant," "Romanian," and "Yugoslav" and pare them back to an older, more universalistic language that discloses their "common humanity."

This is why Romulus, Christina, Hora, Mitru, and the rest are not presented merely as immigrants in rural Victoria of the 1950s, but above all as figures in a timeless tragedy, one that could as easily be taking place in the Greece of Sophocles or Thomas Hardy's Wessex. In Gaita's terms, this is what taking them seriously requires. The terrible things that happen to these people—suicide, madness and unremitting suffering—are seen not in the terms of historical, socio-cultural, or psychoanalytic analysis, but in terms of "fate and character," in the language of religion and metaphysics (124). Gaita makes a strong point of the fact that the vast and timeless Australian landscape in which he grew up, with its ancient weathered hills and twisted gum trees, encouraged a metaphysical view of things. The landscape helped him to understand "the contrast between the malleable laws and conventions made by human beings to reconcile and suit their many interests," and what he calls "the uncompromising authority of morality, always the judge, never merely the servant of our interests" (124). Here, as so often in autobiography, this is so much of a piece with the adult's philosophical views, it is impossible to tell how much he is unearthing the sources of his present self here and how much he is reading that self back into his account of remembered experience. Either way, he makes the landscape in this text a powerful metaphor of his vision of things and one that casts a metaphysical light on the terrible events that shaped his childhood experience. The landscape predisposed him to see these events as tragic: "For that reason tragedy, with its calm pity for the affliction it depicts, was the genre that first attracted my passionate allegiance: I recognised in it the concepts that had illuminated the events of my childhood. They enabled me to see Mitru, my mother, my father and Vacek, living between his boulders, as the victims of misfortune, in their different ways broken by it, but never thereby diminished" (124). The key to the tragedy of Romulus, Christina, and Mitru is that, as Thomas Hardy quotes Novalis as saying in *The Mayor of Casterbridge*, "Character is Fate" (143).

"Character" is "the central moral concept" for Romulus and Hora and, as Gaita puts it, the word means "a settled disposition for which it was possible rightly to admire someone" (101). The local Australians also recognize and admire character—manifest in such qualities as honesty, loyalty, courage, charity, and capacity for hard work (101–2). But some forms of "character," such as his mother's, are not admired; yet the book is working out a notion that is much more complex and ambiguous than this passage allows. At another moment Romulus expresses his fear that Gaita will be like his mother, indicating that like "most Europeans [his father] believed the basic elements of character were inherited" (48). Gaita implies that he has some difference with this view and indeed talks about the ways in which his father's work "both expressed and formed much of his character" (98). And yet Gaita's own characters, like those in a printing press, seem to come into his narrated world already cast into their invariable shapes. As we have seen, when we first strike Romulus at the age of thirteen, his "character" is already strong as steel; he is fearlessly courageous in his defense of principle. Throughout his life, Romulus's word is his bond, and though he treasures a good name, he despises respectability and indeed any merely prudential reasons for acting in a given way. He is also compassionate and un-self-regarding. At the same time, Romulus's behavior shows that such strenuous virtues sometimes have another side, which under certain circumstances can be destructive. His fierce truthfulness, for example, makes him narrow-minded toward anything he suspects of being affected or inauthentic. He is unbending in his hatred of lying and indeed any form of inconstancy. He thrashes his son for a suspected lie and is prepared to kill the lover of a woman who has betrayed his trust.

For such a man sexuality is the destructive element, as it seems to be for the others in the eternal triangle at the centre of the tragedy. Indeed these events convince the adolescent Gaita "that sexual love was a passion whose force and nature was mysterious, and that anyone who came under its sway should be prepared to be destroyed by it" (137). This insight seems to structure the narrative from the beginning. His parents' intense, romantic courtship occurs against the background of the bombing of Dortmund late in the war and, in Gaita's reconstruction of it, is partly formed by "the intoxication that comes from the violent destruction of the symbols of order and continuity." All that "inspired a passionately anarchic way of living which the pressures of responsibility could not touch" (7). Amidst this heady moral chaos, the man of steel loses himself to a beautiful sixteen-year-old girl who turns out to be feckless, irresponsible, undisciplined, and utterly incapable of looking after her infant son. She is also chronically unfaithful, unable to resist adulterous "romances," even after she runs off with the family friend, Mitru. She lacks "character," in other words, which tends to create a tempestuous vortex of wild jealousy and suicidal despair in the men she attaches herself to. Mitru eventually does commit suicide, but for Romulus such impulses seem to have been left behind in the moral chaos of war-time Germany. On Gaita's account, by the time he has got to Australia, he has become both parents to his son and treats his wife with a sort of charitable pity. Just how Romulus gets to such a sagacious detachment from his unfaithful wife is not explained by the narrative. It is curious in a man who will thrash his son for a lie and who will drive to Sydney with the intention of shooting the lover of his Yugoslav fiancée. For some reason, it is this latter woman, Lydia, whom he has never met, who undoes him. It is her faithlessness that drives him into insanity. He becomes paranoid. He is institutionalized and has electric shock treatment. Gaita explains this disintegration by saying that Romulus has the inflexibility of a moral "innocence" which, in the end, breaks under the shocks of life as it is revealed to him. He is driven mad by the failure of human life to meet his exacting demands.

So much for the tragedy of Romulus.[13] I have been arguing that, for Gaita, taking him seriously has involved picturing him not as a victim of an uncomprehending postwar Australian ethos of assimilation but as a figure in a universal drama in which "Character is Fate." In presenting Hora and his father in that way, Gaita has been presenting them in the moral terms in which they see themselves. In other words, if they are "perspectives on the world," then viewing them unpatronizingly, with the respect they deserve, involves seeing them in the light of their own perspectives. But what of someone, such as his mother, who does not view life from the perspective of "character"? What is entailed in viewing her with respect? This is a huge challenge to the writer whose own perspective on the world has been so formed by his father and Hora. And Gaita is aware of it. Gaita's internalization of his father's perspective can be seen partly in the strongly sexualized picture of Christina he presents (6), with focus for example on her beautiful body in a bathing costume (19). At the same time, Gaita tries to free himself from his father's point of view and to create a space in which to see her in her own terms. He finds a vital clue to this in the way in which his mother responds to a friend whose company she enjoys. The man himself is so struck by her as to remember her vividly forty years later, describing her as "very intelligent and a 'woman of substance,' meaning, I think, not merely that she was no scatterbrain, but that she had the arresting presence of someone who experienced the world with a thoughtful intensity" (31). Here we are made aware of serious possibilities in her that might have been realized in a very different sort of setting, and we might be reminded that, as a young woman in Germany, she loved the theater and opera and read Shakespeare in translation. Instead she is destroyed by her "demons" (32), including her chronic addiction to real-life "romances" as they are slightly moralistically termed. What happens to her is truly terrible. In the end she is cruelly, if understandably, rejected by her son. She visits him and, in an attempt to reduce the distance between them, dances in a half-filled café to the tune of "Peggy Sue" played on a jukebox. The scene is memorable in its pathos, not least because of the son's embarrassment. He tells the headmaster that, if she comes again, he does not want to see her. She returns and is told. Something similar happens between her and Romulus. These events occur only a little while before she commits suicide.

The father and son experience harrowing grief and "remorse" at the news of her death. Remorse is a key emotion in Gaita's moral philosophy. Only in remorse does one realize the full meaning of the wrong one has done to the one wronged. Gaita and his father are driven to rethink many things. Gaita questions the very terms of his understanding of her and comes to see that she was "pathologically" ill in a way that "no failing of character" (112) could explain—no language that included such near-to-hand terms as lazy, irresponsible, or unfaithful. In the end he sees her, as his father does, "more as a helpless cause than a free agent of other people's misfortune" (113). Again, Gaita himself has internalized this view of his father's. Early on, he writes powerfully about the limitations of the language of "character" in coming to grips with someone such as his mother: "But for someone like my mother, highly intelligent, deeply sensuous, anarchic and unstable, this emphasis on character, given an Australian accent, provided the wrong conceptual environment for her to find herself and for others to understand her. Tom Lillie's contempt for her was common. It was also emblematic of a culture whose limitations were partly the reason she could not overcome hers" (103–4). Though he does not himself provide the framework for us to see his mother's destruction in different terms, Gaita's instinct is surely right: the vocabulary of "character" is too narrow and indeed is no doubt part of what kills her. We clearly need another sort of moral vocabulary, a more capaciously Romantic one, to capture the tragic dimension of her thwarted vitality. One feels sure that Emily Brontë, Tolstoy, or Jean Rhys would have known how to come to grips with such a figure. What is puzzling, however, is why the narrowness of the *Australian* conception of character is suddenly made so central in her destruction. Even granted that Tom Lillie's contempt of her was "common," and that it no doubt contributed to her final sense of alienation, why is this more important here than the rejection of her son and husband? In short, why is *Romulus's* own intense but constricted (hypergood) conception of character not invoked here at very least as part of what oppresses Christina? In fact, Gaita himself gives us good reason to pose this question. At the very beginning he tells us of Romulus's dismissiveness toward her interest in the arts, which he rejects out of hand as "snobbishness, a fault he detested even then, but indulged in her because he loved her" (6). Being "indulged" can have been little comfort for Christina when something so important to her is "detested" as a moral "fault," a mere manifestation of "snobbishness." It is hard to believe that this difference between husband and wife goes no deeper than Gaita's single sentence implies. Christina complains after her first suicide attempt that nothing she does satisfies her husband. This is undercut in Gaita's narrative by the observation that she hardly ever did the things Romulus is alleged not to like, which is again slating the blame home to her inadequate "character." But her chronic depressive irresponsibility in these matters might also be explicable in other terms, not least in terms of a feeling of demoralized incompetence and worthlessness before so strong, capable, and righteous a husband. The narrative gives us ample space to appreciate the husband's heroic forbearance toward such a wayward wife. What it does not face squarely is the question of her point of view: What would it have been like for such a young woman—she was sixteen when they met—to find herself married to such a man? Granted that she does serious wrong to him, is it beyond question that Romulus has done no wrong to her?

Do we have the right to ask this question?[14] The premise of the book, as we have seen, is that Romulus is a man who would sooner suffer wrong than do it. And nobody alive, it may be presumed, knew the couple better than Gaita. So by what right do we, who know only Gaita's book, question his view of them? The answer is that it is not the historical people who are under question but the textual people, created by Gaita in our imaginations. Gaita has of course drawn deeply on his memory of the historical people. But they are beyond all reference and, in any case, ineffably complex, whereas the people in his text represent *interpretations* of them made from a certain perspective, which includes Gaita's current philosophical interests. It is especially important to make this point in Gaita's case because, as we have seen, he is exploring the sources of those very interests in his own past and not least in the figure of his father. Given what is at stake for the adult narrator, we can legitimately ask whether the narrated lives in the text both support that search for sources and hang together imaginatively in the way in which we might ask of the characters in a novel. Indeed, for a reader there is no significant difference between the existence of Romulus and Christina Gaita and that, say, of Walter and Gertrude Morel in D. H. Lawrence's *Sons and Lovers*. In each case, we are dealing with narrative interpretations of the marriages of the author's parents. The question in both cases is whether we find the understanding we are given of the narrated figures full, deep, and ultimately just.

My point in posing this question is to suggest that there is enough in Gaita's text to indicate that, however bad a wife Christina is to Romulus, he also seems to have been bad for her. Bad, not because he is a bad man, but bad *for her*, not least because of the sort of strenuous hypergood he lives by. As I have said above, another sort of moral language is needed here to articulate the way in which a certain kind of good man may be none the less a bad partner *for a given individual*. The moral language concerned is particularistic, focused not on "common humanity" but on individual "difference." It is what Taylor calls a "Romantic-expressive" moral language, which can allow us to see the force, once again, of Blake's dictum: "One Law for the Lion & Ox is Oppression."

CHAPTER FOUR

The Good Life: Ethical and Aesthetic Value

Raimond Gaita's work raises subtle ethical questions about what is involved in fully recognizing another person. The woman who thought that a Vietnamese mother could get over the death of her child by simply having more children is a case of someone not attending to an other as "another perspective on the world." Gaita explicates this phrase of Simone Weil's in terms of seeing another person as having a perspective on the world rather like one's own. Taking the Vietnamese mother seriously, like taking Romulus, Hora, and the other immigrants seriously, means seeing them in their common humanity, that is, with lives, and especially inner lives, that are morally equivalent—with our own.

But as we see in *Romulus, My Father*, these formulations elide a certain difficulty. Romulus and Hora are Gaita's own first conversation partners, the interlocutors who initiate him into the key languages of spiritual and moral discernment by which, as an adult, he comes to interpret and understand the world. From them he comes to learn what a good man, a good workman, and even a good life mean. He is thankful that he is "able to say" what these things are, since the good lives of Romulus and Hora remain in his memory. Like Augustine, he holds a Platonic view of the role of memory in the constitution of moral being. As Gaita says, "those who love and seek wisdom are clinging in recollection to things they once saw" (74). The particular kind of moral philosopher Gaita becomes, in other words, is shaped and enabled by their example: in recognizing them he is also recognizing himself. And this is partly what makes it so difficult for Gaita to recognize his mother Christina more fully. He is himself "clinging in recollection" to paternal examples of "character," empowered by the moral languages that make "character," with its emphasis on moral seriousness, forthright judgment, and impartiality, a key term in his own view of the world. Such a language cannot get to grips adequately with Christina's tragic situation. Returning to Simone Weil's phrase, it might be said that seeing Christina "as *another* perspective on the world" would mean seeing her view as radically *different*, a perspective that cannot be justly captured in a moral language that places such heavy emphasis on human commonalities.

Jessica Benjamin offers a useful insight on this point in her memorable formulation of the goal of psychic development in terms of a psychology of intersubjectivity. "The intersubjective view maintains that the individual grows in and through the relationship to other subjects. Most important, this perspective observes that the other whom the self meets is also a self, a subject in his or her own right. It assumes that we are able and need to recognize that other subject as different and yet alike, as an other who is capable of sharing similar mental experiences" (19–20). The key point here is a deceptively simple yet profound one: recognizing other subjects fully as such involves discerning them as "*different* yet alike." Benjamin's intersubjective account of moral growth is another way of expressing what we have been calling "empathic identification," an attention to another that discerns likeness with her within difference. In Gaita's case, having been raised by his father and effectively abandoned by his mother, full empathic identification with her is made difficult by a powerful psychic need to see her from the perspective of the somewhat idealized and wronged father. In his own case, Gaita's phrase "*clinging* in recollection" to his father's example has a special precision.

Yet even where this need is not so marked, the full recognition of others, perhaps especially parents, often involves struggling to dislodge habitual constructions of them set solid in childhood. Freud held an influential view of this kind, involving three developmental moments. The first is what he called the "primitive" impulse of the child to introject the often idealized parent along with his or her values, which happens, according to Freud, with the formation of the superego.[1] The second moment is the so-called "regressive" identification of adulthood in which this process is recapitulated, not least by the autobiographer who discovers self-continuity in recollecting the idealized parent in memory. The third moment comes when the autobiographer attempts, sometimes against great inward resistance,[2] to move beyond the symbolic parent in order to try to understand the actual person. This often involves a special form of empathic identification, which is the attempt to imagine the parent in his or her otherness in part by drawing on one's own experiences at a similar stage of life. Emmanuel Lévinas and many others have warned of the dangers of this move, in which I may be reducing the other to the same.[3] The warning is important, but Seamus Heaney's work shows that this kind of empathic identification is far from impossible.

1. Seamus Heaney: Recognizing the Other

In what follows I am considering Heaney as another intergenerational auto/biographer in the belief that such an approach can illuminate both this new sub-genre and a significant aspect of Heaney's own work. At different moments throughout his poetic career Seamus Heaney has kept returning to his childhood and adolescence, and to the significant figures who peopled his first world. This pattern of return is well understood.[4] Less understood is the fact that the different autobiographical moments show a changing understanding of self and of these others, and of the relationships between them. I am going to refer to five of these moments: *Death of a Naturalist* (1966), "Mossbawn" (1973–78) in *Preoccupations* (1980), "Clearances" from *The Haw Lantern* (1987), *Seeing Things* (1991), and his Nobel lecture, *Crediting Poetry* (1995).

The obvious starting point for any examination of Heaney's autobiographies is the poem we have already glanced at, "Digging," from *Death of a Naturalist*, which stands as a kind of poetic manifesto at the gateway to all collected editions of Heaney's poems, including the latest published in 1998. It is time to explore it more fully.

> Between my finger and my thumb
> The squat pen rests; snug as a gun.
>
> Under my window, a clean rasping sound
> When the spade sinks into gravelly ground:
> My father, digging. I look down
>
> Till his straining rump among the flowerbeds
> Bends low, comes up twenty years away

Stooping in rhythm through potato drills
Where he was digging.

The coarse boot nestled on the lug, the shaft
Against the inside knee was levered firmly.
He rooted out tall tops, buried the bright edge deep
To scatter new potatoes that we picked,
Loving their cool hardness in our hands.

By God, the old man could handle a spade.
Just like his old man.
My grandfather cut more turf in a day
Than any other man on Toner's bog.
Once I carried him milk in a bottle
Corked sloppily with paper. He straightened up
To drink it, then fell to right away
Nicking and slicing neatly, heaving sods
Over his shoulder, going down and down
For the good turf. Digging.

The cold smell of potato mould, the squelch and slap
Of soggy peat, the curt cuts of an edge
Through living roots awaken in my head.
But I've no spade to follow men like them.

Between my finger and my thumb
The squat pen rests.
I'll dig with it.

The final line of this poem expresses an act of identification with the skill and the values manifest in the productive labor of his forefathers. In these dug-up memories he finds defining sources of self and imaginative resources that seem to be a key to his poetic identity. It is characteristic of *Death of a Naturalist* that at moments the father and grandfather seem to inhabit a mythical world, their spade a heroic "bright edge," as if wielded by Byrhtnoth or Cuchulan,[5] "buried deep" into the soil. In the poem "Follower," Heaney describes his father ploughing like some great Atlas, "His shoulders globed like a full sail strung / Between the shafts and the furrow." This partly captures the child's view of the father, as the stability of the world, in whose "broad shadow" he follows, and on whose shoulders he rides, "Dipping and rising to his plod"—the last word of which cuts to something antiheroic, of which more in a moment. These poems partly relive and partly valorize the child's narcissistic identification with his father and grandfather: their discovery and premise is that the remembered experiences were and in a way still *are* identity-defining. The poet of memory commemorates in words the values implicit in their work. In this we can see the familiar pattern that was called earlier the narrative of recognition.

For all the admiration these much-anthologized poems have drawn, especially from their early readers, they have seemed to some commentators to construct a poetic identity too exclusively in terms of continuities between child and adult, and above all between the poet and his rural forefathers. David Lloyd, for example, sees Heaney's final resolution to dig with his pen (in "Digging") as occluding important elements of personal and cultural discontinuity. Despite the opening glimpse of separation between father and son—"I look down"—the poet, he says, quickly moves to "forget or annul the knowledge of writing's power both for dispossession and subjection" as well as the "irreducible difference between physical and cultural labour." Lloyd cites Heaney's own commentary on his poetry in his essay "Feeling into Words" collected in *Preoccupations:* "poetry as divination, poetry as revelation of the self to the self, as restoration of the culture to itself; poems as elements of continuity, with the aura and authenticity of archaeological finds, where the buried shard has an importance that is not diminished by the importance of the buried city; poetry as a dig, a dig for finds that end up being plants."[6] Lloyd makes several points in criticism of this, including the following:

> The predicament of a literary culture as a specialised mode of labour is that it is set over against non-cultural labour, yet Heaney's writing continually rests in the untested assumption that a return is possible through writing back to the "illiterate" culture from which it stems and with which, most importantly, it remains at all times continuous. The actual, persisting relation between the literate and the non-literate, at times antagonistic, at times symbiotic, disappears along with such attendant problems as class or ethnic stratification in a temporal metaphor of unbroken development. No irreparable break appears in the subject's relation to his history by accession to culture, nor is culture itself anything but a refined expression of an ideal community of which the writer is a part.[7]

While this might be more or less true of the short passage of "Feeling into Words" cited by Lloyd, it reduces the poem to a monologic tract. In fact, the poem resists such a reading. For a start, the separation established at the beginning is sustained throughout "Digging," nowhere more crucially than in the penultimate stanza: "the curt cuts of an edge/Through living roots awaken in my head. /But I've no spade to follow men like them." The speaker is underlining that digging in the poem is not actual but a memory awakening *in his head* (the word "head" gets emphasized by being placed on the end of the line); this stresses removal from physical work. Also, the spade in his head is sharp—it is an "edge" (also an end-word) making "curt cuts . . . /Through living roots." Digging, but especially this digging in the head, is an action that paradoxically cuts roots as it encounters them. In other words, the speaker is implying that the very act by which he asserts continuity with words is an act of disconnection, which leads into the line that makes discontinuity clearest: "But I've no spade to follow men like them." At this point we can see just how emphatic the separation from these men has been all along. At the beginning of the poem the poet is placed within his study, his father being outside in the garden. The opposition has a long dualistic lineage, and the gap is emphasized by the deliberate beginning and end of stanza two: "Under my window . . . I look down." The "straining rump" and the "coarse boot" seem a long way from the focused inwardness of the writer self-reflexively contemplating his pen, which is figured—a shade melodramatically perhaps—as a weapon of death. What does the pen kill here, if not connection and continuity? Inseparable from the relational story of interconnection is the narrative of authenticity, self-discovery through separation.

The word "follow" is an especially resonant one for Heaney. He has no spade to follow "men like them," but the poem suggests he is following them *in his own way.* As I have argued, the qualification is crucial in "Digging," though it gets eroded at moments in the more monologic "Feeling into Words," for example, where Heaney discloses the "origin" of his clinching last line in a verbal memory he dug up from his unconscious in the moment of composition:

> The pen/spade analogy was the *simple* heart of the matter and *that was simply a matter of almost proverbial common sense.* As a child on the road to and from school, people used to ask you what class you were in and how

many slaps you'd got that day and invariably they ended up with an exhortation to keep studying because "learning's easy carried" and "the pen's lighter than the spade". And *the poem does no more than allow that bud of wisdom to exfoliate,* although the significant point in this context is that at the time of writing I was not aware of the proverbial structure at the back of my mind. (42, my italics)

Revealing though this insight is, the italicized words draw attention to the reductive thrust of Heaney's account. That the poem involves and does very much more than simply allow a bud of folk wisdom to exfoliate is clear from the very organic metaphor that underpins Heaney's account. At least as important as "the proverbial structure" at the back of Heaney's mind when he wrote "Digging" is the structure of Romantic thought and, in particular, the crucial enabling voice of Wordsworth in *The Prelude*—whose centrality as an influence Heaney has acknowledged. "I intend to retrace some paths into what William Wordsworth called in *The Prelude* 'the hiding places.'" Heaney then quotes the familiar passage about the opening and closing of the hiding places of his power, which is a reminder of just how much of a follower of Wordsworth he is, not simply in his discovery of the sources of power but also in his separation from them. Like Wordsworth, Heaney is as much a poet of disconnection as of accession. Becoming what he is in these early poems is ever a double-edged spade, severing roots even as it drives for sources of the buried self. The yearning for what is lost is never far away, as we see in the poignant ending of "Follower":

> I wanted to grow up and plough,
> To close one eye, stiffen my arm.
> All I ever did was follow
> In his broad shadow round the farm.
> I was a nuisance, tripping, falling,
> Yapping always. But today
> It is my father who keeps stumbling
> Behind me, and will not go away.

As we have seen, apart from any metaphorical following the son may achieve in his skilful measuring and turning of verses, the poet must face the fact that the father can never follow him there, leaving him with the nagging longing for a connection that can be neither evaded nor realized. In a poignant reversal of the past, the somewhat heroic father of his childhood has given way to the inconvenient, stumbling figure of "today," who has no hope of keeping up with the young poet beginning to rise to the height of his powers.

Like many of the poems in *Death of a Naturalist*, Heaney's Nobel lecture *Crediting Poetry* is (among other things) a carefully wrought piece of autobiography. It too portrays a self drawn both back and forward at the same time. But there is a significant difference: Heaney's childhood world is now more fully historicized, described as "in suspension between the archaic and the modern" (447). The stress is now less exclusively on tapping into traditional cultural sources and more on what he calls his "journey into the wideness of language" (449), beginning with the radio aerial wire that entered the kitchen window of the thatched farmstead at Mossbawn and that initiated him into the rich but bewilderingly multiple and heterogeneous webs of his linguistic world. If Heaney is able to follow his forefathers *in his own way*, that is because, as *Crediting Poetry* makes explicit, this "journey into the wideness of language" crucially includes the language of poetry as he encountered it at grammar school and university. His poetic interlocutors included Wordsworth, of course, as well as Keats, Dickinson, Frost, Owen, Eliot, Lowell, Rilke, and Stevens, who entice him into a variety of Romantic and modernist languages (450–51). In this lecture the implicit background of the earliest autobiographical poems is filled in, but more than that, *Crediting Poetry* locates Heaney's poetic identity more satisfactorily in the tensions *between* diverse languages, especially "between the archaic and the modern."

This is done in relation to two counterpointed images. One is the wireless that brings home to the child what he calls "the contending discourses" (451–52) of which his consciousness is the site, such as the domestic idiom of his parents and the official idioms of the BBC. But not just the BBC: the air around is "alive and signalling" (447), from Dublin, Oslo, Stockholm, and a dozen other European capitals where he first hears the various "gutturals and sibilants of European speech" (449). He is being initiated into a multilinguistic world, of which the names on the radio dial are capitals, great centres, while the child in his farmhouse listens at the periphery. Exciting as such wavelength surfing may be for the child, further on in Heaney's lecture this multicentered heteroglot world will be linked to the danger of moral and spiritual "relativism."

The second image is the drinking water "that stood in a bucket in our scullery: every time a passing train made the earth shake, the surface of that water used to ripple delicately, concentrically, and in utter silence" (447). At first, this may seem an image of passive receptiveness to external vibrations, but later in the lecture the delicate ripples express responsiveness to both outer *and* inner reality. Here it is made clear that the fluid surface is a figure of the poetic process itself. Heaney credits poetry,

> Ultimately because [it] can make an order as true to the impact of external reality and as sensitive to the inner laws of the poet's being as the ripples that rippled in and rippled out across the water in that scullery bucket fifty years ago. An order where we can at last grow up to that which we stored up as we grew. . . . I credit poetry, in other words, both for being itself and for being a help, for making possible a fluid and restorative relationship between the mind's center and its circumference, between the child gazing at the word "Stockholm" on the face of the radio dial and the man facing the faces that he meets in Stockholm at this most privileged moment. (449–50)

This is a key moment in the lecture in which Heaney gets to the heart of his theme, the value of poetry. Within the multi-discursive world with its dangers of "relativism," the poet can and must find his mind's still "centre." Like Wordsworth, Heaney finds it in remembered childhood experience, which enables a "restorative" relationship with the "circumference"—the faintly Prufrockian grown man, a shade alienated in his "privileged moment" in Stockholm, "facing the faces that he meets." At such a moment, identification with the child gazing at the word "Stockholm" on the radio dial is a spiritual and poetic resource. Here and elsewhere Heaney suggests that everything important was already in that childhood world, "seeded full with the light," as he says in "The Railway Children." Maturity as a poet is growing up "at last . . . to that which we stored up as we grew"—such as the bucket of water, lying there in Heaney's memory as a resonant unconscious symbol, rippling concentrically in utter silence.

The notion of *growing up to* all this is crucially important. The experiences of the Mossbawn world are his center, seed, seed-time of the soul. The word "concentrically" redraws the map: the vibrations (like the radio signals) may originate in the world beyond, but the response centers *here* in the farmhouse, his *omphalos*, as he says in his autobiographical piece "Mossbawn": "the stone that marked the centre of the world" (17). In this sense, it is the great capitals on the radio dial such as London, Dublin, and Stockholm that are at the periphery, in relation to Heaney's autobiographical first place. But this place becomes a center in the fullest sense not simply through passive inheritance, or mere personal archaeology, but through existential choice and active commitment to expression of it—such as this Nobel lecture itself. In giving such centrality to the otherwise peripheral world of Mossbawn, Heaney the adult is precisely *"facing* the faces that he meets" on the world stage at Stockholm. This is the ethical edge of the phrase "grow up to." These places mark out the topography and orientation of a self in *moral* space.

Facing faces is the key to what follows. The image includes a number of ideas, but essentially identity is figured and formed not simply in identification but also in loving contestation with the parent, in facing up to difference, to otherness, and in seeing him or her face to face. Where does this new language of self and other, with its moral edge, come from? It makes its appearance in "Clearances," the moving and beautiful sequence of sonnets Heaney wrote after his mother's death. The prologue begins to probe the subtle ways in which she has been a "source" for him, and indeed *of* him:

> She taught me what her uncle once taught her:
> How easily the biggest coal block split
> If you got the grain and hammer angled right.
>
> The sound of that relaxed alluring blow,
> Its co-opted and obliterated echo,
> Taught me to hit, taught me to loosen,
>
> Taught me between the hammer and the block
> To face the music. Teach me now to listen,
> To strike it rich behind the linear black.

This poem takes us back to "Digging" in locating a key source of poetic identity in the practical wisdom of his forebears. Here, too, the focus is on a handed-down physical skill that is a metaphor for poetic creation: what holds good for the grain of the block of coal holds good for the "linear black" on the page.[8] Here again the poet is an inheritor of know-how that echoes with figural meaning: the poet who can mine its significance from memory may "strike it rich" in the way that Heaney undoubtedly does in these lines themselves. Angle, echo, hit, loosen, music—all ramify richly for Heaney as he listens "beyond silence" for what his mother has taught him. The rest of the sequence will develop what are here only hints, such as the emphasis on striking a "blow," learning from her how "to hit"; on not being too up-tight: her blow is "relaxed," she has taught him how to "loosen," trust in himself; on responsibility: she has taught him to "face the music."

Such images suggest that "Clearances" will be exploring a different kind of identification from the patrilinear one of *Death of a Naturalist*, delineating a process of self-formation that is more intimately intersubjective in Jessica Benjamin's sense. The setting of "Clearances" is not the outer agricultural space of action, the fields, wells, dams, and barns, but the inner domestic space of the kitchen, coal-shed, and washing line. It is the domain of conversation, language, and love in all its manifestations, including the subtlest forms of conflict. Sonnet 4 is central to the sequence in more than one sense:

> Fear of affectation made her affect
> Inadequacy whenever it came to
> Pronouncing words "beyond her". *Bertold Brek.*
> She'd manage something hampered and askew
> Every time, as if she might betray
> The hampered and inadequate by too
> Well-adjusted a vocabulary.
> With more challenge than pride, she'd tell me, "You
> Know all them things." So I governed my tongue
> In front of her, a genuinely well-
> Adjusted adequate betrayal
> Of what I knew better. I'd *naw* and *aye*
> And decently relapse into the wrong
> Grammar which kept us allied and at bay.

On one level the poem is about belonging, identity, and language. His mother's fear of affectation is a fear of transgressing the speech boundaries of her locality and class, of pretending to the more standardized, "better" speech Heaney himself has been educated into. But it is more complex than that, because she evidently is not ignorant of this speech, nor of its cultural trappings, such as the name of Bertolt Brecht. To be safe from affectation, she has to "*affect*/Inadequacy," to err on the side of the "hampered and askew" by actively *performing* her speech-identity. The unnaturalness of this is seen in the precariousness of the performance: "she'd *manage* something hampered and askew/Every time. . . . " This is a most complicated act of simplicity, an artful imitation of artlessness. It is no mere defensive reflex before her educated son, but a highly conscious "challenge," a demonstration for him, showing him that whatever "pride" she may have in his achievements it is more important to have pride in what one is, where one came from. It is of course implicit that "inadequate" dialectal speech, with its "wrong/Grammar," is imbued with class-shame, but her performance is a deliberate refusal to buy into those valuations. There is wisdom in this because for her to be ashamed of herself is to make Heaney ashamed of her—and ultimately of himself. And Heaney, in a mirroring act of complicated fidelity in affectation, takes the point: better to "betray" what "he knew better" than to desert pride in his roots.

To this extent mother and son are "allied," not simply in an unspoken agreement to play this most many-layered of games, but much more deeply. The linguistic and cultural *pietàs* she both models and draws him into is a key source of all he is later to become. We see this when, in a gesture that recapitulates both his life and his poetic career, he begins his Nobel lecture with the child in the farmhouse at Mossbawn. That child, with his deepest roots in this linguistic and cultural place, is identified there as the mind's "centre," and this sonnet suggests his mother's role in forming the orientation in moral space from which that self-defining identification springs. This is one of those decisive deposits that Heaney stored up as he grew and which the man is at last growing up to.

However, sonnet 4 ends in an unstable resolution, achieved by the son learning to govern "his tongue/In front of her." She knows as well as he does that it is a temporary accommodation and that, whatever surface harmony his nawing and ayeing may achieve, she and her son are linguistically and culturally "at bay." Hers is a speech that Heaney cannot yield to in a thoroughgoing way, because he is already culturally bilingual—to an extent that she is not—and cannot help knowing "better." However he may govern his tongue *in front of her,* Heaney is set on a course that will end in the speech of the poem itself, which is narrated in the "well-adjusted vocabulary" of his education. Behind her back, presumably, his ungoverned tongue will be betraying her speech, attempting to form that *"cunning* middle voice" he speaks of in the poem "Making Strange," in Station Island, which advises him to be *both* "adept and . . . dialect." The oblique reference is to Stephen Dedalus finding his own voice ("silence, exile, and cunning"), the suggestion being that Heaney needs to find his distinctive voice, or Bakhtinian "place" *between* two men, one an international visitor and the other a local farmer he has known all his life:

> I stood between them,
> the one with his travelled intelligence
> and tawny containment,
> his speech like the twang of a bowstring,
>
> and another, unshorn and bewildered
> in the tubs of his Wellingtons,
> smiling at me for help,
> faced with this stranger I'd brought him.
>
> Then a cunning middle voice
> came out of the field across the road
> saying, "Be adept and be dialect . . . "

As in sonnet 4 of "Clearances," Heaney finds himself caught between his allegiances to two cultures, that of his childhood and that of his education and poetic vocation. He is inward with, and partly constituted by, the speech of both, the implicit question being *how* shall such a cultural hybrid speak? The first answer, given by the "cunning middle voice" within him, is be *both:* "Be adept *and* dialect. . . . " But the poem ends with a different understanding:

> A chaffinch flicked from an ash and next thing
> I found myself driving the stranger
>
> Through my own country, adept
> at dialect, reciting my pride
> in all that I knew, that began to make strange
> at that same recitation.

I am not the first to find this resolution somewhat evasive. While it is possible to concede Heaney his *donné*, that the stranger's perspective has contributed to the defamiliarization of his "own country," the fact remains that being "adept/*at* dialect" is significantly different from being "adept *and* dialect." The tensions between two linguistic worlds have somehow been dissolved in a verbal sleight of hand. The ending of "Making Strange" offers a merely gestural dialectical synthesis in place of the irresolvably dialogic tensions of sonnet 4 of "Clearances," which I believe deals more adequately with Heaney's double-voiced heritage.

In the sonnet his mother's own way of looking at things provides an intelligent critique of the freight of cultural assumptions and values entailed in educated speech. The poem by no means dismisses her voice, even as it hints at why nawing and ayeing cannot of itself constitute for Heaney an adequate voice of poetry. In fact her "hampered and askew" speech gives his mother a distinctive voice and presence in the poem, a presence inseparable from the moral challenge her words present to any attempt by the boy or the man he became to get above himself, to forget where he came from. Her language of the good, redolent of Wordsworthian natural piety, is a cherished source of who Heaney has become: his fidelity to it is a response to the love he recognizes in the light blow of her challenge. But the poem does not in any sense adopt her voice as it recognizes too that the poet will have to surpass it if he is to enter, as he must, into the wideness of language. The "M.K.H." of the "Clearances" sequence, utterly free of the unfinished business that constricts so much intergenerational auto/biography, is one of the truly memorable realizations of the literature of recognition.

In "Clearances," sonnet 7, Heaney talks about the "pure change" that followed the moment of his mother's death and enabled the poems themselves, with their realistic yet lyrical recollections of the complex intimacy between mother and eldest son. However, because we only get brief glimpses of her in the early poems, it is not easy to say precisely what the "pure change" is.

The same is not true of his father. The volume *Seeing Things*, which followed his father's death in 1986, shows a clear development from the figure in *Death of a Naturalist*. The key poem is "Man and Boy." The poet is no longer the aloof and inward youthful naturalist looking down from his study on the "straining rump among the flowerbeds," but a middle-aged man fondly recalling a man much missed:

I

"Catch the old one first,"
(My father's joke was also old, and heavy
And predictable). "Then the young ones
Will all follow, and Bob's your uncle."

On slow bright river evenings, the sweet time
Made him afraid we'd take too much for granted
And so our spirits must be lightly checked.

Blessed be down-to-earth! Blessed be highs!
Blessed be the detachment of dumb love
In that broad-backed, low-set man
Who feared debt all his life, but now and then
Could make a splash like the salmon he said was
"As big as a wee pork pig by the sound of it."

II

In earshot of the pool where the salmon jumped
Back through its own unheard concentric soundwaves
A mower leans forever on his scythe.

He has mown himself to the centre of the field
And stands in a final perfect ring
Of sunlit stubble.

"Go and tell your father," the mower says
(He said it to my father who told me),
"I have it mowed as clean as a new sixpence."

My father is a barefoot boy with news,
Running at eye-level with weeds and stooks
On the afternoon of his own father's death.

The open, black half of the half-door waits.
I feel much heat and hurry in the air.
I feel his legs and quick heels far away

And strange as my own—when he will piggy back me
At a great height, light-headed and thin-boned,
Like a witless elder rescued from the fire.

The two sections of this poem exemplify the two sorts of identification to which I am drawing attention. "Catch the old one first [. . .] Then the young ones/Will all follow" encapsulates the master-impulse of intergenerational auto/biography. This poem follows the impulse by catching the idiom of his father's speech and drawing from it tacit moral and spiritual continuities between father and son. For all their differences, the young one "follows" the old one. His father's habitual distrust of the fulsome and the lyrical are caught in a speech that, for all *its* exquisite lyricism, is partly fathered by the father's values. We can see this in Heaney's version of the sermon-on-the-mount beatitudes with which he blesses his father's spirit: "Blessed be down-to-earth!" The quality of down-to-earthness, which he associates with two of his poetic interlocutors in *Crediting Poetry*, Frost and Owen, is one of Heaney's own signal qualities, in a whole variety of ways from the literal to the moral. He also talks there about having internalized in his early years a distrust of "any flourish of rhetoric or extravagance of aspiration" (451).

But then, as we see here, the father *could* be expansive and verbally extravagant, and in a verbal gesture in the same spirit Heaney casts off the "lightly checked" quality of their wordless intimacy and expresses his love with an expansive splash of his own: "Blessed be highs!/ Blessed be the detachment of dumb love/In that broad-backed, low-set man." At this point the tribute goes beyond anything we could call "regressive" identification, the process of finding self in the other. The focus is squarely on the other in his beloved otherness: "the detachment of *dumb* love" is not the poet, nor is "broad-backed" or "low-set." This is a different sort of love from that of a little boy for his father: this is the love of the grown man for another man whose quirks, whose very singularity ("*that* broad-backed, low-set man") is what is so cherished and so much missed.

The second section of the poem brings us back to the day on which his father learned of *his* father's death. The concentric soundwaves and the mower leaning "forever on his scythe . . . in a final perfect ring / Of sunlit stubble" introduce a complex circling and closing of time that brings together the grief of father and son in one timeless moment. His father is now a boy whom the middle-aged Heaney himself fathers in tender empathic identification. The son enters the father's experience in imagination so fully that he "feels"—that is, in the *present*—the "heat and hurry in the air" as well as "his legs and quick heels *far away.*"

The last words fade out to his own memory of being carried on his father's back, which clearly recalls "Follower," but here the effect is quite different. Gone is the tense interplay between childlike idealization of the father and the uneasy Oedipal separation occasioned by the young poet's power. In "Man and Boy" imaginative power connects, and in a new way. The whole effect is altogether more complex: here on his father's shoulders he feels "light-headed and thin-boned / Like a witless elder rescued from the fire." In a flash, time has circled: the son is now the elder Anchises being rescued by Aeneas from the flames of Troy. That is, the strong young father of memory rescues the ageing poet—from grief, from death? But in another flash time circles again as we realize that all this is a figure for the son Heaney rescuing his father from the flames of oblivion. It is he, the writer, who has returned to the Underworld of lost time through the golden bough of ever-renewing art. That is the significance of the timeless present that this whole section creates.

The references to the Underworld and the golden bough are far from gratuitous. *Seeing Things* is prefaced by Heaney's own translation of book 6, lines 98–148, of the *Aeneid*. Aeneas is told of the golden bough and expresses his overwhelming desire "for one look, one face-to-face meeting with my dear father." This points forward to the poem in the volume that is itself called "Seeing Things." It recalls a moment in Heaney's childhood in which the father has fallen into the river. He had gone spraying and Heaney had wanted to go with him and was peeved to be denied.

> But when he came back, I was inside the house
> And saw him out the window, scatter-eyed
> And daunted, strange without his hat,
> His step unguided, his ghosthood immanent.
>   . . . That afternoon
> I saw him face to face, he came to me
> With his damp footprints out of the river,
> And there was nothing between us there
> That might not still be happily ever after.

The vision of the father at the end of the poem differs markedly from that of the disappointed, rebellious son throwing stones in anger. *That* father might have perished in the whirlpool, whereas the "undrowned father" has as it were passed through a sort of Styx and come out on the other side, his "ghosthood immanent." In this epiphanic apparition, his mortality is suddenly visible to the child. The "scatter-eyed/and daunted" father is not the stumbling nuisance at the end of "Follower," nor an Atlas with globed shoulders figuring the stability of the world, but a man whose whole being went "tumbling off the world." The father appears in his vulnerable humanity: the son sees him, not through the dark glass of either Oedipal rebellion or of "re-gressive" identification, but clearly, "face to face," in his otherness. To the retrospective vision of the poet, the moment is a sort of vision: "he came to me." The poet has his last "face-to-face meeting" in the Underworld. The poem ends with a sense of completion; nothing is left unresolved.

Once again, the last word is given to art: "happily ever after." At crucial points in both this poem and "Man and Boy," memory becomes imagination, under the pressure of which autobiography is pushed toward what Bakhtin called "novelness." The parent ceases to be the psychic symbol of the author's child-need but is imagined, like Frank McCourt's mother Angela, having lost her baby daughter and crying out in her distinctive voice, "Oh, Jesus, Mary and Joseph, help me this night. I'll go mad, so I will, I'll go pure mad" (Angela's Ashes, 37). In such moments figures in autobiographies exist as unfinalized others, as they do in great novels, according to Bakhtin. The most significant of these texts, in other words, are creations of the dialogic imagination.

For Heaney the Nobel Prize winner, growing up to what he stored up as he grew meant facing up to moral relativism by centering himself in the values of his remembered childhood world. This involved facing up also to the complexities of his cultural heritage, owning that it was a world in transition between the archaic and the modern and valuing it in a way that acknowledged its limitations within a wider world. Growing up to his parents meant coming face to face with them in memory with a loving attention that includes a searching intersubjective understanding of them, at once fondly comic and down to earth, both affectionate and clear-eyed. Face to face, with its Pauline overtones, implies beatitude, but it also suggests the equality of adults and, at moments, loving contestation. These auto/biographies are some of the most moving and powerful poems the Nobel Prize winner ever wrote. Part of their power is their complex attitude to their subjects, the work of a man who is at once filial and utterly grown up.

It is, in other words, work of moral maturity, without any shadow of such un-worked-through feelings as *ressentiment* that intergenerational auto/biography is peculiarly prey to.

I choose the example of *ressentiment* to recapitulate an earlier moment in which I noted Walter Kaufmann's defense of Nietzsche's autobiography *Ecce Homo* on the grounds that it too was free from *ressentiment*. As a matter of fact, I think that Kaufmann is empirically wrong: Nietzsche is far from having come to terms with Wagner, or the neglect of his German contemporaries. But the point is the form of Kaufmann's argument. He uses his reading of the *ethical* attitude embodied in Nietzsche's life narrative as a defense of its *aesthetic* worth. I have done exactly the same in my account of the greatness of Heaney's more recent auto/biographical poems about his parents. I try to capture my sense of that greatness by attempting to find language for the complex attitude they manifest toward these figures, an attitude I sum up in the phrase "moral maturity." This is a way I believe most of us tend to think and speak when we are not thinking and speaking theoretically but as ordinary readers, when we say, for example, that a life narrative is "good."[9] Like Nietzsche, when he describes his own books as "good," we usually mean something at once ethical and aesthetic.

In fact these two adjacent domains of value are intimately connected. Wittgenstein, as we have seen, makes this point with memorable force when he says that "ethics and aesthetics are one." This dictum may be somewhat hyperbolic, but it poses important questions about the precise interrelations between the two that are explored in a collection of essays edited by Jerrold Levinson, *Aesthetics and Ethics: Essays at the Intersection* (1998). The essay in the collection that explores the present issue is called "The Ethical Criticism of Art" by Berys Gaut. Here Gaut outlines a position he calls "ethicism," which is defined thus: "Ethicism is the thesis that the ethical assessment of attitudes manifested by works of art is a legitimate aspect of the aesthetic evaluation of those works, such that, if a work manifests ethically reprehensible attitudes, it is to that extent aesthetically defective, and if a work manifests ethically commendable attitudes, it is to that extent aesthetically meritorious" (182). The thesis is carefully elaborated by Gaut. Some very important words in the definition are "to that extent," which make it clear that "manifesting ethically admirable attitudes *counts toward* the aesthetic merit of a work, and manifesting ethically reprehensible attitudes *counts against* its aesthetic merit." But there is no implication that either ethically admirable or reprehensible attitudes constitute a *necessary* condition for the aesthetic merit or demerit of a work. A great work of art can still manifest, for example, anti-Semitic attitudes, but it is, to that extent, flawed. The examples Gaut gives are T. S. Eliot's early poetry and Wagner's Ring Cycle. Nor, to the contrary, do ethically admirable attitudes constitute a *sufficient* condition for aesthetic merit, as we can see, says Gaut, from the example of *Uncle Tom's Cabin*. Ethicism denies both necessity and sufficiency since there is a "plurality of aesthetic values, of which the ethical values of artworks are but a single kind" (183). The view that ethical values constitute the one and only kind of aesthetic value is *moralism* (200), and the difference between this and ethicism will be evident from the examples already cited. Works can display formal genius and expressive power and at the same time they may trivialize the issues they raise for the audience's reflection. For the ethicist, the latter will count against the aesthetic merit of the work, while the former will count for it. According to the ethicist, aesthetic judgments are made in an "all things considered" way, in which the work's manifest ethical attitudes are weighed in the balance.

Some of Gaut's careful elaborations of his position are made for the sake of a readership of philosophers and will be familiar to literary scholars. The "manifest ethical attitudes" of a work of art are of course not necessarily those explicitly stated in it even by speakers who may seem in some ways authoritative. Nor are the final attitudes of a work necessarily those the work may claim to possess. The attitudes it *really* possesses—for example, misogynist ones—may be unconscious and these may only be elucidated by careful, subtle, and informed critical analysis. Nor does the ethicist thesis entail the causal claim that aesthetically "good" works are necessarily morally improving for their audience. Ethicism has nothing to say on the question of whether art with pernicious attitudes—for example, condoning gratuitous violence—is morally corrupting. The ethicist thesis has no implications either for or against censorship.

An important aspect of ethicism for Gaut is the notion that works "prescribe" responses to the situations or the life they represent, but the important question is whether or not these responses are found by the viewer/audience/reader to be "merited." An unfunny comedy would be an example of one way in which a prescribed response is unmerited. But a more interesting case is the one in which the quality of the prescribed response is in question. When we find a work manipulative, sentimental, or crude, we may be responding to "a mismatch between the response the work prescribes a reader to feel and the response actually merited by the work's presentation of the fictional situation" (195). This sort of case becomes most relevant to Gaut's argument when the mismatch comes about because we find the prescribed response unethical. For example, the Marquis de Sade's *Juliette* prescribes that we find arousal, even enjoyment, in scenes depicting the sexual torture of a victim. Most of us will feel some very different response, such as disgust. This sort of failure to elicit the response a work prescribes is, Gaut argues, an *aesthetic* failure in a work, but an aesthetic failure directly related to the *ethical* attitudes manifested by the work. The work has given us no reason to respond in the prescribed way. By the same token, where the prescribed responses to an imagined situation are commendable, we have reason to adopt those attitudes ourselves. Such responses are therefore merited, and the work will be aesthetically meritorious to that extent. Gaut concludes: "So ethicism is true" (196).

Gaut's argument, it should be noted, implies an ethics, such as Aristotle's, in which attitudes, feelings, and responses are morally relevant. Such considerations will not have much force within an ethics, such as Kant's, that gives exclusive moral significance to conscious deliberation, choice, and action. Gaut's work makes sense, in other words, where the key ethical question is not *What is it right to do?* but *What is it good to be?* The latter question is of course central for me, as it has been for recent Anglo-American philosophers such as Martha Nussbaum and Bernard Williams, for whom literature constitutes an important mode of ethical inquiry. At the same time, compared with the language of these philosophers, I find Gaut's ethical vocabulary sometimes insufficiently nuanced, as if the relevant cases were always about unambiguously "commendable" or "reprehensible" attitudes. For literary and life writing texts, the attitudes most relevant to ethical analysis may be destructive or transformative in more subtle psycho-moral ways. That reservation aside, I believe that Gaut is broadly right. Ethicism is true in that it captures something about the reading practices and responses of most of us. We do tend to react against books where we find in the attitudes manifested by them some lack of integrity, or moral shallowness, inconsistency, sentimentality, or insensitivity. Such things do tend to count against the aesthetic value we ascribe to a life narrative, even if we find other reasons to value it.

◡

The only mention of the aesthetic dimension of life writing[10] in Smith and Watson's landmark *Reading Autobiography: A Guide for Interpreting Life Narratives* (2001) comes in a discussion of the canon of life narratives (119ff.). Smith and Watson tell what has become a highly familiar story in literary studies. Over time there comes to be agreement among critics and scholars that certain texts represent "the best" produced by the culture. These texts come to acquire cultural authority. They become models; they determine the content of the curriculum. They are assigned what Griselda Pollock calls "transhistorical aesthetic value" (qtd. 120). The autobiographies of Augustine, Rousseau, Franklin, Goethe, Mill, Newman, Thoreau et al. are treated as "timeless" monuments of human achievement. And yet, as Smith and Watson argue, these canonical life narratives tend to privilege a certain teleological pattern of development in which there is some conclusive epiphany of self-understanding, seen in terms of individual autonomy and separateness. The assumptions underpinning this pattern turn out to be time-bound and culturally relative; they now seem conservative in relation to certain struggles of contemporary cultural and gender politics.

Smith and Watson's story about the canon of autobiography is hard to deny. What needs to be questioned, however, is the reflex association of the aesthetic with timelessness and "transhistorical" value. If ethicism is true, then ethical shifts over time are likely to be associated with complementary shifts in the aesthetics of art works. This idea would be broadly familiar to literary scholars, for example, of eighteenth century British poetry, where changes of moral feeling toward the rural poor begin to herald the aesthetic shifts we associate with Romanticism. In the field of autobiography, we have seen a relatively recent shift of moral feeling away from the attainment of autonomous authenticity as the highest achievement of the human spirit toward a much more other-centered ethic in which self is understood in relation to the recognition of significant others.

In earlier chapters, I have argued that life writing has been a significant site of a "relational" turn in ethics that has spawned the recent growth of a virtually new form, the intergenerational auto/biography, where authorial self and significant others tend to be co-subjects. My argument is based on an account of the historical growth of modern Western identity in terms of the self's complex search for moral ideals to live by. This pictures the modern Western self in Taylor's terms as pulled between hybrid ideals largely derived from Judeo-Christianity, Romantic expressivism, and Enlightenment rationalism. For the life writer, the key poles of conflict are likely to be what Taylor calls the ethics of "authenticity" and those of "recognition," which pull the writer between narratives of autonomy and narratives of relationality. In contemporary practice, since writers cannot but feel the pull of both ethical demands, the two narratives may be intertwined, as they are in autobiographies by Heaney and Carolyn Steedman. The recent tendency, however, is to give formal emphasis to the relational narrative. Hence the current vogue for the slashed auto/biography, which represents a clear departure from the structural pattern of the "canonical" autobiographies with their teleological unfolding into epiphanies of the autonomous self. If we can see this latter pattern as part of an aesthetic of autonomy, then a relational aesthetic will look very different.

2. J. M. Coetzee's *Boyhood*: Toward an Aesthetics of Life Narrative

The difference can be appreciated by looking at the ending of one of the most distinguished memoirs of the past decade, J. M. Coetzee's *Boyhood: Scenes from Provincial Life* (1998). This is no auto/biography, but a "memoir," as the subtitle on the cover of my Vintage edition proclaims. The two subtitles, together with the use throughout of the third person in relation to the protagonist, proclaim a clear impulse to displace the narrated self as much as possible from center stage. At the same time, the aesthetic of autonomy draws the text strongly toward the "canonical" teleology. The classic rhythm of Joyce's *Portrait of the Artist as a Young Man* exercises its tidal pull, with its structuring imagery of family, religious, and political relationships as "nets" designed to hold the creative soul back from flight, and its proclamation of "silence, cunning and exile" as the artist's weapons of escape. The human drama in *Boyhood*, however, has clear echoes of another classic struggle for autonomy, that of Paul Morel in *Sons and Lovers*, who must put behind him, if he can, the engulfing love of an unfulfilled and self-sacrificing mother.

When Coetzee's protagonist contemplates the moment when he will have to assert himself in an act of separation from his mother, he is quick to imagine her anguish, and guilt holds him back:

> Feeling her hurt, feeling it as intimately as if he were part of her, she part of him, he knows he is in a trap and cannot get out. Whose fault is it? He blames her, he is cross with her, but he is ashamed of his ingratitude too. *Love:* this is what love really is, this cage in which he rushes back and forth, back and forth, like a poor bewildered baboon. What can ignorant, innocent Aunt Annie know about love? He knows a thousand times more about the world than she does, slaving her life away over her father's crazy manuscript. His heart is old, it is dark and hard, a heart of stone. That is his contemptible secret. (122–23)

From the ethicist point of view, part of the aesthetic power of this memoir, as with Lawrence's, is the even-handed clarity with which the inexorable emotional logic of the family drama works itself out before the reader. The parents are finished sexually, and the mother is using her love for her eldest son and his for her as a weapon against the father. It is an unnatural, displaced love, full of distorted intensities. The question "Whose fault is it?" strikes to the center. Mother and son blame the father; the father blames both; and the son blames both in turn. But the memoir, with its just and clear-eyed comprehension of all the figures, teaches the reader to see that, in the end, it is nobody's fault. It is a common garden tragedy of an ill-matched couple like the Morels, helplessly destroying each other and themselves in their unhappiness. The father's feckless alcoholism and the mother's iron-willed sacrifices for the family are symbiotic and dysfunctional.

What they combine to produce for the eldest son is a "cage." The Dedalus-like logic of this metaphor is implicit in the trajectory of the larger autobiographical enterprise of which *Boyhood* is only the first step. In *Youth* (2002), the second part, the protagonist has escaped the cage and fled to London. Here he seems to be following the path of many colonial memoirists of an earlier era for whom the inevitable escape route from a stultifying provincial life led to the higher intensity of a great metropolitan center. But the similarities with the likes of Randolph Stow (1968) and Jill Ker Conway (1992) are only superficial. Rather than ending with the gesture demanded by the aesthetic of autonomy, a relieved kicking of the provincial dust off the feet, Coetzee achieves something altogether different by intertwining his fate with that of his Aunt Annie. At first, it might seem that her fruitless devotion to the deranged outpourings of a tyrannical father is simply set up for contrast. The boy thinks of himself as burdened by a darker, more tragic knowledge than any she could possibly possess: "He knows a thousand times more about the world than she does. . . . art is old, it is dark and hard, a heart of stone." This is where the reader needs to be careful, as Gaut reminded us, to distinguish the protagonist's attitudes from those of the memoir itself. The boy does perhaps know something about being the guilt-ridden child of a demanding parent that Annie may not have known. He certainly knows about his own particular emotional cage very well. But this is hardly knowledge "of the world." In fact, the language in which he contemplates his cold-hearted disillusionment has an edge of Romantic excess, of the *poète maudit,* faintly reminiscent of Stephen Dedalus at some of his own epiphanic moments of dark knowledge. But the boy's is partial knowledge at best, and it is as yet ignorant of something that Aunt Annie knew a lot about, the importance of "leaving something behind" (119). He will only begin to grasp the importance of this at the very end of the memoir.

From the point of view of an ethicist reading, it is critical to note that, for all the celebrated vividness with which the boy protagonist's experience is evoked, the memoir has a broader, steadier, and more complex comprehension of the relevant ethical issues than his. The aesthetic power associated with this comprehension emerges clearly in the penultimate chapter. Coetzee is winding toward his conclusion, as boyhood begins to give way to adolescence. The chapter begins with "Something is changing" (151). The something is partly hormonal, but also partly psychological and moral. The boy observes with shame the unforgettable step-by-step decline of his father into debt, alcoholism, and despair. He also sees how, at every step, his mother girds her loins for yet more self-sacrifice and becomes stronger and more resolute. He sees with horror where, from his point of view, that spirit of sacrifice will lead: she is building even stronger bars for a cage of love from which he will seemingly never escape. In a way this represents a final triumph over his father, but a hollow one: "Yet at the same time he wishes he were not here, witnessing the shame. Unfair! he wants to cry: I am just a child! He wishes that someone, a woman, would take him in her arms, make his wounds better, soothe him, tell him it was just a bad dream" (160). The protagonist has become the site of a psycho-moral battle. The "child" in him, at the center of his ego-world, wants to protest at the injustice that all these grotesque events are happening *to him,* a child, who can bear no responsibility for them. He wants to regress into denial. But at the same time he cannot hold off moments of decentered vision, when he glimpses a world beyond the defenses he has erected around himself:

> Sometimes the gloom lifts. The sky, that usually sits tight and closed over his head, not so near that it can be touched but not much further either, opens a slit, and for an interval he can see the world as it really is. He sees himself in his white shirt with rolled-up sleeves and the grey short trousers that he is on the point of outgrowing: not a child, not what a passer-by would call a child, too big for that now, too big to use that excuse, yet still as stupid and self-enclosed as a child: childish; dumb; ignorant; retarded. In a moment like this he can see his father and his mother too, from above, without anger: not as two grey and formless weights seating themselves on his shoulders, plotting his misery day and night, but as a man and a woman living dull and trouble-filled lives of their own. The sky opens, he sees the world as it is, then the sky closes and he is himself again, living the only story he will admit, the story of himself. (160–61)

These moments of clarity are truly epiphanic in the Joycean sense. The protagonist catches glimpses of himself, not from the self-righteous perspective of the heavily defended child-self, but as anyone would see him from the outside. From that perspective the view is as grotesque in its way as the events he is recoiling from: he is half-way to being a man, yet is still posing as a child, living out a false excuse for a responsibility he should be beginning to assume. At the same time he sees "the world as it really is." Crucially this means his parents, seen not as half-paranoid projections of his own misery, "plotting" his unhappiness, but as they are in themselves, "living dull and trouble-filled lives of their own." They are what George Eliot in *Middlemarch* called an "equivalent centre of self, whence the lights and shadows must always fall with a certain difference" (146). Like Heaney's parents, this is what they look like when they cease to be the child's psychic symbols, but are seen as they, in their "difference," would see the world themselves.

This is a very important issue for an ethicist account of autobiography. As we have seen with *Landscape for a Good Woman* and *Romulus, My Father*, texts will tend to be aesthetically more powerful to the extent that the figures of parents or other parental figures cease to be mere psychic symbols of the wounded child but can be viewed in their "difference." This is central because many autobiographies are written by people who were wounded children, some of whom really have been harmed by figures who continue to merit their anger. Aesthetically stronger texts, nonetheless, will tend to have a perspective that transcends the child's blame and anger. In Coetzee's case, the mother is very much more than the woman whose love is a cage for her elder son:

> His mother stands at the sink, in the dimmest corner of the kitchen. She stands with her back to him, her arms flecked with soapsuds, scouring a pot, in no great hurry. As for him, he is roaming around, talking about something, he does not know what, talking with his usual vehemence, complaining.
>
> She turns from her chore; her gaze flickers over him. It is a considered look, and without any fondness. She is not seeing him for the first time. Rather, she is seeing him as he has always been and as she has always known him to be when she is not wrapped up in illusion. She sees him, sums him up, and is not pleased. She is even bored with him. (161)

Once again, this vision of his mother is more than the child can bear:

> He fears the cool thoughts that must be passing through her mind at moments like this, when there is no passion to colour them, no reason for her judgment to be anything but clear; above all he fears the moment, a moment that has not yet arrived, when she will utter her judgment. It will be like a stroke of lightning; he will not be able to withstand it. He does not want to know. So much does he not want to know that he can feel a hand go up inside his own head to block his ears, block his sight. He would rather be blind and deaf than know what she thinks of him. He would rather live like a tortoise inside its shell.
>
> This woman was not brought into the world for the sole purpose of loving him and protecting him and taking care of his wants. On the contrary, she had a life before he came into being, a life in which there

was no requirement upon her to give him the slightest thought. At a certain time in her life she bore him; she bore him and she decided to love him; perhaps she chose to love him even before she bore him; nevertheless, she chose to love him, and therefore she can choose to stop loving him. (161–62)

Escaping the mother's potentially entrapping love is something the son must do to become an autonomous person and to become a man. But, as Jessica Benjamin shows, this move is fraught with the danger of "false differentiation," in which she will become a fantasized object. "She is not seen as an independent person (another subject), but as something other—as nature, as an instrument or object, as less than human" (76). As the above passages make clear, the figure of the mother exists precisely in this memoir as "another subject," with her own particular perspective on the world that precedes his existence and in which he is neither essential, central nor even always especially interesting. If these passages, as I have argued, represent a significant epiphany for the protagonist, it is not an epiphany simply of autonomy, of male separateness. It is an epiphany of "recognition" in Benjamin's terms, in which the parent is seen intersubjectively as both other and alike. She is significantly alike in the sense of being a subject, with her own separate interests and desires, just like the narrated self. The recognition has been there all along in Coetzee's text, from the moment in chapter 1 in which she buys the bicycle in order to try to escape the trap of suburbia. The child, with great ambivalence, may join his father in mocking her, but the adult narrator's perspective, in registering her frustration, is more complex and psycho-morally fuller. The form of male differentiation into which the child is being led by his father—and later comes to reject—is very different from that implied in the voice of the narrating self. In fact, ethicism will turn out to be more useful in literary studies if it complements its moral vocabulary of the "commendable" versus the "reprehensible" with a consideration of the developmental or therapeutic value of attitudes manifested by literary texts.

I have been arguing that it is only in the epiphanic passages near the close of the book that the narrated "he" begins to glimpse the world with the fuller, more intersubjective vision that has been the narrator's all along. If so, this pattern of development still has much in common with the classic teleology we might expect with the aesthetic of autonomy. The memoir does not end there, however. It ends instead, in a somewhat unexpected turn, neither with a focus on himself nor on his most significant others, but with an account of the death of Aunt Annie. The final chapter begins with the boy's "usual vehemence" and "complaining" (161). He does not want to go to the funeral; Aunt Annie is old and ugly, which fills him with disgust. He asks why old people, with their ugly bodies, cannot simply be disposed of in a hole in the garden of the old folk's home (163). There has been talk of a "special bond" (116) between the old woman and the boy, but he wants to objectify her, partly to hurt his mother and partly because there is more to this special bond with her than he can currently handle. Only at the end, as they leave the coffin by itself in the rain, is he touched by a deeper feeling. He recollects what she has said of him:

> "You know so much," Aunt Annie once said to him. It was not praise: though her lips were pursed in a smile, she was shaking her head at the same time. "So young and yet you know so much. How are you ever going to keep it all in your head?" And she leaned over and tapped his skull with a bony finger.
>
> The boy is special, Aunt Annie told his mother, and his mother in turn told him. But what kind of special? No one ever says. (165)

This is an important moment. The shaking of her head tells us that this is not the random gushing of a maiden aunt. It is a carefully considered, even somewhat unwilling observation. And the tapping of his "skull" with her "bony finger" is an oblique reminder of the all-important context: the seemingly immortal boy (164) may be denying his own commonality with her, but in the narrator's eyes they share the common human fate of mortality. In this perspective, one that goes well beyond the here and now, the view that he is "special" is a significant act of recognition. He has some gift that must be used.

The last few paragraphs keep the same sure-footed poise that Coetzee achieves in these final chapters. The boy drags his feet unwillingly into a broader vision of things. He is embarrassed that his mother asks for a lift to town in the hearse. He notes that the undertaker is a Scottish immigrant, ignorant of South Africa and people like Aunt Annie; and he is to boot the hairiest man the boy has ever seen. But the man makes a crucial comment on Aunt Annie, who has been a schoolteacher for forty years. "Then she left some good behind," says the undertaker, "A noble profession, teaching" (166). The comment cuts through all the boy's meiopic self-preoccupation, prejudice, and fastidiousness, which are the forms his regressive impulse has been taking. It prompts him to glimpse the idea that there is a larger perspective than a single life—and a special dignity in a life lived in the service of others. From these thoughts comes the intuition of responsibility on which the book ends:

> "What has happened to Aunt Annie's books?" he asks his mother later, when they are alone again. He says books, but he only means *Ewige Genesing* in its many copies.
>
> His mother does not know or will not say. From the flat where she broke her hip to the hospital to the old age home in Stikland to Woltemade no. 3 no one has given a thought to the books except perhaps Aunt Annie herself, the books that no one will ever read; and now Aunt Annie is lying in the rain waiting for someone to find the time to bury her. He alone is left to do the thinking. How will he keep them all in his head, all the books, all the people, all the stories? And if he does not remember them, who will? (166)

Hints about the "special bond" between the boy and his aunt come to fruition here in his consciousness, together with a dim recognition of his "special" gift. The boy's gift and the responsibility that goes with it is to remember, to hold what he knows in his head: the books, Aunt Annie, and the rest may come to exist only in his memory. At another level the writer is clearly reflecting on his own gift and responsibility, which are continuous with the boy's and issue in the very book we are reading. For the memoirist, the books, the people, the stories in *Boyhood* are important because they all meet in him and in fact to some degree constitute him. They constitute what Bakhtin called his "speaking position," his unique place in discourse. For Bakhtin, realizing this uniqueness involves a form of answerability. Coetzee is answerable to the books, others, and stories partly because only he can remember them, speak of them and speak for them. There is a special responsibility to remember and to speak, to write, which is both a responsibility to himself, to define and realize that which is unique in him; and at the same time he is responsible to those books, those others, and those stories. These are not two responsibilities but one.

What Coetzee is defining in this final epiphany in the book is the interlocutive identity of the relational autobiographer, for whom self cannot be understood without those constituting others, books, and stories. Given that few things are as important in a life narrative as the question of where and how it ends, it is clear that Coetzee's ending departs from the powerful canonical models of Joyce and Lawrence in their fictional memoirs. In place of solitary flight, Coetzee puts an intuition of connection, which draws the hero out of solitude. If it makes sense to call the modernist model an aesthetic of autonomy, then the aesthetic shaping of *Boyhood* is ultimately relational. I say ultimately because, if we take Charles Taylor's account of the rise of the modern Western identity seriously, there is no escaping at least some thread of the developmental drama of autonomy. That is, there is no escaping it for a post-Romantic Western autobiography such as *Boyhood*. The "relational turn" of the past thirty years is a change of moral feeling which, conceding the thrust of ethicism, must have aesthetic implications. It certainly does so in Coetzee's case, where the final chapters dwell on the importance of recognition in growing up—of both being recognized by significant others and of recognizing them. But, according to Jessica Benjamin, the fullest truth about the "differentiation" that children, boys especially, need to go through involves "the reciprocity of self and other, the balance of assertion and recognition" (25). If this is so, it will not be altogether surprising if, in contemporary memoirs, a relational aesthetic coexists with an aesthetic of autonomy.

Articulating the Good

I began by giving some preliminary answers to the question, why write a book on life narrative and the good? The nub of a fuller answer latent in my argument is that, as Taylor says, goods "only exist for us through *some* articulation" (91). One of Taylor's examples is that universal rights only came into being for us because of the talk and writings of such people as revolutionaries and philosophers. An important strand of his argument, which I re-deploy here, has been that individuals are initiated into languages of moral and spiritual discernment by conversation partners. As we have just seen, J. M. Coetzee clearly indicates how the moral languages of others are instrumental in suggesting the new moral horizon that reorients his protagonist at the end of *Boyhood*. At the boy's uncomprehending dismissiveness of his aunt's labors in printing her father's book, his mother explains how one can be proud of a man "who left something behind him," and who "did something with his life" (119), which is reinforced by the undertaker at the very end when he learns of his aunt's profession: "Then she left some good behind. . . . A noble profession, teaching" (166). These "thick" value-concepts, which recast his aunt's life in a new narrative for him, lay the foundations for the writerly vocation the boy glimpses at the end. Without such words from others, the young Coetzee's new sense of responsibility would not have been an option for him. Articulation was a necessary though not sufficient condition for his ethical development, enabling him to see his life as a wholly new kind of story.

New moral horizons can be mediated equally through writing, not least life writing. As we saw with John Stuart Mill, the Romantic vision of the good that changed his life came to him through Wordsworth's *Prelude* and "Intimations of Immortality." These provided a new language of the good that Mill found morally empowering, enabling him to discern possibilities in experience that were previously opaque to him. Like St Augustine and Edmund Gosse, he encountered literary interlocutors who enabled him to reconfigure his life in a new narrative. New moral languages are resources for life.

Given the transformative impact of life writing on Mill and others, it is clear that the genre can be a significant mode of moral articulation, making it potentially a rich resource for ethical development in many lives. Of course, it may not realize this potential. A book such as Coetzee's *Boyhood* could be read in many ways that would obscure the perspective that I am bringing to it here. In fact, given the persistence of sociological paradigms in life narrative studies, that may well happen in many contemporary classrooms where the book is likely to be read. One obvious way of aiming to maximize the impact of life writing as an ethical source is by reading the book within a framework such as Taylor's. This kind of reading is only likely to be taken up, however, with a metadiscursive articulation, such as the one I have outlined in this book: of the case for reading life-writing texts as narratives of the good.

The kind of reading needed has come to be called "ethical criticism." Given the ambiguities attendant on the word "ethical," however, it is worth spelling out once again precisely what sort of reading and articulation I have in mind. I do not mean an interest in the question, *What is it right for the life writer to do?* but an interest in the writer's, narrator's, and protagonist's engagements with the question, *What is it good to be?* I have said this often, here and elsewhere, and I have given many examples, but there is still need for further clarification. Returning to the end of Coetzee's *Boyhood*, we find a telling example— already discussed—of a protagonist undergoing repression of moral insight. The interest of the passage concerns his ethical being: "In a moment like this he can see his father and his mother too, from above, without anger: not as two grey and formless weights seating themselves on his shoulders, plotting his misery day and night, but as a man and a woman living dull and trouble-filled lives of their own. The sky opens, he sees the world as it is, then the sky closes and he is himself again, living the only story he will admit, the story of himself" (161). This passage is worth looking at again because it raises the important question of agency. If insight comes and goes like the sky opening and closing, what is especially *ethical* about the processes Coetzee is concerned with here?

To put the question differently: if deliberation and moral choice are not involved, surely the processes that are going on here are best thought of as *psychological?* I put it that way partly to invoke once again Iris Murdoch's critique of the spiritual tendency of modernity to locate the ethical purely in moments of conscious choice, the rest of psychic life being consigned to a "sea of scientific facts, and morality escaping from science only by a wild leap of the will" (26). The question is, how fully can "science" account for the sort of movements of the psyche Coetzee is interested in—or that Murdoch herself analyzes in her famous meditation on M pondering her daughter-in-law D? The answer is this: whatever insights developmental psychology might have to offer about the young Coetzee, the writer's interests are not merely in processes conceived as morally neutral "stages." He is also interested in the *values* attached to them. Coetzee's writing about the boy is what Murdoch calls "normative-descriptive" (31) language. Without the "normative" element, we would lose the fact that is crucial to Coetzee, namely, that seeing "the world as it is" is a fuller, more mature way to respond to it than withdrawing into "the only story he will admit, the story of himself." Coetzee is deploying a "thick" language of the good, in other words, and his interest is ethical in a way that is similar to Iris Murdoch's interest in the value of moral "attention."[1]

This link between Murdoch and Coetzee is worth pursuing, because it helps to clarify another important aspect of articulating the good. "Seeing the world as it is" is strongly reminiscent of Plato's allegory of the Cave and the difficulty the eye has, being inured to the half-darkness of the firelight, in looking directly at the sun. Toward the end of *The Sovereignty of Good*, Murdoch gives a memorable interpretation of the allegory:

The fire, I take it, represents the self, the old unregenerate psyche, that great source of energy and warmth. The prisoners in the second stage of enlightenment have gained the kind of self-awareness which is nowadays a matter of so much interest to us. They can see in themselves the sources of what was formerly blind selfish instinct. They see the flames which threw the shadows which they used to think were real, and they can see the puppets, imitations of things in the real world, whose shadows they used to recognize. They do not yet dream that there is anything else to see. What is more likely than that they should settle down beside the fire, which though its form is flickering and unclear is quite easy to look at and cosy to sit by? (98)

I do not think it is drawing too long a bow to say that the "story of himself" to which the boy Coetzee is so powerfully attached has some similarities with the flickering fire of what Murdoch calls "the old unregenerate psyche." This is an example of what Taylor means when he talks about how ancient "empowering images and stories" continue to operate as "moral sources" in the disenchanted universe of modernity. He has Murdoch's book in mind when he explains how the Cave inspires moral feeling and insight about the value of seeing things truly, even though we have lost belief that values are part of the frame of things. "No one today can accept the Platonic metaphysic of the Ideas as the crucial explanation of the shape of the cosmos. And yet the image of the Good as the sun, in the light of which we can see things clearly and with a kind of dispassionate love, does crucial work for [Murdoch]. It helps define the direction of attention and desire through which alone, she believes, we can become good" (96).

Part of articulating the good is recognizing that, as the allegory of the Cave reminds us, not all seeing or telling of life stories is done in a spirit that attends to life justly and with a kind of dispassionate love. Attention is, as Murdoch says, an "endless task" (27), and not something achieved without moral effort and maturity. Many life narratives tend to be confined, like Coetzee's boy, to the story of self in the limiting sense, where life is seen by the warming but partial flames of the old unregenerate psyche. What Murdoch calls "great art" is rare in life writing as in drama or painting, but we tend to know it when we see it in work such as Heaney's and Coetzee's, work that teaches "something about the real quality of human nature, when it is envisaged, in the artist's just and compassionate vision, with a clarity which does not belong to the self-centred rush of ordinary life" (63–64). What follows from this is that although, as I have argued, all autobiographers necessarily define themselves in relation to strongly valued goods, not all autobiographical texts have significant value in the ethicist sense. To take what may seem an extreme example, *The Sexual Life of Catherine M.* is constructed on an ethics of being free, totally liberated from sexual taboos and the bourgeois hypocrisy of conventional morality. There is a clear language of the good, in other words, and the possibility cannot be ruled out that this could be transformative for some readers. I would not hope for this to happen, not because of the book's sexual license, but because it is deeply narcissistic, and the sexual act is never the gateway to loving another person. A longing for a hint of the great artist's "just and compassionate vision" is never going to be satisfied.

Articulating the good, as I have argued, implies recognizing that we all tend to make ethicist judgments about life narratives. But because making judgments is so often confused with being *judgmental*, there is need for a further distinction. Coetzee's child is judgmental when he sees his parents "as two grey and formless weights seating themselves on his shoulders, plotting his misery day and night," but not when the sky opens and he sees them "as a man and a woman living dull and trouble-filled lives of their own." The latter vision of them is nonjudgmental; it has the beginnings of the just and compassionate vision by which the adult Coetzee has, all along, comprehended the boy. "Judgmentalism," as I have called it in an earlier book, is a particular constricted form of moral consciousness—or rather unconsciousness. The story I used to define the meaning of the term was the story in the gospel of St John, chapter 8, of the woman taken in adultery. The turning point in the story comes when Jesus says to the Pharisees, "let him who is without sin cast the first stone." Up till then, they have been in the grip of a rigid binary code: they are within the Law; therefore they are the righteous; the woman is a sinner; therefore, she is outside, Other, forfeiting her claim to membership of the tribe. This rigid binarism is what I mean by the word "judgmental." Jesus's words call this binarism into question. The woman's accusers are forced to look into their own consciences and to admit that they are not simply "different" from her; they look within themselves and find an element of *similarity* to her, which presumably convinces them that they do not belong to another moral universe at all. The point needs to be underlined that Jesus is not refusing to make judgments *per se:* the woman is still guilty of this serious sin, which presumably the Pharisees are not. What he is implicitly objecting to is an ethic of difference that obliterates any sense of common humanity. It is this element of commonness, the fact they are sinners too, that the Pharisees, in the grip of their rigid binary code, appear to have forgotten.

Judgmentalism, in short, is a form of unconsciousness, of moral obliviousness. Carl Jung would go further and argue that the Pharisees are externalizing their psychic "shadow"—that is, the darker side of themselves that resists the moral law by which they try to live. Jung's point, of course, is that they can only silence the accusations of the shadow within by projecting them onto some scapegoat beyond themselves. The aim of Jungian therapy here is to bring the patient to embrace all that he or she is, which must include *both* the binary terms in question, the good and the evil, whatever they are. In *Psychology and Alchemy* Jung makes the very incisive point that intense commitment to any good is fraught with psychic danger: "In the last resort there is no good that cannot produce evil and no evil that cannot produce good" (31). Those in Plato's Cave may be intensely driven by a vision of the good, unable to perceive the shadow in their judgments of others.

There are a couple of implications here for the project of articulating the good. The first is that if it entails, as any form of criticism does, the discernment of hierarchies of value, then this need not mean judgmental binarism. The last thing one would wish to see is a rigid division of the corpus of life writing on the basis of some form of "ethical correctness." It should be observed, however, that this danger is no more endemic in ethical criticism than it is in forms of political criticism, where "correctness" is a similar tendency. Pharisaism, it seems, is a permanent possibility of the human spirit, and a world divided into sheep and goats is sometimes easier to achieve than the just and compassionate spirit of nonjudgmental criticism.

Another implication is that articulating the good needs to be, for want of a better term, psycho-ethical. That is, it needs to be in touch with forms of moral inattention or unawareness that I have called the "ethical unconscious." We have looked at examples of this in earlier chapters. The authors of *The Accidental Asian* and *Inside Outside*, championing universalistic moral languages, discover the extent to which, all along, they have been repressing moral feeling of particularistic kinds. In *Landscape for a Good Woman* the case is somewhat the reverse: in framing the lives of her mother and herself within the particularistic moral language of social class injustice, Steedman is not aware of the extent to which she is moved by an ethics of care. But then, as I have argued, we are all almost necessarily living by many more forms of the good than we can be aware of, let alone articulate. It is the virtue of Taylor's historical argument in *Sources of the Self* to bring the multiplicity and mutual tension between these goods to our awareness.

One of Taylor's early chapters is called "Ethics of Inarticulacy," in which he explains why it is that we moderns tend to repress the whole realm of value and the good, mostly under the sway of hypergoods of various Enlightenment-derived and neo-Nietzschean kinds. This is what I was exploring in chapter 1 with a comparison of the self-account of Wang Shih-min with that of Roland Barthes, showing how the Ming scholar-gentleman enjoyed an explicit understanding of the goods at the heart of his identity that was not possible to the neo-Nietzschean scholar-critic of the modern West. Barthes is an extreme illustration of what Taylor calls "the cramped postures of suppression" (107) of our contemporary civilization. The moral orientation Barthes professes under the banner of neo-Nietzschean "preferentialism" is shown to be self-obscuring and self-refuting by the life narrative he cannot help telling, in which he displays clear implicit allegiances to strongly valued goods. Preferentialism is a creed that is not possible for him or indeed anybody of relative normality to live by, which points to the deep incoherence of many modernists and post-modernists in their thinking about values and about the ethical. Frederic Jameson is another example when he argues that the whole realm of the ethical is nothing but a discourse of oppression. Not only is this, like preferentialism, based on a highly tendentious reading of Nietzsche, it also obscures the way in which Jameson's own argument is driven by tacit ethical demands such as equality of respect.

This brings us back to the most basic reason for articulating the good in a study of life narrative. There is a clear epistemic gain in moving beyond the deeply incoherent neo-Nietzschean theoretical paradigms that underpin much of the identity politics still current in life writing studies. What is needed is a new reconstructive paradigm to bring to focus the suppressed structures of value that constitute the ethical lives that we moderns cannot avoid living, whichever way we turn. This new paradigm would make it clear that such central terms in life narrative as self and identity cannot be fully understood outside moral space—that is, outside a space of questions about what it is important, admirable, or valuable to be. Such a paradigm would enable us to see "the full range of goods" brought into play in life narrative, inevitably manifest in key transitions of moral experience and moments of moral crisis and development. It would enrich our historical understanding of how present life narrative draws on deep moral sources and enacts perennial moral conflicts within Western civilization. It would also help to realize the transformational potential of life narrative, by opening us readers and students "to our moral sources, to release their force in our lives" (107). Last but not least, such a paradigm would point to a quite new and fruitful meeting place between life writing studies and moral philosophy—a place where a whole range of new questions is waiting to be explored.

Notes

Introduction: Life Narrative and the Good

1. I generally prefer "life narrative" to "autobiography," even though the latter term refers more unambiguously to the kind of narratives in which I am mostly interested—those written by and principally about a given author. I am persuaded by recent discussions, notably that of Sidonie Smith and Julia Watson, that "life narrative" is preferable because it does not connote a narrow range of canonical texts that tend to produce a particular kind of "autonomous self" (Smith and Watson, chap. 1).

2. The phrase is the title of chapter 2 of Charles Taylor, *Sources of the Self.* I have chosen this out of the many metaphors Taylor uses in his book because it encapsulates the argument of my book with great economy—namely, that self can only be understood in the domain of values, that is, in moral space. The analogy between spatial orientation and orientation in moral space is spelled out in my exposition of Taylor's essential argument against value antirealism in chapter 1. No special reference is intended to physical space or place, though a place may be so important in the life of a given individual we could say that it constitutes one of his or her points of moral reference. This would certainly be true of Wordsworth and Seamus Heaney.

3. See Eakin, "Breaking Rules," 123.

4. The work of these scholars gives attention to the roles played by the virtues and by values in moral life and so is closer to my emphasis than are the others in the Eakin collection. Barbour pays attention, for example, to aloneness as a virtue in *The Value of Solitude* and Freadman to decency in "Decent and Indecent." Barbour's *Versions of Deconversion* focuses on the autobiographer's change of values in the process of loss of religious faith.

5. Murdoch's thoughts on this subject are elaborated in the early chapters of her *Metaphysics as a Guide to Morals.*

6. These include Bernard Williams, *Ethics and the Limits of Philosophy*, and Martha C. Nussbaum, *Love's Knowledge.*

7. Ruth Abbey notes Taylor's indebtedness here to Mikhail Bakhtin in her *Charles Taylor*, 67. The basic debts, however, in Taylor's "dialogical" view of language are to Herder and Humboldt, as we see in *Philosophical Arguments*, 79–99.

8. The current understanding of self as relational rather than autonomous owes a lot to the work of John Eakin, *How Our Lives Become Stories,* chap. 2, and Nancy K. Miller, "Representing Others."

9. As I argue in "Inhabiting Multiple Worlds," the interlocutive self can help us to understand the extended relationality that can exist between people of very different cultures in a globalized world.

10. Richard Freadman argues this case very persuasively in his review of *Reading Autobiography* in *Biography.* See also Philip Holden, "Other Modernities," for a related argument.

11. *Tractatus,* 6.421. Iris Murdoch discusses this view of Wittgenstein's at length in *Metaphysics as a Guide to Morals,* chap. 2.

12. I agree with John Gardner on the need for heroes to embody moral ideals: "from God comes the standard; it is enacted by a hero and recorded by the poet" (*On Moral Fiction,* 28).

13. I have in mind the kind of interpretation James Olney gives in *Metaphors of Self,* 232ff.

14. George Eliot is referring not to a parent but to Dorothea's husband, but this classic passage perfectly expresses the need, felt by Dorothea for the first time, to overcome an immature projection of her own impulses and to see the real other.

1. Life Narrative and Languages of the Good

1. This is a fundamental belief of Plato's, found throughout his work, inherent in his theory of Forms. Knowledge of reality, as opposed to mere opinion, is knowledge of the Forms. Similarly, knowledge of true goodness, as opposed to non-moral goods such as reputation and wealth, is knowledge of the "Form or essential nature of Goodness," *Republic,* 6:508.

2. Nietzsche's main target is not Platonism, of course, but Christianity.

3. This view is almost all-pervasive, but an interesting case in literary studies is an article by John Carey proclaiming "An End to Evaluation." He takes it for granted that values are human projections: "Modern man is quite used to the idea that . . . good and evil and other such ephemera were created by the human mind in its attempt to impose some significance on the amoral flux which constitutes reality," 204.

4. Williams, *Ethics and the Limits of Philosophy,* 139ff.

5. As Taylor argues elsewhere, evaluations that repose on *reasons* are ipso facto not grounded purely on radical choice. *Human Agency and Language,* 29. Nietzsche's own practice shows that his evaluations of Christian *ressentiment,* for example, are based on reasons: for him, *ressentiment* is self-destructive. It is not a bad thing for him simply because he, Nietzsche, chooses it to be so. In *Human Agency and Language,* Taylor takes Sartre to task for an allied self-contradiction, 29ff.

6. He argues this at greater length in *Human Agency and Language,* 18ff.

7. Williams, *Ethics and the Limits of Philosophy,* 140ff.

8. Gilbert Ryle, *The Concept of Mind;* Clifford Geertz, *The Interpretation of Cultures.*

9. Williams, *Ethics and the Limits of Philosophy,* 140.

10. Donald Davidson, "Mental Events," in *Essays on Action and Events,* 216.

11. Confucius, *The Analects*, 2.14.
12. De Bary, *Self and Society in Ming Thought*, 149.
13. King and Bond, "The Confucian Paradigm of Man: A Sociological View," 31.
14. John Eakin, *Touching the World*, 14–23.
15. Richard Freadman, *Threads of Life*, 114–16.
16. In Greek philosophy an *aporia* is an *impasse*, an apparently insoluble difficulty, at which philosophical reflection should begin. In postmodern thought the *aporia* has a more particular significance. It refers to the moment in deconstructive argument when a given text is revealed as contradicting itself, subverting the very binary oppositions around which it is organized. I am employing the term in this latter sense as an ironic way of pointing out the self-undermining nature of Barthes' postmodern text.
17. John Eakin, in *Touching the World*, cites a number of readers who experience the same paradox at moments such as these—that "Barthes emerges as an autobiographer in spite of himself" (17).
18. John Eakin cites the same passage for analogous reasons in *Touching the World*, 10.
19. It is in writing of his mother that Barthes' resistance to autobiography is at its most fragile. It is a resistance that seems to break down entirely in *Camera Lucida* (1981), the moving memoir he writes after her death, which reads like a kind of remorseful palinode to his whole intellectual career.
20. This is very much the Barthes of *The Pleasure of the Text* (1975), both in its privileging "jouissance" and in its eschewal of finalizing discursive and narrative form.
21. Taylor makes a powerful case of this kind in relation to Michel Foucault in *Philosophy and the Human Sciences*, 152–84.
22. The key works here are too well known to require extended citation, but they must include Jacques Derrida, *Of Grammatology*, Michel Foucault, *The History of Sexuality*, and Jean-François Lyotard, *The Postmodern Condition*.
23. In his chapter on Foucault in *Philosophy and the Human Sciences*, Taylor shows clearly how Foucault obscures the issue of the ethics of liberation in his own work.
24. This shift is particularly pronounced in the later work of Barthes, *Camera Lucida* (1981); Derrida, "The Politics of Friendship" (1988), *Adieu à Emmanuel Lévinas* (1997); and Foucault, "The Ethics of the Concern for Self as a Practice of Freedom" (1984), and "What Is Enlightenment?" (1984).
25. See, for example, Simon Critchley, *The Ethics of Deconstruction* (1992).
26. This process is ably described—as well as manifested—in one of the most popular accounts of this shift, Terry Eagleton's *Literary Theory* (1983).
27. A notable exception is Terry Eagleton in his recent book, *After Theory* (2003), which has lengthy chapters titled "Truth, Virtue, and Objectivity" and "Morality."
28. Like Derrida, Foucault, and Barthes, Jameson had second thoughts about some matters, including ethics. A more nuanced view of the ethical emerges from his essay on Alasdair MacIntyre in *The Ideologies of Theory*, 1:181–85.
29. Wittgenstein, cited in Berkowitz, *Nietzsche*, x.
30. The problem is that Taylor does not distinguish the words in this way. Following his thought as closely as I do makes it next to impossible to avoid his usages—such as my very title, *Self in Moral Space*. I would guess that Taylor

feels he needs to draw on a rhetorical power in the word "moral" that "ethical" does not always possess.

31. Berkowitz, *Nietzsche*, 48.
32. The phrase alludes to the title of chapter 1 of *Sources of the Self:* "Inescapable Frameworks."
33. At the same time, as Walter Kaufmann points out in his compelling *Nietzsche: Philosopher, Psychologist, Antichrist* (408–9), *Ecce Homo* is partly modeled on Socrates' *Apology*.
34. See Foucault's "Technologies of the Self," 227ff.
35. Aristotle, *The Nicomachean Ethics*, 4:3.
36. Nehamas, *Nietzsche*, chap. 1.
37. I am thinking of the critique of modernity in Allan Bloom, *The Closing of the American Mind*.
38. Williams, *Ethics and the Limits of Philosophy*, 67.

2. The Full Range of Goods, Judeo-Christian and Romantic

1. Kant, *Grounding for the Metaphysics of Morals*, 16.
2. James O'Donnell in his biography, *Augustine*, notes the contrast between Augustine's early life when he was surrounded by close friends and his later life in which there were no new friends, though "friendship remained valuable to him . . . in a new key," 103.
3. James Olney says that "there still remained somewhere in [Augustine's] memory the fact that his carnal loves *had* been sweet" (*Memory and Narrative*, 31).
4. Simon Haines makes this point in his *Poetry and Philosophy from Homer to Rousseau*, 60.
5. O'Donnell calls it Augustine's "most original and nearly single-handed creation," 296.
6. Olney also notes that self-continuity through memory in *The Confessions* has a similarity with Wordsworth: "[I]n Augustine's development, the child was father of the man, his days being bound each to each by the natural piety of friendship" (*Memory and Narrative*, 38).
7. Coleridge, in "Frost At Midnight."
8. Edmund Charteris, *The Life and Letters of Sir Edmund Gosse*, 444.
9. Taylor criticizes this aspect of the poststructuralist account of language in *Human Agency and Language*, 11.
10. Blake, "The Marriage of Heaven and Hell," plate 24.
11. Quoted in Thwaite, *Edmund Gosse*, 432.
12. The full meaning of this phrase, from my book *Ethics, Theory, and the Novel*, will be developed in later chapters.

3. The Full Range of Goods, Universal and Particular

1. Kwame Anthony Appiah makes a closely related point in *The Ethics of Identity* (2005): that militant identity politics can make collective identities

straitjackets. "Demanding respect for people *as blacks* and *as gays* can go along with notably rigid strictures as to how one is to be an African American or a person with same-sex desires. In a particularly fraught and emphatic way, there will be proper modes of being black and gay: there will be demands that are made; expectations to be met; battle lines to be drawn. It is at this point that someone who takes autonomy seriously may worry whether we have replaced one kind of tyranny with another," 110.

2. Gilroy is referring in the first instance to the work of W. E. B. Du Bois, which he says spread out in its impact "across the black Atlantic world" to inspire many European writers moved by questions of race. In fact, for Gilroy the phenomenon becomes even more complex in a way that prefigures my later argument in this chapter. "Double consciousness emerges from the unhappy symbiosis between three modes of thinking, being, and seeing. The first is racially particularistic, the second nationalistic in that it derives from the nation state in which the ex-slaves but not-yet-citizens find themselves. . . . The third is diasporic or hemispheric, *sometimes global and occasionally universalist*" (*Black Atlantic*, 126–27; my italics).

3. In some ways Liu comes close to what Appiah calls "liberal cosmopolitanism" (*The Ethics of Identity*, 258). The distinctions he draws between cosmopolitanism and universalism are interesting but not altogether germane to my argument.

4. *The Examined Life.*

5. This doubleness is somewhat like that of Richard Wright, as discussed by Paul Gilroy, the condition of having "two warring souls in one black body" (*Black Atlantic*, 161).

6. In a study of women of mixed race, Maureen Perkins writes how these women also tend to identify their concerns in "universalist" terms ("Thoroughly Modern Mulatta," 113). Perkins is borrowing the term from Françoise Lionnet's *Postcolonial Representations*, 5.

7. What I refer to as "the vastly extended range of others that self encounters in a globalized world" in "Inhabiting Multiple Worlds," my introduction to the special issue of *Biography* (vi), is taken up by various other contributors—in relation to travel (Barbour and Besemeres), multinational publishing (Whitlock and Tridgell), migration (Fan, Freadman, and Prosser) and electronic media (Rak and Jolly). Several essays on similar themes are found in Rosamund Dalziell's collection, *Selves Crossing Cultures.*

8. *Global Culture/Individual Identity*, 19ff.

9. Masao Miyoshi likewise argues that although in contemporary culture studies "every literary and cultural system is [supposedly] different, . . . power, however, is nearly always introduced as the constitutive factor—effectively casting every ethnic or gender minority in a more or less similar light, the light, for instance, of victimology" ("Turn to the Planet," 33).

10. Guy Rundle, "The Processes of Globalisation," 141.

11. Coming from a very different direction, Paul Gilroy also reaches for an ethics of impartiality when he argues for the renunciation of a particularist politics of race. "The deliberate wholesale renunciation of 'race' proposed here even views the appearance of an alternative, metaphysical humanism premised on face-to-face relations between different actors—beings of equal worth—

as preferable to the problems of inhumanity that raciology creates." *Against Race*, 41. He is in favor of what he calls a "planetary humanism" or a "strategic universalism," 327ff.

12. The high respect in which Gaita holds both Murdoch and Simone Weil is plain in several of Gaita's writings, for example, *A Common Humanity*, 276–77.

13. His story doesn't end there. In the end he meets a woman who shares his final years with him happily enough.

14. Gaita himself read an earlier version of this section on *Romulus, My Father* and raised some objections to my line of argument. He argued, incorrectly I believe, that I am challenging the referentiality and truthfulness of his memoir. My point is rather about the ways in which his perspective on his mother may be biased by his commitment to his father's point of view and the ethical values underpinning it. See Gaita's "*Romulus, My Father*: A Reply" and my "Reply to Raimond Gaita."

4. The Good Life: Ethical and Aesthetic Value

1. Sigmund Freud, *The Ego and the Id*, 18–29.
2. See J.M. Coetzee's *Boyhood*, 161–62.
3. See Seàn Hand, ed., *The Levinas Reader*, 38–54.
4. See Frances Dixon, "Circling the Terrain."
5. Michael Parker makes this connection in his biography, *Seamus Heaney*, 63.
6. Seamus Heaney, *Preoccupations*, 41.
7. David Lloyd, "Pap for the Dispossessed," 163–65.
8. Frances Dixon explores this metaphor in "Circling the Terrain," 217–18.
9. When we move from theory and scholarship to our reading and teaching practices, we make aesthetic judgments and evaluations of life writing texts all the time. New texts are reviewed, and reviews partly shape what is read, along with the word of mouth buzz surrounding newly published books, especially in the form of advice from friends: "You must read this, it's good." The word "good" belongs to those "thick," anthropocentric languages of value that we cannot do without in practice, whether we're talking about movies, restaurants, or the work of fellow scholars. By a "good" life narrative we may mean a range of things, depending on what we value as an individual. We may partly mean a book's cultural politics, its unusual point of view, or its daring form. But for most of us, I daresay, these are hardly likely to justify the word "good" if we find the author vain and self-preening or his prose over-written and pretentious.

   Our students tend to be much the same as we are, perhaps in a way even more so. The life narratives we teachers put on our courses, either because they are historical "landmarks" in the genre, or we think them "good," or because we think there is something "interesting" to say about them, usually have to compete for the students' interest against the texts on other courses, say on the contemporary novel, or Renaissance drama. In this cut-throat marketplace Jean-Jacques Rousseau, Benjamin Franklin et al. do not always stack up so well against the likes of Toni Morrison or Shakespeare. Students are often disarmingly quick to complain that they find the great canonical figures of autobiography comically self-regarding, narcissistic, hypocritical, or exploitative of others. The students seem to be searching for something or someone to admire, which they typically find, thank goodness, in Frederick Douglass, Malcolm X, or Maxine Hong Kingston. For them, John Gardner's dictum *On Moral Fiction* seems particularly apt: "from God comes the standard; it is enacted by a hero and recorded by the poet" (28). Many students seem to be looking for poets and heroes, writers with imaginative power and models of identity who embody some ideal of life or conduct. We are doing no favors to our specialization if we ask them to read too many texts where the autobiographer's moral feet of clay are all too obvious.

10. Aesthetics is so remote from the forefront of contemporary scholarly attention in the field of life writing that there is no entry for it in Margaretta Jolly's otherwise exhaustive *Encyclopedia of Life Writing* (2002). The reason for this lack of attention is not difficult to see. If it has a place at all, aesthetics would seem to belong to the prehistory of serious theorization in the field, to the age of the New Criticism when autobiography was fighting for attention against the dominance of fictional narrative forms.

Conclusion: Articulating the Good

1. I am assuming a distinction here and throughout my book between humanistic forms of psychology such as psychoanalysis, with its teleological good of achieving insight by working through repressions, and modern experimental psychology, which does its best to proceed in a value-free space like physics. The former kind I draw on in my term "the ethical unconscious"; the latter kind we tend to take at its own estimate as morally neutral, which encourages the split in our thinking that Iris Murdoch is arguing against. Murdoch says, as I point out, that analytical philosophy instinctively tends to conceive of ethical experience as consisting exclusively of moments of deliberation and choice, and consigns the remainder of psychic life to the moral neutrality of processes as described by behaviorist psychology. My argument is that life narratives embody the goods writers live by and do not tend to construe the "remainder" of psychic life in such morally neutral terms. In fact, such narratives proceed in the domain of what I call the "psycho-ethical" in which a significant element of my detailed analysis is focused—that is, on bringing to light various repressions from awareness of goods that autobiographers show commitment to in their writing. It can be said that Taylor too draws on a humanistic psychology when he describes various goods as being "repressed" from modern consciousness, the point of his work being to return them to awareness.

Bibliography

Abbey, Ruth. *Charles Taylor.* Teddington, UK: Acumen, 2000.

Ang, Ien. "On Not Speaking Chinese: Postmodern Ethnicity and the Politics of Diaspora." *New Formations* 24, 1 (1994): 1–18.

Appiah, Kwame Anthony. *The Ethics of Identity.* Princeton: Princeton University Press, 2005.

Aristotle. *The Nicomachean Ethics.* Translated by J. A. K. Thomson. Harmondsworth: Penguin, 1953.

Augustine. *Confessions.* Translated by R. S. Pine-Coffin. Harmondsworth: Penguin, 1961.

Bakhtin, M. M. *The Dialogic Imagination: Four Essays.* Edited by Michael Holquist. Translated by Caryl Emerson and Michael Holquist. Austin: University of Texas Press, 1981.

Barbour, John D. *The Conscience of the Autobiographer: Ethical and Religious Dimensions of Autobiography.* London: Macmillan, 1992.

——. *Versions of Deconversion: Autobiography and the Loss of Faith.* Charlottesville: University Press of Virginia, 1994.

——. *The Value of Solitude: The Ethics and Spirituality of Aloneness in Autobiography.* Charlottesville: University of Virginia Press, 2004.

——. "Judging and Not Judging Parents." In *The Ethics of Life Writing,* edited by P. J. Eakin, 73–98. Ithaca: Cornell University Press, 2004.

——. "The Ethics of Intercultural Travel: Thomas Merton's Asian Pilgrimage and Orientalism." *Biography: An Interdisciplinary Quarterly* 28, 1 (Winter 2005): 15–26.

Barthes, Roland. *The Pleasure of the Text.* Translated by Richard Miller. New York: Hill and Wang, 1975.

——. *Roland Barthes by Roland Barthes.* Translated by Richard Howard. Basingstoke: Macmillan, 1977.

——. *Camera Lucida: Reflections on Photography.* Translated by Richard Howard. New York: Hill and Wang, 1981.

185

Benjamin, Jessica. *The Bonds of Love: Psychoanalysis, Feminism, and the Problem of Domination*. London: Virago, 1990.

Berkowitz, Peter. *Nietzsche: The Ethics of an Immoralist*. Cambridge, Mass.: Harvard University Press, 1995.

Besemeres, Mary. "Anglos Abroad: Memoirs of Immersion in a Foreign Language." *Biography: An Interdisciplinary Quarterly* 28, 1 (Winter 2005): 27–42.

Blake, William. *The Complete Writings*. Edited by Geoffrey Keynes. London: Oxford University Press, 1966.

Bloom, Allan. *The Closing of the American Mind*. New York: Simon and Schuster, 1987.

Booth, Wayne C. *The Company We Keep: An Ethics of Fiction*. Berkeley: University of California Press, 1988.

Carey, John. "An End to Evaluation." *TLS* 4013 (22 February 1980): 204.

Charteris, Evan. *The Life and Letters of Sir Edmund Gosse*. London: Heinemann, 1931.

Clark, Maudemarie. "On the Rejection of Morality: Bernard Williams's Debt to Nietzsche." In *Nietzsche's Postmoralism: Essays on Nietzsche's Prelude to Philosophy's Future*, edited by Richard Schacht, 100–22. Cambridge: Cambridge University Press, 2001.

Coetzee, J. M. *Boyhood: Scenes from Provincial Life*. London: Vintage, 1998.

——. *Youth*. London: Secker and Warburg, 2002.

Coleridge, Samuel Taylor. *Poems*. Edited by J. B. Beer. London: Dent, 1963.

Confucius. *The Analects*. Translated by Simon Leys. New York: Norton, 1997.

Couser, G. Thomas. "Making, Taking, and Faking Lives: Ethical Problems in Collaborative Life Writing." In *Mapping the Ethical Turn: a Reader in Ethics, Culture, and Literary Theory*, edited by T. Davis and K. Womack, 209–26. Charlottesville: University Press of Virginia, 2001.

Critchley, Simon. *The Ethics of Deconstruction: Derrida and Levinas*. Oxford: Blackwell, 1992.

Dalziell, Rosamund, ed. *Selves Crossing Cultures: Autobiography and Globalisation*. Melbourne: Australian Scholarly Publishing, 2002.

Davidson, Donald. *Essays on Action and Events*. Oxford: Oxford University Press, 1980.

Davis, Todd F., and Kenneth Womack, eds. *Mapping the Ethical Turn: a Reader in Ethics, Culture, and Literary Theory*. Charlottesville: University Press of Virginia, 2001.

de Bary, W. M. Theodore. *Self and Society in Ming Thought*. New York: Columbia University Press, 1970.

Derrida, Jacques. *Of Grammatology*. Translated by G. C. Spivak. Baltimore: Johns Hopkins University Press, 1974.

——. "The Politics of Friendship." *Journal of Philosophy* 85, 11 (November 1988): 632–44.

——. *Adieu à Emmanuel Lévinas*. Paris: Galilée, 1997.

Dixon, Frances. "'Circling the Terrain': The Pattern of Seamus Heaney's Poetic Discovery." Canberra: Doctoral Thesis, Australian National University, 1991.

Eagleton, Terry. *Literary Theory: An Introduction*. Oxford: Blackwell, 1983.

——. *After Theory*. London: Allen Lane, 2003.

Eakin, Paul John. *Touching the World: Reference in Autobiography*. Princeton: Princeton University Press, 1992.

——. "The Unseemly Profession: Privacy, Inviolate Personality, and the Ethics of Life Writing." In *Renegotiating Ethics in Literature, Philosophy, and Theory*, edited by J. Adamson, R. Freadman, and D. Parker, 161–80. Cambridge: Cambridge University Press, 1998.

——. "Breaking Rules: The Consequences of Self-Narration." *Biography: An Interdisciplinary Quarterly* 24, 1 (Winter 2001): 113–27.

——, ed. *The Ethics of Life Writing*. Ithaca: Cornell University Press, 2004.

——. *How Our Lives Become Stories: Making Selves*. Ithaca: Cornell University Press, 1999.

Eliot, George. *Middlemarch*. New York: Norton, 1977.

Fan, Kit. "Imagined Places: Robinson Crusoe and Elizabeth Bishop." *Biography: An Interdisciplinary Quarterly* 28, 1 (Winter 2005): 43–53.

Finnis, John. *Natural Law and Natural Rights*. Oxford: Clarendon Press, 1980.

Foucault, Michel. *The History of Sexuality: An Introduction*. Translated by Robert Hurley. Harmondsworth: Penguin, 1981.

——. "Self Writing." In *Ethics: Subjectivity and Truth*, edited by P. Rabinow, 207–22. New York: New Press, 1997.

——. "Technologies of the Self." In *Ethics: Subjectivity and Truth*, edited by P. Rabinow, 223–51. New York: New Press, 1997.

——. "The Ethics of the Concern for Self as a Practice of Freedom." In *Ethics: Subjectivity and Truth*, edited by P. Rabinow, 281–301. New York: New Press, 1997.

——. "What is Enlightenment?" In *Ethics: Subjectivity and Truth*, edited by P. Rabinow, 303–19. New York: New Press, 1997.

Freadman, Richard. "Moral Luck in Paris: *A Moveable Feast* and the Ethics of Autobiography." In *Renegotiating Ethics in Literature, Philosophy, and Theory*, edited by J. Adamson, R. Freadman, and D. Parker, 134–60. Cambridge: Cambridge University Press, 1998.

——. *Threads of Life: Autobiography and the Will*. Chicago: University of Chicago Press, 2001.

——. Review of *Reading Autobiography: A Guide for Interpreting Life Narratives* by Sidonie Smith and Julia Watson. *Biography: An Interdisciplinary Quarterly* 26, 2 (Spring 2003): 298–306.

——. "Decent and Indecent: Writing My Father's Life." In *The Ethics of Life Writing*, edited by P. J. Eakin, 121–46. Ithaca: Cornell University Press, 2004.

——. "The Bonds of Civility Cut Asunder: Arnold Zable as Post-Holocaust Life Writer." *Biography: An Interdisciplinary Quarterly* 28, 1 (Winter 2005): 117–129.

Freud, Sigmund. *The Ego and the Id*. Translated by Joan Riviere. New York: Norton, 1962.

Gaita, Raimond. *Romulus, My Father*. Melbourne: Text Publishing, 1998.

——. *A Common Humanity: Thinking about Love and Truth and Justice*. Melbourne: Text Publishing, 1999.

——. "*Romulus, My Father*: A Reply." *Critical Review* 41 (2001): 54–65.

Gardner, John. *On Moral Fiction*. New York: Basic Books, 1978.

Gaut, Berys. "The Ethical Criticism of Art." In *Aesthetics and Ethics: Essays at the Intersection*, edited by Jerrold Levinson, 182–203. Cambridge: Cambridge University Press, 1998.

Geertz, Clifford. *The Interpretation of Cultures: Selected Essays*. New York: Basic Books, 1973.

Gilroy, Paul. *The Black Atlantic: Modernity and Double Consciousness*. London: Verso, 1993.

——. *Against Race: Imagining Political Culture beyond the Color Line*. Cambridge Mass.: Belknap Press, 2000.

Godwin, William. *Enquiry concerning Political Justice*. Oxford: Clarendon Press, 1971.

Goldberg, S. L. *Agents and Lives: Moral Thinking in Literature*. Cambridge: Cambridge University Press, 1992.

Gosse, Edmund. *Father and Son: A Study of Two Temperaments*. Edited by Peter Abbs. London: Penguin, 1983.

Haines, Simon. *Poetry and Philosophy from Homer to Rousseau: Romantic Souls, Realist Lives*. Basingstoke: Palgrave Macmillan, 2005.

Hand, Seán, ed. *The Levinas Reader*. Oxford: Basil Blackwell, 1989.

Hardy, Thomas. *The Life and Death of the Mayor of Casterbridge: A Man of Character*. London: Macmillan, 1974.

Harpham, Geoffrey Galt. *Getting It Right: Language, Literature, and Ethics*. Chicago: University of Chicago Press, 1992.

Heaney, Seamus. *Opened Ground: Poems, 1966–1996*. London: Faber and Faber, 1996.

——. *Preoccupations: Selected Prose, 1968–1978*. London: Faber and Faber, 1980.

Hillis Miller, J. *The Ethics of Reading: Kant, de Man, Eliot, Trollope, James, and Benjamin*. New York. Columbia University Press, 1987.

Holden, Philip. "Other Modernities: National Autobiography and Globalization." *Biography: An Interdisciplinary Quarterly* 28, 1 (Winter 2005): 89–103.

Jameson, Fredric. *The Political Unconscious: Narrative as a Socially Symbolic Act*. Ithaca: Cornell University Press, 1981.

——. *The Ideologies of Theory: Essays 1971–1986*, Volume 1: *Situations of Theory*. London: Routledge, 1988.

Jolly, Margaretta, ed. *The Encyclopedia of Life Writing: Autobiographical and Biographical Forms*. London: Dearborn, 2002.

———. "E-mail in a Global Age: The Ethical Story of 'Women on the Net.'" *Biography: An Interdisciplinary Quarterly* 28, 1 (Winter 2005): 152–65.

Joyce, James. *A Portrait of the Artist as a Young Man*. Harmondsworth: Penguin, 1960.

Jung, Carl. *Psychology and Alchemy*. Translated by R. F. C. Hull. Princeton: Princeton University Press, 1968.

Kant, Immanuel. *Grounding for the Metaphysics of Morals*. Translated by James W. Ellington. Indianapolis: Hackett, 1981.

Kaufmann, Walter. *Nietzsche: Philosopher, Psychologist, Antichrist*. New York: Vintage, 1968.

Ker Conway, Jill. *The Road from Coorain*. London: Minerva, 1992.

King, Ambrose Y. C., and Michael H. Bond. "The Confucian Paradigm of Man: A Sociological View." In *Chinese Culture and Mental Health*, edited by Tseng Wen-Shing and David Y. H. Wu. Orlando: Academic Press, 1985.

Lasch, Christopher. *The Culture of Narcissism: American Life in an Age of Diminishing Expectations*. New York: Norton, 1978.

Leiter, Brian. *Nietzsche on Morality*. London: Routledge, 2002.

Levinson, Jerrold, ed. *Aesthetics and Ethics: Essays at the Intersection*. Cambridge: Cambridge University Press, 1998.

Liu, Eric. *The Accidental Asian: Notes of a Native Speaker*. New York: Vintage, 1999.

Lionnet, Françoise. *Autobiographical Voices: Race, Gender, Self-Portraiture*. Ithaca: Cornell University Press, 1989.

———. *Postcolonial Representations: Women, Literature, Identity*. Ithaca: Cornell University Press, 1995.

Lloyd, David. "'Pap for the Dispossessed': Seamus Heaney and the Poetics of Identity." In *New Casebooks: Seamus Heaney*, edited by Michael Allen. London: Macmillan, 1997.

Lyotard, Jean-François. *The Postmodern Condition: A Report on Knowledge*. Translated by Geoff Bennington and Brian Massumi. Manchester: Manchester University Press, 1984.

MacIntyre, Alasdair. *After Virtue: A Study in Moral Theory*. Notre Dame: University of Notre Dame Press, 1981.

McBride, James. *The Color of Water*. Sydney: Sceptre, 1997.

McCourt, Frank. *Angela's Ashes: A Memoir*. New York: Scribner, 1996.

Malone, Cynthia Northcutt. "The Struggle of *Father and Son*: Edmund Gosse's Polemical Autobiography." *a/b: Auto/Biography Studies* 8, 1 (1993): 16–32.

Mathews, Gordon. *Global Culture/Individual Identity: Searching for Home in the Cultural Supermarket*. London: Routledge, 2000.

Mill, John Stuart. *Autobiography*. Harmondsworth: Penguin, 1989.

Miller, Alice. *The Drama of the Gifted Child and the Search for the True Self*. London: Faber and Faber, 1983.

Miller, Nancy K. "Representing Others: Gender and the Subjects of Autobiography." *Differences* 6, 1 (1994): 1–27.

——. *Bequest and Betrayal: Memoirs of a Parent's Death*. New York: Oxford University Press, 1996.

Millet, Catherine. *The Sexual Life of Catherine M.* Translated by Adriana Hunter. New York: Grove, 2002.

Miyoshi, Masao. "Turn to the Planet: Literature, Diversity, and Totality." In *Globalization and the Humanities*, edited by David Leiwei Li, 19–35. Hong Kong: Hong Kong University Press, 2004.

Morgan, Sally. *My Place*. Fremantle: Fremantle Arts Press, 1987.

Murdoch, Iris. *The Sovereignty of Good*. 2d ed. London: Routledge, 2001.

——. *Metaphysics as a Guide to Morals*. 2d ed. London: Vintage, 2003.

Nagel, Thomas. *The View from Nowhere*. New York: Oxford University Press, 1986.

Nehamas, Alexander. *Nietzsche: Life as Literature*. Cambridge, Mass.: Harvard University Press, 1985.

Nietzsche, Friedrich. *The Gay Science*. Translated by Walter Kaufmann. New York: Vintage, 1974.

——. *On the Genealogy of Morals*. Translated by Walter Kaufmann and R. J. Hollingdale. New York: Vintage, 1989.

——. *Ecce Homo*. Translated by Walter Kaufmann. New York: Vintage, 1989.

Nozick, Robert. *The Examined Life: Philosophical Meditations*. New York: Simon and Schuster, 1989.

Nussbaum, Martha C. *Love's Knowledge: Essays on Philosophy and Literature*. New York: Oxford University Press, 1990.

O'Donnell, James J. *Augustine: A New Biography*. New York: Harper Collins, 2005.

Olney, James. *Metaphors of Self: The Meaning of Autobiography*. Princeton: Princeton University Press, 1972.

——. *Memory and Narrative: The Weave of Life-Writing*. Chicago: University of Chicago Press, 1998.

Parker, David. *Ethics, Theory, and the Novel*. Cambridge: Cambridge University Press, 1994.

——. "Introduction: The Turn to Ethics in the 1990s." In *Renegotiating Ethics in Literature, Philosophy, and Theory*, edited by J. Adamson, R. Freadman, and D. Parker, 1–17. Cambridge: Cambridge University Press, 1998.

——. "Reply to Raimond Gaita." *Critical Review* 41 (2001): 66–67.

——. "Life Writing as Narrative of the Good: *Father and Son* and the Ethics of Authenticity." In *The Ethics of Life Writing*, edited by P. J. Eakin, 53–72. Ithaca: Cornell University Press, 2004.

——. "Inhabiting Multiple Worlds: Auto/biography in an (Anti-) Global Age." *Biography: An Interdisciplinary Quarterly* 28, 1 (Winter 2005): v–xv.

Parker, Michael. *Seamus Heaney: The Making of the Poet*. Iowa City: University of Iowa Press, 1993.

Perkins, Maureen. "Thoroughly Modern Mulatta: Rethinking 'Old World' Stereotypes in a 'New World' Setting." *Biography: An Interdisciplinary Quarterly* 28, 1 (Winter 2005): 104–16.

Peterson, Linda H. *Victorian Autobiography: The Tradition of Self-Interpretation.* New Haven: Yale University Press, 1986.

Plato. *The Republic.* Translated by F. M. Cornford. Oxford: Clarendon Press, 1941.

Prosser, Jay. "Sim Koh-Wei, My Jewish Grandmother." *Biography: An Interdisciplinary Quarterly* 28, 1 (Winter 2005): 130–37.

Rak, Julie. "The Digital Queer: Weblogs and Internet Identity." *Biography: An Interdisciplinary Quarterly* 28, 1 (Winter 2005): 166–82.

Riemer, Andrew. *Inside Outside: Life between Two Worlds.* Sydney: Angus and Robertson, 1992.

Robertson, Roland. *Globalization: Social Theory and Global Culture.* London: Sage, 1992.

Rundle, Guy. "The Processes of Globalisation." In *Globalising Australia*, edited by Christopher Palmer and Iain Topliss, 141–55. Melbourne: Meridian, 2000.

Ryle, Gilbert. *The Concept of Mind.* London: Hutchinson, 1949.

Siebers, Tobin. *The Ethics of Criticism.* Ithaca: Cornell University Press, 1988.

Singer, Peter. *One World: The Ethics of Globalization.* New Haven: Yale University Press, 2002.

Smith, Sidonie, and Julia Watson. *Reading Autobiography: A Guide for Interpreting Life Narratives.* Minneapolis: University of Minnesota Press, 2001.

Sollors, Werner. *Beyond Ethnicity.* New York: Oxford University Press, 1986.

Steedman, Carolyn. *Landscape for a Good Woman.* London: Virago, 1986.

Stow, Randolph. *The Merry-go-round in the Sea.* Harmondsworth: Penguin, 1968.

Taylor, Charles. *Human Agency and Language: Philosophical Papers I.* Cambridge: Cambridge University Press, 1985.

——. *Philosophy and the Human Sciences: Philosophical Papers II.* Cambridge: Cambridge University Press, 1985.

——. *Sources of the Self: The Making of the Modern Identity.* Cambridge: Cambridge University Press, 1989.

——. *The Ethics of Authenticity.* Cambridge, Mass.: Harvard University Press, 1991.

——. "The Politics of Recognition." In *Multiculturalism: Examining the Politics of Recognition*, edited by Amy Gutmann. Princeton: Princeton University Press, 1994.

——. *Philosophical Arguments.* Cambridge, Mass.: Harvard University Press, 1997.

Thwaite, Ann. *Edmund Gosse: A Literary Landscape, 1849–1928.* London: Secker and Warburg, 1984.

Tridgell, Susan. *"From the Land of Green Ghosts*: Commodifying Culture, Downplaying Politics?" *Biography: An Interdisciplinary Quarterly* 28, 1 (Winter 2005): 77–88.

Weil, Simone. *First and Last Notebooks*. Translated by Richard Rees. London: Oxford University Press, 1970.

Whitlock, Gillian. "The Skin of the *Burqa*: Recent Life Narratives from Afghanistan." *Biography: An Interdisciplinary Quarterly* 28, 1 (Winter 2005): 54–76.

Williams, Bernard. *Ethics and the Limits of Philosophy*. Cambridge, Mass.: Harvard University Press, 1985.

Wiltshire, John. "The Patient Writes Back: Bioethics and the Illness Narrative." In *Renegotiating Ethics in Literature, Philosophy, and Theory*, edited by J. Adamson, R. Freadman, and D. Parker, 181–98. Cambridge: Cambridge University Press, 1998.

Wittgenstein, Ludwig. *Tractatus Logico-Philosophicus*. Translated by D. F. Pears and B. F McGuinness. London: Routledge and Kegan Paul, 1974.

Wordsworth, William. *The Fourteen-Book Prelude*. 1850. Edited by W. J. B. Owen. Ithaca: Cornell University Press, 1985.

Wu, Pei-yi. *The Confucian's Progress: Autobiographical Writings in Traditional China*. Princeton: Princeton University Press, 1990.

Index